Trustee Investment Strategy
for Endowments and Foundations

Trustee Investment Strategy
for Endowments and Foundations

Chris Russell

John Wiley & Sons, Ltd

Copyright © 2006   John Wiley & Sons Ltd, The Atrium, Southern Gate, Chichester,
West Sussex PO19 8SQ, England

Telephone   (+44) 1243 779777

Email (for orders and customer service enquiries): cs-books@wiley.co.uk
Visit our Home Page on www.wiley.com

Other Wiley Editorial Offices

John Wiley & Sons Inc., 111 River Street, Hoboken, NJ 07030, USA

Jossey-Bass, 989 Market Street, San Francisco, CA 94103-1741, USA

Wiley-VCH Verlag GmbH, Boschstr. 12, D-69469 Weinheim, Germany

John Wiley & Sons Australia Ltd, 42 McDougall Street, Milton, Queensland 4064, Australia

John Wiley & Sons (Asia) Pte Ltd, 2 Clementi Loop #02-01, Jin Xing Distripark, Singapore 129809

John Wiley & Sons Canada Ltd, 22 Worcester Road, Etobicoke, Ontario, Canada M9W 1L1

Wiley also publishes its books in a variety of electronic formats. Some content that appears
in print may not be available in electronic books.

Library of Congress Cataloging-in-Publication Data

Russell, Chris.
    Trustee investment strategy for endowments and foundations / Chris Russell.
        p.   cm.
  Includes bibliographical references and index.
  ISBN-13: 978-0-470-01196-6 (cloth)
  ISBN-10: 0-470-01196-3 (cloth)
  1. Endowments—United States—Finance.   2. Investments.   3. Portfolio
  management.   I. Title.

HV97.A3R87 2006
332.67′253—dc22   2006011224

British Library Cataloguing in Publication Data

A catalogue record for this book is available from the British Library

ISBN 13   978-0-470-01196-6 (HB)
ISBN 10   0-470-01196-3 (HB)

Typeset in 10/12pt Times by TechBooks, New Delhi, India
Printed and bound in Great Britain by Antony Rowe Ltd, Chippenham, Wiltshire
This book is printed on acid-free paper responsibly manufactured from sustainable forestry
in which at least two trees are planted for each one used for paper production.

Contents

Foreword

The invested assets of endowments and foundations are a major resource of society, both in the US and the UK. They support education and scientific research, as well as cultural and charitable institutions. Endowments of colleges and universities in the US total more than $250 billion, and US foundation assets are now more than $500 billion. While the size and scope of similar institutions in the UK is not nearly as large, endowments and foundations are very important resources for the same activities there. There are 60–70,000 organizations involved, and a very large number of Trustees who have assumed fiduciary responsibility for investing their assets by serving as a member of a finance or investment committee.

Forty years ago, when I was a young officer of TIAA-CREF*, I became aware that most college and university endowment funds were not being well managed. Endowments then were usually managed by committees of trustees who met periodically to choose specific stock and bond investments, which they did not monitor closely thereafter. Investment results were poor.

Working with William C. Greenough, then Chairman of TIAA-CREF, and aided greatly by studies sponsored by the Ford Foundation, in 1971 we established a new service called The Common Fund for Nonprofit Organizations (known as the Commonfund Group today) to pool endowment investments, and bring them high quality, full time professional management of their investments. This proved to be much more effective, and eventually led to a basic change in the way all endowments were managed. Professional investment management, which was rare in the 1960's, has become virtually universal today. The role of trustees has evolved from choosing investments to selecting and monitoring professional managers, as well as setting guidelines for investment policy and asset allocation.

These are neither simple nor easy tasks, and are made more difficult by the fact that it is quite common for membership on Finance or Investment Committees to rotate every few years. Trustees who assume the fiduciary responsibility for the management of an endowment or foundation need to have a clear understanding of what their responsibilities are, as well as what aspects of investment management are more appropriate to delegate to professional managers. There are probably something of the order of 250,000 individuals who find themselves serving on such committees, and perhaps as many as 50,000 are new to the task each year. These are typically people who have had success in business and professional careers, but may have had limited experience with the daunting challenge of successful investment management.

---

* TIAA-CREF provided a nationwide retirement program for US colleges & universities

When Chris Russell first spoke with me about writing this book two years ago I was very supportive, because I knew from experience how much it was needed. I have shared with him the insights I have gained from helping establish and manage the Commonfund programs, and working with hundreds of trustee groups for many years.

TRUSTEE INVESTMENT STRATEGY is a valuable resource and reference for all trustees of endowments and foundations. Chris Russell brings the knowledge and perspective gained from a successful career in professional investment management with the Robert Fleming group in London, and later in managing a large international investment program formed jointly by Flemings and T. Rowe Price in the US. His clients included a number of prominent endowments and foundations, and he has experience serving as director and trustee himself. He has done an outstanding job of distilling this knowledge and experience into a clear and comprehensive summary of the important principles and concepts that will help trustees discharge their responsibilities effectively, and avoid some of the mistakes that others have made. He has labored long and hard, and produced a valuable work that deserves to be on the bookshelf of every trustee who has fiduciary responsibility for the investment of endowment or foundation assets.

George F. Keane, University Park, Florida
President Emeritus, The Commonfund Group

Preface

Do what you will, the capital is at hazard. . . . All that can be required of a trustee to invest is that he shall conduct himself faithfully and exercise a sound discretion. He is to observe how men of prudence, discretion and intelligence manage their own affairs, not in regard to speculation, but in regard to the permanent disposition of their funds, considering the probable income, as well as the probable safety of the capital to be invested.

JUSTICE SAMUEL PUTNAM in the judgment in the administration of the estate of John McClean of Boston in 1830 and the origin of the 'Prudent Man Rule'.

This book is written for people who are responsible for the stewardship of endowment fund assets: trustees, governors or directors, members of a Committee, Board of Regents, Court or Council of any entity that has been given assets to generate a return to support some purpose. The entity may be a trust, a charity, a foundation or other 'not-for-profit' organization established to fulfill a need, educational, social or cultural, which is a fundamental motivation for giving. Those who have mastered the content of this book should be in a better position to satisfy the requirements of the law in respect of their responsibilities, including recognition of what can be spent and yet sustain an endowment, and better equipped to ask the key questions to help to make the right decisions.

The Uniform Management of Institutional Funds Act in the USA defines an endowment fund as 'an institutional fund, or any part thereof, which is held in perpetuity or for a term and which is not wholly expendable by the institution'. Implicit in the definition is the continued maintenance of all or a part of the endowment. In practice, a distinction is made between 'Foundations' and 'Endowments'. Foundations, whether private or community organizations, are endowed with a capital sum for a given purpose but typically have no other sources of income. 'Endowments' often receive periodic gifts and bequests and may have other sources of income. They are also treated differently for regulatory and tax purposes. In the USA there are many public supported colleges that have also created separate foundations.

The investment principles described in this book apply to all types and sizes of foundations and endowments, whether they are the largest charities or the smallest family trusts, whether the need is educational, social or cultural, or whether the time horizon is finite or perpetual. This book is about understanding, developing and implementing good policies and practices in investment strategy for endowment funds. Investment strategy is about selecting and combining classes of asset, investment themes and styles of management to create a portfolio that reliably generates spendable investment return to fund the objective of the endowment institution over the whole of its anticipated life. Strategy, however, involves more than simply combining the prospective return and risk of a number of asset classes. It must be integrated with spending rules, with other sources of income and with policy on non-financial issues such as socially responsible investing.

Spending rules are therefore an integral part of that overall strategy. The formula for spending cannot be divorced from the long-term return on the endowment. The amount that can safely be spent, as a proportion of the endowment, is often a misunderstood element of endowment fund policy. The legal requirement for foundations to spend at least 5% of their assets, irrespective of long cycles of inflation and deflation, could well lead, in any extended period of low inflation or, more especially, in a deflation environment, to the eventual demise of some foundations that were established to provide philanthropy in perpetuity. That could be a serious challenge for trustees of foundations and endowments.

Strategy is that part of the investment process that has the greatest impact on the financial risk and return. The focus of this book is therefore on the strategic decisions about which trustees should concern themselves rather than on security-specific questions that can sometimes take an inordinate and inappropriate amount of time at trustee meetings. Trustees have ultimate responsibility for endowment assets – a responsibility interpreted as a 'duty of undivided loyalty to the beneficiaries'. Trustees can also become personally liable for loss in respect of decisions made during their term of office, even after they have relinquished their role. In most US States, however, voluntary trustees are protected from civil liability other than gross negligence.

Trustees' responsibility was once interpreted as requiring them to choose specific investments, but today they can delegate the detailed portfolio management of their assets to professional managers. What cannot be delegated is trustees' ultimate responsibility for the assets under their stewardship. Trustees are required to exercise 'reasonable care, skill and caution' either in the management of assets or in the selection and monitoring of an agent who manages on their behalf. Monitoring means asking the right questions and making the right judgments. In a word it means governance, 'a hand on the tiller', in the original sense of the Latin word *guberno* 'I steer'.

Trustees are not expected to have the same degree of knowledge, skill and experience in investment as investment professionals, although as the financial world becomes ever more sophisticated there is increasing demand for professional training. In the UK 'non-professional' trustees of pension funds are already becoming required to be trained and this could begin to extend to endowments and foundations. In the USA, the Uniform Prudent Investors Act makes a clear distinction between amateur and professional trustees of non-institutional funds, placing a higher burden of responsibility on the latter.

This book therefore tries to bridge the comprehension gap, usually made wider by jargon and mathematics, between those who carry the ultimate responsibility for, and those who usually manage, the investments of endowment funds. In a famous UK legal case (Cowan v. Scargill 1984), Justice Megarry commented:

> The duty to seek advice on matters which the trustee does not understand, such as the making of investments, is not discharged merely by showing that the trustee has acted in good faith and with sincerity. Honesty and sincerity are not the same as prudence and reasonableness.

In other words, the trustee must exercise 'prudent and reasonable' judgment in interpreting the advice given by those who provide it.

Some trustees, especially those who have established foundations, may have strong views on investment strategy. They may be high-powered business leaders who have created their own wealth and established an endowment or foundation of which they may also be one of a number of trustees. Trustees who have donated funds and whose personal success is testimony to their financial ability and independent judgment may have more difficulty than most in accepting some of the advice of consultants and investment managers.

They may often be right. There is sometimes a presumption that experts are infallible and that their advice must be sought before due judgment can be made on almost any matter. This has, in some endowment funds, reached a point where independent decision-making has become frozen, especially where the inclination is to action that may run counter, or at least at a tangent, to professional advice.

We will see, when we touch on the subject of behavioral finance in Chapter 3 that professionals do not have a monopoly of wisdom and can be caught by herd mentality. Professionals cannot sometimes see the forest for the trees; they are too close to the 'noise' of markets, and can be carried along by the psychological certitude of persons rather than the logical certainty of propositions. Winston Churchill's description of an economist as 'someone who will explain tomorrow why the events he forecasted yesterday did not happen today' applies as well to asset managers.

That said, investment is always about an uncertain future. Judgment on the future can be a humbling experience for even the most experienced and successful, except perhaps for those armchair investors who possess that perfect insight of 20/20 hindsight. Many investment managers would subscribe to Tennyson's words: 'there lives more faith in honest doubt, believe me, than in half the creeds.' Investment is not about perfect foresight, which is given to none. It is about decisions that are intuitive and rational in the sense of sound judgment, not in the Keynes's sense of 'there's nothing so disastrous as a rational investment policy in an irrational world'.

Understanding is the key issue. It is a cardinal rule of investment that one should only invest in that which one understands, but understanding is different from simply having knowledge. It is the use of knowledge that is the whole issue, but this begs the question of what kind and what level of knowledge is needed in a world of financial concepts and products that daily becomes more sophisticated. This book is designed to help trustees to gain knowledge of the principles that lie behind these sophisticated concepts and products as they apply in the management of an endowment fund. Trustees do not have to be investment professionals to gain a sufficient level of understanding to be able to ask the right questions, even it is useful to have some investment professionals on the board or on an investment committee.

Understanding the investment principles on which strategy should be based is understanding principles that outlive investment fashions. Fashions change; human nature does not but the foibles of human nature are a prime short-term driver of deviation of market price from underlying value wherein lies potential for excess return. New investment technologies and vehicles emerge but the underlying principles remain obstinately the same. The pricing of futures and forward contracts in wool contracts in Europe in the fourteenth century demonstrated a level of financial understanding that had not yet begun to be quantified in mathematical theory, but the principles of time value of money and volatility were still understood even if they were not articulated.

Understanding the principles of investment is not reinventing them. As Sir Robert Megarry commented in his judgment in Cowan v. Scargill 1984:

> There are some who are temperamentally unsuited to being trustees, and are more fitted for campaigning for changes in the law. This, of course, they are free to do; but if they choose to become trustees they must accept that the rules of equity will bind them in all that they do as trustees.

Justice Megarry went on to say:

> If trustees make a decision upon wholly wrong grounds and yet it subsequently appears, from matters which they did not express or refer to, that there are in fact good and sufficient reasons for supporting their decision, then I do not think that they would incur any liability for having decided the matter on erroneous grounds, for the decision itself was right.

Herein lies one important aspect of understanding by trustees of their ultimate responsibility for investment decisions. In investment what is obviously right so often proves to be wrong and vice versa. It is an Alice-Through-The-Looking-Glass-World where everything is not always what it seems to be. Expectation is as important a factor as reality in determining investment returns. So this book is designed to help to give trustees confidence in recognizing the rules that should apply to investment decision-making, whatever the grounds on which the decision may be made.

A message from the teaching of art applies equally to investment: 'one must learn the rules before one can break them properly' – not 'learn the rules properly before one can break them' as is often misquoted and not, of course, rules as in regulation but in method. As in chess, it is strategy and an understanding of the rules – then 'breaking' properly the apparently established patterns of behavior – that can lead to success in achieving an objective. In investment such success then facilitates and enhances, by value creation, the prime underlying purpose of an endowment organization, but such moves generally need confidence in the manager and moral support from the trustees.

Alastair Ross Goobey, a Governor of the largest endowment in the UK, the Wellcome Trust, observes that trustees often wish for three mutually incompatible outcomes: (1) consistent outperformance of a benchmark index; (2) outperformance of a peer group; and (3) never lose money. In other words, the instruction to managers is to outperform the competition and an unmanaged index portfolio but do not take any risk. This is an impossible request. As we will see, the art of managing assets is not to avoid but to manage risk and to seek opportunities that may not even exist in a benchmark or peer group universe.

Therefore, trustees also need to understand the potential for thinking 'out of the box', as well as the practical parameters of investment: what is feasible and what is not and where it can, and will, go wrong. There is often an assumption that experts must always be right but much of investment is a moving target and moving in unpredictable timeframes. Even the finest investors can prove to be wrong over significant periods of time and they must be given leeway to prove their judgment over a sufficient period of time, especially in the case of an endowment that has the luxury of a perpetual time horizon.

One of the great investment books of all time, *The Intelligent Investor*,[1] shows in the appendices the investment records of a number of the most successful investment managers of the 1950s to 1980s. They all have periods, sometimes up to four years running, of substantial underperformance of benchmark indices against which their results are compared. But in every case the long-term record of wealth creation is outstandingly higher than what would have been achieved by investing in an index rather than their actively managed portfolio. These are classic examples of how a mindset of rewarding short-term performance and punishing failure would have had the opposite effect to the one required. They are examples of the power of compounding high rates of return over longer time periods and they are proof of one of the messages of this book – that is, conventional approaches to benchmarks and measurement may not achieve the desired result.

Another message of the investment records of some of the great investors of the twentieth century was that the returns were achieved without fear of occasional loss. One of the greatest challenges for trustees is to avoid the mentality of hoarding cash, not required for operations, in order to avoid any sense of failure of financial duty. We will see that an overcommitment to cash is one of the sources of failure of an endowment to sustain itself in the long term. Overexposure to cash, and overdistribution of return, are the two main contributory factors to the long-term diminution in the power of an endowment to sustain, and even more to enhance, itself over time.

Good investment performance requires patience, and time is one of the great assets that most endowments enjoy. Too often, however, trustees feel goaded into making decisions over time horizons that are not appropriate. How often have trustees sacked managers at the bottom of a cycle, reinvested in last year's winner and compounded the error when last year's lion becomes this year's dog? Better a live dog than a dead lion.

The aim of this book is not only to provide a bridge between trustee and professional manager but also to bridge the gap between trustees of an organization today and between those of today and the same organization in the future. An endowment may have an investment time horizon of several generations, even if trustees may only serve for a three-year term. Investment managers may last longer in their position than the trustees who appointed them. Yale Professor Emeritus James Tobin described endowment stewardship in the following terms: 'trustees of an endowed institution are the guardians of the future against the claims of the present. Their task is to preserve equity among generations.'[2]

Professor Tobin was describing generations of beneficiaries but this also applies to generations of trustees. The trustees or their advisers may feel a need to 'make a difference' during their occupation of the role, but so often in investment management the right decision is to do nothing. Doing nothing constructively, with knowledge and understanding, can be as important as doing something. The advice should sometimes be: lie down until the feeling for action goes away.

The understanding of investment principles by trustees does not need familiarity with jargon or ability to conceptualize through the mathematical equations that may grace the pages of professional investment journals. Most people see and make practical judgments without precise quantification. Every spectrum of light within a rainbow is measurable in ångström units, but it is sufficient for most practical purposes, even if only for searching for the elusive pots of gold, to detect them by eye and describe the gradations of color.

So it is with investment. Where jargon or mathematical explanation is alluded to in this book, a fuller explanation can be found in the glossary of investment terms toward the end of the book. The glossary could prove to be a useful *aide-mémoire* for trustee investment meetings. Sensible investment is not rocket science even if some of the investment products are designed by rocket scientists. And even the rocket scientists can get it wrong. One of the most spectacular financial crashes in the last decade of the twentieth century was an investment entity, called Long Term Capital Management, created by investment professionals, which numbered among their executives some Nobel prize-winners in the field of finance. Trustees should not be overawed by the jargon of investment professionals. They must engage in debate with the confidence of understanding the fundamentals behind the jargon even if they cannot quite remember the technical words that describe the situation.

Through not being in the day-to-day mêlée of financial market activity, trustees are well placed to question the direction in which the advisers wish to take the endowment fund. Developing a sense of what determines the future in investment risk and return, and developing a confidence to back an unconventional view, is 'learning the rules', is being on the road to investment enlightenment, to becoming a proper guardian of the future and not just an agent of corporate governance. The goal of this enlightenment is enhanced resources to meet ever-present needs and the potential for enhanced practical benevolence in future.

It is therefore hoped that this book will help to demystify the investment experience and give trustees more confidence in asking professional advisers to justify their positions; to test the judgments of professionals for consistency of argument; to understand where the professionals may have failed in their homework or their performance and why; to understand the unpredictability of markets; to encourage calculated risk by taking a mature view of inevitable, if hopefully only occasional, failure. But even failure is a prerequisite for ensuring ultimate success in managing money. Piet Hein's 'Grook' on life applies also to investment: 'The road to wisdom? Well it's plain and simple to express: err, and err again; but less and less and less.'

Acknowledgments

If I have seen further... it is by standing upon the shoulders of Giants.

ISAAC NEWTON (1642–1727). Letter to Robert Hooke. 5 February 1676

The author has certainly seen no further than other investment professionals, even if he has been looking for over 30 years. But he has had the enormous privilege, during a life in the investment business, of meeting, working with and reading the wisdom of various giants of the profession.

A proverb may be 'the wisdom of many and the wit of one' but so is a book such as this which draws shamelessly on the wealth of knowledge and experience of many giants in the world of investment. They have generously shared their experience and their ideas through publications, lectures and private conversation.

Due acknowledgment is therefore made throughout this book, together with specific references to further recommended reading on various topics. Profound apologies to any who may have been responsible for impressions that have formed judgments that are part of the book but who have not been remembered, and to any others who may have made an unacknowledged contribution, either directly or indirectly.

First and foremost, George Keane has helped generously with his knowledge of the history and development of US endowment investment, having made some of that history in the founding of the Commonfund. He has kindly written the foreword to this book and has helped with advice and comment on the book's various drafts. He has also assisted with introductions to others in the endowment field.

Tom Ingram, Stephen Watson and Andrew Fleming have also helped by constructive comments on a draft of the book. Charles Gave has inspired some of the thinking behind this book over many years with perceptive comment on economies and financial markets. Louis Gave is taking on Charles's mantle and has kindly helped by providing thoughts and charts with the help of Pierre Gave.

Hugh Acland contributed to the construction of the glossary; and Rodney Marian-Green and Tony Golding gave some helpful early advice. In the US endowment and foundation fund field those who have especially assisted, through interview mainly, include Rick Legon of the Association of Governing Boards of Universities and Colleges (AGB); Verne Sedlacek of the Commonfund; Wayne Pearson of the Meyer Memorial Trust; Dr Allan Bufferd of MIT; Jay Morley and Bill Dillon of the National Association of College and University Business

Officers (NACUBO); Harry Turner of Park Street Capital; and Keith Ferguson, Susan Ball and Garth Reistad of the University of Washington. Those in the UK who commented at an early stage on the proposed framework of the book included Professor Robert Mair, Master of Jesus College, Cambridge, and Charles Nunneley, formerly Chairman of the National Trust. Helpful comment also came from Alastair Ross Goobey, a Governor of the Wellcome Trust Ross Goobey and Adviser to Morgan Stanley.

The New York Public Library, the libraries of the Institute of Chartered Accountants in England and Wales and the Royal Society of Arts have all provided practical assistance in various ways. Meanwhile the internet remains a wonderful source of material that has all been acknowledged in the text and is a medium through which to buy the book and contact the author: www.tisef.com.

Last, but far from least, must be acknowledgment of the unseen contribution of tolerance and support for this project from my wife, Tory, and my four children, Emy, John, Kate and Alice.

1

Introduction

An investment in knowledge always pays the best interest.

BENJAMIN FRANKLIN (1706–1790)

Endowments and foundations are entities that have been given assets to generate a return to support some purpose. Each endowment entity is unique in terms of its needs and financial resources, which implies that each endowment must have a unique investment strategy.

The largest pools of non-profit endowment assets today are to be found in the USA, representing educational, social, cultural, political and religious organizations such as museums, hospitals, orchestras, religious, universities and colleges and charities. The Giving USA Foundation estimates that Americans gave some $248.5 billion to charity in 2004, an amount approximately equal to the national incomes of Norway or Indonesia. The largest foundation was that of Bill and Melinda Gates with assets at the end of 2004 just short of $29 billion. The largest financial endowment of any academic institution was that of Harvard, which was nearly $23 billion at the end of the fiscal year 2004. As long ago as the early 1930s the annual income from philanthropy in the USA was only exceeded by the incomes of the US and UK governments. Endowed assets in the USA at that time exceeded the estimated wealth of many nations.[1]

US endowment funds as a whole may not have been the first to exist but, apart from being the largest in the world, they are the most advanced in their investment thinking. This is probably due to the twentieth-century emergence of pension, insurance and mutual funds which all led to the demand for an intellectual foundation for good policies and practices.

Some of the oldest endowments can be found in Europe. Among the earliest examples was the gifting of agricultural land to the Church so that the income from tithes (a tax levied in kind of one-tenth of the annual produce of the land) and from rents and the sale or barter of produce would help to support the institution. Later examples include the medieval trade and craft guilds, called Livery Companies, of the City of London. They still exist today and some have their origins in the eleventh century. Other examples are the early universities and colleges, a number of which were started by the Church or were established following the dissolution of the monasteries in the sixteenth century when the tithe passed from ecclesiastic to lay hands. Yet others include the philanthropic, cultural and charitable organizations created out of the industrial wealth of the eighteenth and nineteenth centuries.

The largest endowment in the UK is the Wellcome Trust with assets of approximately $18 billion. The Trust was created in 1936 by the Will of Sir Henry Wellcome in which the entire share capital of his pharmaceutical company, The Wellcome Foundation Ltd, was vested in trustees (now known as Governors) to distribute the income principally to support 'scientific research which may conduce to the improvement of the physical conditions of mankind'. The shares were sold in tranches over the 1980s and 1990s to diversify the asset base of what is now the largest endowed medical research charity in the world.

What is particularly notable about the oldest endowments in the UK is that few if any seem to have grown to a size that might have been expected given their long history and the power of compounding money over long periods of time. This is probably due to return being essentially in the form of income and all income being spent. The trade-off between current spending and the growth of an endowment, and therefore of the ability to grow spending power in the future, is one of the key factors in developing investment strategy. This is a message for trustees today and for governments if they wish for more of the burden of supporting need in society to be carried by philanthropic organizations.

1.1   ENDOWMENT FUND CHARACTERISTICS

Endowments may be 'True Endowments' (USA) or 'Permanent Endowments' (UK), where the trustees have no power to invade principal. They may be 'Quasi-Endowments' (USA) or 'Expendable Endowments' (UK), where they may make that conversion, albeit in the UK subject to certain constraints. A 'Term Endowment' is designed to expend capital over some period and therefore is not designed to exist in perpetuity.

Endowments are about claims on the future as much as the present. Whatever the underlying motivation for endowing a charity, trust or foundation, the main purpose of providing a lump sum of capital is to provide a return for supporting the activities for which the endowment was established, as defined in its constitution, and to ensure continuity in the activities of that entity over its anticipated life, whether or not that is very long term.

One characteristic of endowed entities, therefore, is their dependence on investment return, both to finance their current consumption and to maintain, or even improve, their asset base for the future. While pension funds can fall back on their sponsoring operating companies to fund them if returns are insufficient to meet their liabilities, and insurance companies can raise new money from shareholders, some endowments such as foundations do not have the luxury of alternative sources of funds. As Charles D. Ellis has written[2]: 'most of the world's great educational and cultural institutions – universities, colleges, libraries, museums and foundations – depend, to varying degrees, on their endowments and the spendable funds they produce.'

While endowments share investment characteristics with some other long-term funds, they are also different from them in another respect. Most endowments are established in perpetuity. Few other types of fund have an infinite investment time horizon and most other funds have constraints either through profit motive or through different regulations. Such funds do not therefore form a part of the consideration of this book even though most of the investment principles generally apply.

Some endowed organizations, such as most foundations, have no income other than that from investment. Most others have additional sources of finance, such as donations, subscriptions, legacies, fund-raising events, trading activities and fee income that may partially cover immediate consumption or be donated to capital. For instance, a university may rely for the majority of its operation on tuition and other fees. The endowed assets may simply provide a subsidy to those fees such as for specific scholarships to qualifying individuals to support eminent scholars or to fund research. Where an endowed institution has other income, this will be an integral part of investment strategy.

Organizations that may spend all or nearly all of their other income as it arises must still develop a strategy for investment of funds. But the strategy will depend on the role the endowment plays in the organization. If there is little income to fund an endowment's mission other than the investment return on the endowed assets themselves, there is a simple trade-off.

That trade-off is between providing a more or less predictable level of shorter term realizable investment return to fund current expenses against a higher but more variable endowment value as a legacy for the future.

The future legacy is known as 'intergenerational equity'. This phrase implies an endowment maintained for future generations sufficient to allow a level of well-being no less than that of the current generation. In the endowment world, intergenerational equity means preserving the capital required to maintain, in real terms, the mission of the endowment.

What is the right balance between current and future demands? The trustees must make that judgment if it is not already mandated in the endowment's constitution. But they must make it knowledgably. That means understanding what any decision to spend now really means for growth of ability to spend in the future, and the implications in terms of the endowment's fundamental objectives.

The following financial formula, where the numbers are all expressed as a percentage of endowed assets at the beginning of the period, is a key message of this book. The formula says that the total return on the endowment over time must equal or exceed both the spending rate and inflation if it has no other income. If the endowment return exceeds the spending rate and inflation over time, then it will grow in real terms and so will spending:

$$Investment\ return + Other\ income = Spending\ rate + Fund\ growth$$

We will call this Micawber's Rule, reflecting the Dickensian quotation at the beginning of Chapter 5 entitled 'Spending Rules', and we will see in that chapter that investment strategy is not just about creating investment return, the first term of the formula. All four terms of the formula are interrelated. If other income is zero, if investment return is 8% per annum and if 5% of the endowment is spent each year, then the endowment fund, and the spending growth, will automatically grow each year by 3%.

If 7% of the endowment's 8% return is spent each year, then the growth of the fund, and therefore the growth of spending in future, will be only 1% per annum. However, given the same numbers and inflation at 3%, an 8% per annum nominal return is only 5% real (inflation adjusted). If 6% per annum of the endowment is spent, the fund, and future spending, will grow by 2% per annum in nominal terms. In real terms, however, fund growth and spending must by definition decline by 1% per annum.

Investment strategy cannot therefore be decided independently of other factors and we will look more closely at this equation in Chapter 5. We will see that the formula helps to discipline spending and decisions on the balance between current spend and intergenerational equity.

While the four components of Micawber's Rule may be inextricably linked, in many endowments the four elements are considered separately. In larger endowments the elements may each be represented by different committees, such as investment, finance, fund-raising, budget and charitable committees. The maths, however, is such that the outcome of (and input to) each committee must be consistent. The two sides of Micawber's Rule must be equal. If nothing changes on the left of the equation (income and financial return) and current spending rises, future growth (of both endowment and spending) must inevitably fall. If current spending as a percentage falls with no change in the return or other income, future growth must rise. Determining the balance is the responsibility of the governing body.

Endowments are therefore different from other long-term funds. Other funds generally have finite lives and have behind them a 'lender of last resort'. Endowments generally have infinite time horizons and depend to a greater or lesser degrees on the investment return generated by a fund of assets; they may or may not have other sources of income.

Endowments as considered here are not-for-profit entities. Pension funds are part of a profit-generating environment that has a different priority and creates other specific issues, especially of a regulatory nature. The same applies to insurance companies that can ultimately fall back on shareholders for funding. Not-for-profit endowments do not have any financial conflicts between either the benefactor or the beneficiary. Pension funds and insurance companies, other than mutual insurance companies, are funded by shareholders to meet contractual and regulatory requirements. Shareholders are subject to profit and loss considerations at the possible expense of beneficiaries and vice versa.

Another sense in which endowments are different is in respect of intergenerational equity issues. There is a special tension between meeting today's needs and providing benefits for a perpetual future. This tension, between current spending and maintenance of funds for the future, is greater when the policy of the endowment is not restricted simply to spending the income but making available for consumption the total return of the fund. Many trustee bodies, not unnaturally, tend to focus more on the needs of today rather than the distant future of the next generation. But, in the words of David Salem, trustees must 'delicately balance the concrete and often very vocal demands of current stakeholders against the amorphous and very silent demands of future stakeholders'.

A long-term perspective can provide opportunity to an endowment that other institutions cannot even contemplate. Endowments should be the last institutions to suffer from the timing pressures generated by short-term investment performance. If they do suffer, then investment and spending strategies have not been properly integrated.

1.2   CONSTRAINTS ON ENDOWMENTS

The tax and regulation surrounding endowments, touched on in Chapter 7, 'Legal, Social and Ethical', are one area of potential or actual constraint. In the USA, for instance, the Internal Revenue Service requires foundations to spend 5% per annum of their asset base in order to maintain their charitable status. Charities in the UK are subject to the Trustee Investment Act and the rules of the Charity Commissioners. As far as tax is concerned, UK charities are generally exempt from tax but there are important tax considerations in the structuring of the endowment from the point of view of cost recovery and trading activities.

While endowment funds are different in a general sense from most other long-term funds, they are also different in a specific sense: each is constrained by its own particular purpose and needs. In the UK, the landmark law of the Trustee Act 1925 provides that trustees have an absolute duty to carry out specifically the terms of their trust. The same applies in the USA. Committing or allowing breach of that trust could leave trustees personally liable. The investment strategy of each endowment will therefore be unique where the needs are uniquely different from that of others. This has important implications for performance assessment and benchmarking, as we will investigate later.

Each endowment has its own quantum and type of resources that may, in turn, be covenanted to be consumed in a way that is defined by its constitution. In the case of Yale University,[3] for instance, some four-fifths of its funds constitute true endowments where donors have specified the objectives: 23% of donors have specified that their gift is to be used for professorships, teaching and lecturing; 18% for scholarships, fellowships and prizes; 4% for maintenance; 3% for books; and 31% for various other specified purposes. Only 21% of the donations are unrestricted.

These differences of purpose are reflected in different patterns of expenditure. An endowment designed to fund long-term research will have a different pattern of expense from an endowment established to provide scholarships. Equally, the constraint may be in the form of restriction of sale of the asset donated, not constriction of the purpose. An endowment that has been funded with cash to be invested with no restraint on consumption of income or capital, or on the asset classes in which funds may be invested, will be different from an endowment that has, as its principal asset, illiquid real estate. Apart from its unmarketability, real estate can be left to an endowment constrained by a term of the bequest that the real estate should not be sold.

The starting point for the investment and consumption of the resources of any endowment must be the governing document, or constitution, that defines its purpose and initial funding. This governing document may be a trust deed; a letter of wishes; the memorandum and articles of a company; the minutes of a meeting; the mission statement of a benefactor. Once the characteristics, aims, objectives and restrictions of an endowment are clearly defined, then, and only then, can an investment objective and a subsequent investment strategy be framed properly and resources spent wisely.

That is the point at which the interplay between constitution and investment strategy becomes iterative. An entity can only consume, now or in the future, what its resources can in reality provide. Expectations must therefore be tailored to reality. When markets have provided many years of double digit returns, trustees have been known to believe that this is sustainable indefinitely and change policy just at the moment when valuations revert to a lower mean. A classic example is a period of secular disinflation when a Government bond of long maturity offers a guaranteed future nominal income yield of, say, 4%, having fallen in yield to that figure from double figures and having thereby provided a historic double figure rate of total return.

The other side of the iterative process is the constant assessment of expected returns, and the way in which that return may be delivered. This involves the tailoring of asset structures to endowment needs as much as the tailoring of expectation to investment reality. For example, if an endowment is established to provide scholarships annually, then an investment and consumption strategy should be framed to provide funds annually that rise in value with the increase in academic fees, not just the general rate of inflation. Too many scholarships awarded now means fewer in the future.

But what constitutes too many now? Is 'too many' a short-term judgment, because of volatility of markets, or a longer term one, because of permanent diminution in wealth? And if those scholarships are funded by an institution in one country to provide places at universities in another, then the trustees must take this into account subject to any conditions in the constitution. The mission of one foundation in Hong Kong, for instance, is to provide scholarships for local students to go to universities all over the world. The trustees of this institution therefore define their strategy in terms of the currency in which the scholarship is consumed, not in terms of the currency in which the endowment is provided. The mission sets the currency and the type of asset class of investment.

Trustees can only invest endowment assets within the scope of the governing document otherwise they may be liable for losses. If there is no governing document, or the document is silent on investment, then, in the UK at least, the trustees automatically have a general power of investment into any kind of investment, excluding land. This general power, which is in addition to other powers expressly given in the governing document or given by statute, is defined in the UK by the Trustee Act 2000. This act also defines a general duty of care of investment by trustees. In the USA, trustees have broad latitude in selecting investments provided prudence is used.

The social objective of the endowment will rarely be defined in financial terms so it will be the duty of the trustees to translate the social objective into a financial one. This means a financial plan. This in turn means costing the objective: how much does it cost to run an orchestra or to send students to university? How much will or can the endowment provide toward meeting a sum of money? Such a plan needs a vision beyond the immediate future and some definition of continuing real or nominal liabilities. The plan must define a working operational and intergenerational framework.

The resources of the fund determine the ability to meet the need. Does the endowment have one fund generating all the return that drives the activities? Or are most of the activities funded by new money inflows and the fund is merely a back-stop reserve? The answers to these sorts of question have an impact on the allowable percentage of consumption to return on assets over any significant period of time. But it also begs the question of the nature of total return itself. It is not only the level of the return over time (in real terms) but it is also the pattern that matters, especially given some trade-off between level and volatility of return.

The extent to which the objectives can be achieved will of course be a function of the return on the endowment. But the future return will be partly dependent on the growth of the endowment. As Micawber's Rule shows, the growth (of the endowment and equally therefore of the ability to spend) will be the rate of investment return less the rate of the spend, both expressed as a percentage of the value of the fund. So before we can begin to look at endowment strategy we must look in turn at return on investment, then at risk – which is indissolubly linked to return – and to spending policy. Only then can we begin to understand the principles of strategy and only subsequently be in a reasonable position to implement.

1.3   HISTORY RHYMES

Dionysius of Halicarnassus said 'history is philosophy teaching by examples'. He may not have had investment philosophy in mind when he wrote those words in the first century BC but past experience forms the bedrock of investment as well as others beliefs. Investment philosophy is as fundamental to what drives investment management as vision and mission is to the purpose of an endowment.

Lived examples together represent experience. The experience of some of the older endowments proves the message that 'history may not repeat itself but it rhymes'. Human nature may itself be a constant but the behavior that arises from it seems almost predictably cyclical. An understanding of the past may at least help to alleviate the behavioral tendency to repeat past errors and to avoid the cardinal sin of compounding them.

Early endowments in the UK were in the form of land rather than money so the activities of the endowment were simply financed by rents or tithes, which was a form of tax in kind. In many cases these tithes moved from ecclesiastic to lay hands with the dissolution of the monasteries. In 1836, tithes were commuted for a rentcharge that was based on an index of the price of wheat, barley and oats averaged over the previous seven years. From endowment of land grew a tradition – which was embedded in laws and lasted until the second half of twentieth century – that income was for spending and capital was for preserving the purpose of the endowment. Common stocks and other forms of investment, particularly mortgages and bonds, did not form a significant part of endowment fund portfolios until the twentieth century.

In the first half of the twentieth century one of the leading economists of the period provided evidence to a Royal Commission on Tithe Rentcharge in his capacity as Bursar of King's College, Cambridge. The economist was John Maynard Keynes who managed to make, and to lose through leverage – then to make again in larger size and grow over subsequent years – a personal fortune from his investment activities. But his skills as an investor touched the fortunes of King's College, Cambridge, and of Eton College, Windsor. Keynes was bursar of King's between the 1920s and 1940s. The least constricted of the funds he managed at King's was the Chest Fund. This fund grew a remarkable 11-fold under his stewardship between 1920 and 1945 – a period over which the London Industrial Share Index rose 60% and the US Standard & Poor's index rose 90%.

Keynes first became involved with the financial affairs of King's College, Cambridge, after his election as a Fellow in 1909 when he became an Inspector of Accounts. His influence really began to be felt after his appointment as Second Bursar in 1919 and then First Bursar in 1924 until his death after the Second World War.

Through both his involvement with an insurance company, and as bursar of a Cambridge College, Keynes was responsible for a significant commitment by those long-term institutions to equities, rather than just bonds and real estate, long before this became common practice in the UK. Equities were simply regarded as too risky but Keynes also invested in commodities as well as currencies. There was one famous occasion with an investment in wheat on behalf of King's College in 1936 when he was about to take delivery of one month's supply for the whole of the UK. He estimated the cubic capacity of King's College Chapel and found it was too small!

Keynes's credo was to commit funds in a large way to those investments he knew about rather than to diversify across a multiplicity of investments he did not follow closely. He referred to the latter as 'carrying eggs in a great number of baskets without having time to discover how many have holes in the bottom'. He believed 'a speculator is one who runs risks of which he is aware and an investor is one who runs risks of which he is unaware.'[4]

Keynes also argued that 'the object of an investment policy is averaging through time' compared to an insurance policy that is 'doing that a little bit but on the whole is averaging of a number of items which are in the same position in time but in different positions in place'. And his concern was to avoid 'stumers ... I mean by this definite mistakes where the fall in value is due not merely to valuations but to an intrinsic loss of capital.'[5]

In a post mortem on investment in 1938[6] Keynes wrote that successful investment depended on three principles:

1. A careful selection of a few investments based on actual and potential intrinsic value in relation to alternative investments;
2. Holding them in fairly large units through thick and thin until they have fulfilled their promise or their purchase has proved to be a mistake;
3. A balanced investment position, i.e. a variety of risks and if possible opposed risks (e.g. a holding of gold shares among other equities since they are likely to move in opposite directions when there are general fluctuations).

He also commented in the post mortem that it was:

a mistake to sell a £1 note for 15 shillings in the hope of buying it back at 12 shillings and sixpence and a mistake to refuse to buy a £1 note for 15 shillings on the grounds that it cannot really be a £1 note (for there is abundant experience that £1 notes can be bought for 15 shillings at a time when they are expected by many people to fall to 12 shillings and sixpence).

Keynes's investment philosophy was to exploit relative value – a message that coincided with that of Benjamin Graham in the USA. Benjamin Graham is one of the icons of investment management, having co-authored in 1934 with David Dodd the classic book on value investing,

Security Analysis. He then published in 1949 *The Intelligent Investor*, which is described by Warren Buffet as by far the best book on investing ever written.

Keynes also pre-empted the key message of portfolio diversification formalized in modern portfolio theory. He stated that optimal diversification is achieved not simply by averaging risk across many numbers but by combining securities that are not correlated with each other. Keynes's investment philosophy of seeking relative value, of diversification by non-correlation of risk and of averaging risk over time all permeate our thinking on investment strategy in this book.

1.4   THE US ENDOWMENT EXPERIENCE

A study in 1932[7] of the endowment assets of the 30 leading universities and colleges, with reported endowed assets amounting to 74% of those of all institutions of higher education with assets more than $5 million, was illuminating. It was published three years into one of the worst bear markets in history, during which common stocks had fallen 75% from their highs. It was a period over which endowments 'suffered so severely as to be forced to reduce their teaching staffs, to lower salaries, to discontinue various courses, to close buildings and to curtail activities to a degree which threatens to minimize their efficiency in the field of higher education'.

Of the aggregated portfolios, bonds and preferred stocks were 58% of assets, real estate mortgages 13.5%, directly owned real estate 13.1% and common stocks 10%. Mortgages were not marketable but were regarded as secure streams of income. Agricultural real estate was considered speculative and the whole focus of strategy was on improving the quality and level of income yield and extending duration. Endowments lived off income. Capital preservation was sacrosanct but Government bonds yielded little, the value to endowments of their marketability was limited and the price paid for high security and high liquidity was considered 'a needless sacrifice of income'. They were worth more to other investors with liquidity needs.

Despite the investment conditions at the time, the particular nature of endowments was recognized as being different from other long-term funds, such as insurance companies. It was understood that the endowment income must be related:

> to the uses to which it necessarily is put . . . this obviously suggests that certain investment media, such as selected common stocks in ably managed, essential companies, which become more productive in periods of rising prices, have their place among university investments alongside of the traditional bonds and mortgages.[8]

Endowments still had to contend with the same issues as Keynes in allocating funds between asset classes, even if the focus was primarily on analysing and selecting fixed income assets by type, duration and level of security. Yale University acknowledged the difficulties of tactical asset allocation and thought it had an answer to the problem of sustaining and then growing the income that provided a large percentage of the total needed to operate the institution in the 1930s.

The 'Yale Plan', as it was known, created a long-term strategic benchmark allocation, and when markets took the asset values outside a range around that allocation, simply rebalanced the fund, subtracting from equities and adding to bonds when the equity percentage rose beyond a given percentage and vice versa. This was a formula for naturally selling a rising asset value into one that had fallen and worked perfectly for a while when markets see-sawed around a mean level. However, during the 1940s and 1950s Yale continually rebalanced in favor of fixed income that continued to lose real value. This is one of the issues of a 'regression to the mean' policy in terms of market values or returns in a trend-change environment. As we will see, there is another regression to the mean policy of rebalancing assets that is based on relationships rather than fixed values and provides a more effective way of managing strategy.

A shift back to equity, and a growth stock era, led to a change in view away from a centuries old concept that only income is consumable. A Ford Foundation report in 1962[9] acknowledged that 'The Foundation has not only expended all of its income but has invaded its capital . . .'. The report added: 'The Trustees are prepared to continue invading capital, as necessary, to respond to opportunities for making advances on the vital problems of the period ahead.' The policy was to continue to reduce the reliance on Ford Motor Company stock and not to be governed in grant-making by 'short-term increases or decreases in its capital or income'.

The Ford Foundation, established in Detroit in 1936 and subsequently increased substantially in size by bequests from the estates of Henry Ford and Edsel Ford, played a major role in the late 1960s in raising the level of sophistication of endowment management with attention on the funding and financial management of higher education. McGeorge Bundy, who had been a star figure in the Kennedy administration, became head of the Foundation in 1966 at a time when few colleges had professional managers of money. Prompted by George Keane and Bill Greenough of TIAA–CREF, the Foundation commissioned a report that was published in 1968 entitled *The Law and Lore of Endowments*. A second study entitled *Managing Educational Endowments* was completed a year later.

The second study concluded that the focus of endowment investing should be on total return and not on income yield, as had been the tradition of endowment investment based on accounting practice and the continuing need for realized cash flow to fund activities. The 20 years following the end of the Second World War had seen the combination in equity markets of growth in earnings and dividends. Low interest rates both enhanced return on risk capital and helped to translate that earnings growth into capital gain because low interest rates ensured a higher present value of growth. The new focus on total return had a dramatic effect on investment strategy thereafter to the present day. Total return investment underlies thinking on financial return, on risk assessment and on spending rules.

The publication of the Ford Foundation studies and the establishment of The Common Fund for Non-profit Organizations influenced the development of a new law in the United States known as the Uniform Management of Institutional Funds Act (UMIFA). This was first proposed by the National Commission on Uniform State Laws and subsequently adopted by most state legislatures. Following on a lead by Yale, this officially sanctioned the 'total return' concept and authorized spending of a 'reasonable portion' of an endowment fund. It essentially ended the time-honored practice of spending only dividends and interest without spending the corpus or principal of the endowment.

The Ford Foundation also supported the establishment of what is now known as Commonfund (formerly the Common Fund for Non-profit Organizations), an initiative that has grown into one of the most successful specialist investment management operations in the USA, providing a broad range of advice and investment capability to educational endowments and other non-profits in the USA. The Commonfund was established to provide a safe and professional way for colleges to invest through a pooled process. There were some 2,000 colleges and about 1,500 community colleges in 1971 but only some 600 had significant endowments.

The Ford Foundation agreed to pay $2.1 million toward operating costs for the first three years of the Commonfund's life, including an additional $500,000 grant to support research. TIAA–CREF, the nationwide pension system for higher education institutions, offered space for the first board of 10 trustees to meet. The trustees were selected by Bill Greenhough, Chairman and CEO of TIAA–CREF, on criteria that included representation by size and by geographic location of potential contributory endowments.

George Keane, who helped to conceive the idea of a cooperative professional investment management program during his 10 years as an officer of TIAA–CREF, was chosen to run the Commonfund as its founding President. He opened an office in New York on January 1, 1971.

During 1970 the Board of Trustees conducted extensive analysis of equity strategies and managers and on July 1, 1971, the Commonfund established an equity fund to invest across a spectrum of large and small capitalization, value and growth, using specialist managers for each category. Diversifying the equity portfolio across a range of styles and managers was revolutionary at the time, especially because one style, growth stocks, had performed so well since 1945. In due course this approach became broadly accepted by nearly all such institutions to great beneficial effect on their investment returns.

Once the Equity Fund was established, George Keane also realized that many colleges had money from tuition fees that was being held in checking accounts that earned no interest. So in 1972 the board approved a research study that recommended the creation of a short duration cash/bond fund to offer to colleges for the management of their operating funds. The board was reluctant to begin a second fund until the IRS were prepared to issue a tax exemption on these funds. Tax exemption was granted in mid-1974 and the second fund was launched in October 1974. The fund was managed by Fisher, Francis, Trees & Watts (FFTW), a start-up firm that had worked with George Keane on the project.

The formula for this 'cash plus' fund, which has consistently provided higher returns than cash on deposit for the past 30 years since inception, was to credit participating colleges monthly with the current yield on 90-day Treasury Bills but to invest in varying durations depending on the outlook for interest rates. At the end of each quarter the total return on the fund would be assessed and half of any excess return would be credited to the colleges and half to reserves. If interest rates rose, then funds would be extracted from reserves.

The Commonfund's short-term fund was a novel concept for education. It smoothed the volatility of return over time and was the first commingled approach to providing a general operating reserve asset class for educational institutions. It was the first time a vehicle for raising return on cash became available to such institutions and has grown to become the largest of the many investment programs provided today by the Commonfund Group.

Although the Commonfund struggled during the difficult stock market in the first half of the 1970s, by the time it reached its tenth anniversary in mid-1981 it had clearly demonstrated the advantage of diversified professional investment management. By the late 1980s the Commonfund was receiving $1 billion a year in new money from endowments. Membership grew from 200 to more than 1,000 institutions during the 1980s and assets rose from $500 million to $10 billion. Additional investment programs were added for bonds, international equities and private capital market investments. Today the number of non-profit investors exceeds 1,600 institutions, and assets under Common Fund management total more than $35 billion.

The Commonfund established a sister organization in Canada and the success of the Commonfund has inspired other similar organizations that were started for particular types of endowment. For example, the Christian Brothers Investment Fund was started as a program for religious organizations. The CIO of this entity was Frank Haines who had worked for George Keane. Another fund was started specifically for hospitals and is now run by the Commonfund.

The Investment Fund for Foundations (TIFF) was created to serve the large and growing number of charitable foundations in the USA.

Harvard University, by contrast to Yale, had made a major and unprecedented move from fixed income assets to common stocks in the mid to late 1940s. Harvard's endowment had traditionally been managed by State Street Investment Management (not to be confused with the trust bank), an officer of which was Paul Cabot who had served as Treasurer of Harvard.

George Putnam, who succeeded Paul Cabot in 1974, decided that the management at Harvard should change, and that Harvard was large enough to have its own manager. The Harvard Management Company (HMC) was therefore established in 1974. Putnam's original concept was to employ a diversified group of managers for a portion of the endowment fund, along similar lines to the Commonfund, but to manage the bulk of the funds with an internal staff. Outsourcing fund management proved not to be successful and Harvard decided to bring most of its investment management in-house.

Jack Meyer, who came in to head up the Harvard Management Company in 1990 introduced the 'policy portfolio' concept into the management of the endowment.[10] Meyer was skeptical of managers' ability to time market moves, although he allowed some deviation of weight from the neutral policy portfolio in anticipation of short-term market moves. The main thrust of the investment strategy, however, was to add value from mispricing within each of the asset classes that comprised an overall diversified portfolio. While identification of this mispricing had been mostly in-house under Putnam, and in the early 1990s only 15% of the assets was being managed externally, by the year 2000 external management had increased to 35%. Most of this allocation was to real estate, private equity and timberland.

In 1967, Yale had also been one of the first institutions to adopt the concept of 'total return'. This policy went hand-in-hand with a change in their spending policy. Until that time the Endowment's contribution to the operating budget of the university was simply the income yield from dividends, interest and rents. Yale realized, however, that this policy could result in a bias in investment strategy toward yield at the expense of growth – a bias that was expensive in total return terms for much of the 1950s and 1960s when growth stocks outperformed value. In the latter part of the 1980s, Yale also adopted, under the leadership of David Swensen, an unconventional approach to asset management with considerable success. The approach was based on absolute return with a heavy commitment to 'alternative assets' such as hedge funds and private equity.

By June 2004,[11] only 7.4% of the Yale endowment was in fixed income and the balance in equity-type assets. Of the 92.6% in equity-type assets, however, only 14.8% was in domestic-listed equity. This compared with over a third in domestic equity with many other educational institutions in 2004 and over three-quarters of Yale's own portfolio in US stocks, bonds and cash only 20 years before. The rest of the 92.6% comprised private equity, international equities, real estate, other real assets such as timberland and oil and gas.

The Ford Foundation's Report, which encouraged of endowments to become more aggressive and imaginative, was published at the end of the 1960s just as a long bull market was coming to an end. A large part of the Foundation's own resources was invested in equity assets. The endowment and its annual grants more than halved in value from 1972 to 1974 and then recovered in 1975. The universities that followed the advice suffered similarly. The 1970s was one of the poorest decades for stock and bond returns in the twentieth century and endowment fund contributions to operating expenses shrank. Over the longer term, however, the recommendations of the Ford Foundation have been validated and the results have helped to produce fundamental changes in the way all endowment funds are managed.

The 1980s and 1990s, by contrast, saw a boom in asset prices as inflation and interest rates fell and growth was stimulated. But inevitably boom led to excess in a number of areas. Those bull market returns then led once again to siren voices for higher payouts from endowments. The US economist Robert Shiller published his book *Irrational Exuberance* in 2000[12] which analyzed the latest bull market and foretold the subsequent setback in equity prices. He wrote:

> ... colleges and foundations with endowment funds invested in the market should consider, when possible, substantially lowering their payout rates. This conclusion stands in sharp contrast to some recent recommendations about endowment payout rates. For example, the National Network of Grantmakers, an organisation of progressive foundations, issued a report in 1999 urging all foundations to increase their payout from the 5% of assets mandated by US law to 6% ... For endowments heavily exposed to stock market risks, these recommendations are pointing in the wrong direction.

It was only a short time before Robert Shiller was proved right. William Dietel said in a talk to the Institute for Philanthropy in June 2002: 'There is abundant and serious bad news to confront today. The endowments of our largest foundations with few exceptions have been seriously diluted by the failure of the financial markets of the recent past.' He mentioned in particular the Packard Foundation where the portfolio value, with 70% invested in the founder's Hewlett–Packard common stock, fell from a high of $15 billion to under $5 billion at the bottom of the market.[13] Staff were laid off, grant-making was curtailed and extended over a greater number of years.

While the pioneers of absolute return strategies with diversified portfolios, such as Harvard and Yale, escaped the worst of the bear market which began in 2000, this was the second time in 30 years that endowments with more conventional exposures to equity assets had suffered a major setback to their ability to fund their collective stated purpose.

Academic studies have shown that nine-tenths of the variation in return of a portfolio is due to asset allocation. History has shown that we are condemned to repeat our errors, or as Machiavelli said, history is always the same and never the same. Can we use this experience of the past to create an architecture of endowment investment strategy to prevent setbacks to achieving an endowment's mission in the future? Prevent, no; manage and minimize, yes. That is the purpose of this book.

1.5   STRUCTURE OF THE BOOK

Chapter 2, 'Language of Return', looks at definitions of investment return, of time- and money-weighted return, of arithmetic and geometric return, whether nominal or adjusted for inflation. We see that not everything is what it seems and we discover Einstein's eighth wonder of the world: compound interest. Chapter 2 introduces the concept of the Nobel prize-winning economist, Sir John Hicks, who defined income as what a person can spend and expect to be as well off at the end as at the beginning. The Hicks concept is that income is simply the wealth that can be consumed in a year and leaves unchanged the original quantum of wealth to generate the same income in the following year. The amount that is generated to be consumed, which is income in his words, is equivalent to total return adjusted for inflation. The quantum of wealth left unchanged to generate the same income in the following year is equivalent to intergenerational equity – a concept that is at the heart of endowment fund management.

In Chapter 3, 'Elements of Return', we look behind investment return to see what creates it. It is only by understanding what creates return, rather than simply by extrapolating past returns, that one can hope to make reasonable judgments for the future. This chapter outlines the macroeconomic forces and circumstances that favor different asset classes. The chapter also looks at some of the indicators that give clues to the type of financial environment that is created by governments and the 'animal spirits' of rational and irrational economic agents.

The chapter draws on research by Dimson, Marsh and Staunton of the London Business School,[14] and other sources, in looking at historic returns. The Dimson, Marsh and Staunton study of listed financial market returns in 15 different countries over the twentieth century and into the twenty-first is by far the most comprehensive published work in this area to-date. The twentieth century saw a wide range of economic conditions in which investment return has been generated: global war and peace; communist and capitalist political systems; worldwide inflation and deflation; monetary attachment to, and detachment from, gold; fixed and managed currencies. No other era has been such a testbed for return or, indeed, for risk. Certainly no other era has those factors so well documented in financial terms.

Knowledge is of no use without understanding. So what created those returns? What were the underlying factors that caused periods of above-average and below-average investment return. Are those factors sustainable and, if so, over what time period? How do we identify and monitor them? And even if we monitor them, how can we be sure that what was true in the past will also be true in the future? We cannot, but we can make shrewd judgments of most likely outcomes by analysis of the drivers of change. History may not repeat itself but it rhymes, and as GaveKal also reminds us occasionally, 'this time it's different' are four of the most expensive words in the English language.

If there is one message that should be taken from Chapter 2, 'Language of Return', and Chapter 3, 'Elements of Return', it is that endowments that have the luxury of a longer term perspective have an advantage over the multitude of funds driven by shorter term needs. These chapters help to show that long-term superior wealth creation can be achieved by compounding positive return, and avoiding major total portfolio downside. This needs to focus on the strategic exploitation of longer term signals rather than the short-term noise often created by high-frequency and volatile short-term economic and financial market data.

Chapter 4, 'Understanding Risk', is second only to understanding return in importance for strategy. The Chinese written expression for risk is formed from two characters: the first means danger, the second means opportunity. The two together mean risk, suggesting that risk and opportunity are inextricably linked. This is true in financial markets especially when markets are being driven by those two fundamental forces of human nature: fear and greed.

The western view of risk is often expressed more in terms of danger, of downside, of failure to achieve expectation, of loss. Peter Bernstein in his most readable history of risk, *Against the Gods*,[15] has argued that measuring and controlling risk has been at the center of western economic development through the ability to assess the future and weigh the consequences of actions and events. Bernstein argues that all the tools we use today for analyzing decisions and making choice stem from the developments of probability theory in the sixteenth and seventeenth centuries, from the concept of regression to the mean in the nineteenth century and from modern portfolio theory in the twentieth century.

Chapter 4 looks at how these developments in statistics influenced the practical application of theories of risk. The chapter looks at the key to investment diversification: the co-movement of investments resulting from factors that are common between them. It focuses on risk as failure to meet liability driven benchmarks and formulates a concept of endowment fund risk based on failure to meet a minimum level of need.

After risk and return comes the creation of a sustainable spending rule for the consumption of return. Chapter 5, 'Spending Rules', considers this process which is an iterative part of determining strategy. Whatever the endowment's aims and objectives, the limits of reasonable expected return from any asset class must constrain the desired quantum of spending and the balance between current and future consumption.

Chapter 5, therefore draws on what we have understood from return and risk to generate a sustainable spending strategy. This strategy is defined by the resources of the endowment fund in the context of the economic and financial environment. It dwells on what can be spent and what needs to be reinvested to sustain the activity of the endowment in the longer term.

Chapter 6, 'Assets for Strategy', defines two major asset classifications based on asset class usage: operational reserves and intergenerational reserves. The first are assets that can provide for defined near-term (up to five years) operational needs with a high degree of certainty. The near-term operational needs include those of the organization in meeting grant-making and administrative needs as well as those of the investment manager when managing the assets to reduce portfolio risk by reducing portfolio duration.

The second classification, intergenerational reserves, incorporates all the longer duration assets available to meet intergenerational needs. Defining asset classes, such as equities, bonds and real estate, is more a question of asset class characteristic than of nomenclature. It is about finding factors that are common, as sources of risk and return, to all investments in that asset class. Some fixed income bonds, for instance, can behave like real estate; real estate can behave like equities and equities like commodities. Investment styles such as 'growth', 'value' and 'momentum' are also about characteristics: each has factors in common.

Chapter 7, 'Legal, Social and Ethical', touches on non-financial issues as they bear on investment strategy for endowments. The chapter is not designed to be the definitive word on the legal obligations of trustees, but it touches on codified and case law in respect of fiduciary obligations. The focus of this chapter is then on governance and the areas of social and ethical responsibility and how they relate to investment strategy.

Probity and trust have always been 'top of the agenda' in matters of money, but corporate governance and socially responsible investment have become more of a general issue for trustees. Some religious groups have always had constraints on the type of asset in which investment can be made. These include the Quaker constraints on investing in defence- and alcohol-related stocks or the Muslim obeyance of Sharia Rules. But non-financial issues have become a much higher profile for all trustees in the twenty-first century.

To the extent that legal, social and ethical issues feature in the vision of an endowment, they should be integrated with overall policy and the ground rules of strategy. It is too late to consider these issues until the strategy has been determined and to paste an ethical screen over a predetermined investment policy. As Sir Robert Megarry established in his judgment in Cowan v. Scargill 1984, 'campaigning for changes in the law' on ethical matters is a different matter to following the law in responsibility to beneficiaries. The constitution of an endowment should make clear the ground rules for trustees to interpret.

Chapter 8, 'Understanding Strategy' and Chapter 9, 'Implementing Strategy' form the kernel of the book. Chapter 8 brings together the characteristics, aims and objectives of endowments, the anticipation of investment risk and return and the appropriate spending strategies into one coherent whole. It demonstrates that the jigsaw puzzle of appropriate strategy is incomplete without each of those pieces.

Chapter 8 is not just an holistic approach to the issue of marrying resources with the achievement of objectives. It is about ways of thinking, of considering different scenarios created by different conditions and not simply relying on one best estimate of future expectations. It is then about structuring portfolios in the light of resources and both operational and intergenerational needs. It is about scenario analysis for intergenerational assets, avoiding asset classes which protect against risks that do not exist and diversifying among those that do.

Scenario analysis is akin to weather forecasting, looking beyond the next weather frontal system and understanding the long-term, stratospheric weather patterns. It is having 'what if' scenarios in case the forecast is wrong: if the approaching depression deepens to a serious storm or, alternatively, 'fills in' to a more benign outcome. It is beneficial to be aware of the best estimate or the most likely forecast. However, the trustees must also be aware of the likelihood of different outcomes and the consequences in case things go wrong.

Chapter 8 considers the questions on investment risk and return that trustees should be asking their investment experts, the consultants and managers to whom the day-to-day advice on strategy and management of investments may be outsourced. Trustees should be satisfied that the investment strategy being followed is consistent with the endowment's requirements and timeframes.

Too often an endowment that has a genuine 20- or 30-year perspective is being managed by an expert on the basis of quarterly returns, and this is usually due to the trustees' monitoring method. It may also be more due to the perceived risk to the manager of losing the business of the endowment – as a result of being spectacularly wrong for a period of time – than to the real financial and portfolio risk to the endowment fund. As Roger Murray said, managers should be measured on a quarterly basis but the time period should be a quarter century not a quarter of the year.

The chapter looks at the difference between strategic and tactical asset allocation, between the framework for asset allocation within parameters determined by the objectives of the endowment and shorter-term judgments about the most likely next scenario. The latter must be integrated into the former for the proper fulfillment of the objectives of an endowment. A football field defines the limits of a game, and occasionally strategy might move the goal posts, but it is then tactics within the strategy, as effected by the team of players, that achieves the ultimate goal.

Finally, this chapter considers the issue of moving the strategy goal posts by rebalancing asset classes when relative performance changes their relative weights within the portfolio. It looks at different approaches and suggests 'relationship rebalance' as the optimal end game of investment strategy.

Chapter 9, 'Implementing Strategy', is the practical application of 'Understanding Strategy.' It considers the practical impact of philosophy and principles and the structure and process through which strategy is effected. It is about forging good policies and practices. It is about investigating the selection of investment consultants and investment managers. It covers Charters and Investment Policy Statements, the structuring of operational and intergenerational reserves, the formation and operation of investment committees, and the costs, fees, and performance monitoring over appropriate timescales.

The conduct of trustee meetings is a critical part of the overall process. Good governance at these meetings will focus on the strategic and tactical areas and not dwell on specifics of security selection. Too long spent on the past performance of an individual security sometimes indicates more of a personal investment interest by the trustee than necessarily an independent concern for the fund. Even with a focus on strategy, too much time can be spent on justifying the immediate past. Too little time is often spent on the future which is represented in the portfolio as it stands, too little time in considering different possible scenarios rather than a manager's single best guess of what will happen next.

Chapter 10, as the title 'Synopsis' suggests, summarizes the chapters and the key messages of the book. While the book covers varied ground, there are some overriding messages for endowment trustees. Finally, there is a References and Reading Matter section and a Glossary. The references section includes suggested reading other than just those publications from which quotes and ideas have been taken and acknowledged. The glossary is more of an *aide-mémoire* than a detailed and definitive explanation of investment terms, and tries to avoid economic or accounting terms unless they are specifically investment related.

2

Language of Return

I know you believe you understand what you think I said, but I am not sure you realize that what you heard is not what I meant.

ALAN GREENSPAN, Chairman of the Federal Reserve

This chapter concerns one of the commonest but least understood words in the language of investment: return. Nominal return is income and capital gain and real return is nominal return adjusted for inflation. The economist Sir John Hicks defined the word income as: 'the wealth which can be consumed in a year which leaves unchanged the quantum of wealth left to gener- ate the same income in the following year.' The quantum of wealth that is left at the end of that year to generate return in the following year is underlying capital; the amount that is available to be consumed during the year, which Hicks calls income, is economic return. The Hicksian 'unchanged quantum of wealth' is known as 'intergenerational equity'. This chapter also looks at absolute and relative return – relative that is to a benchmark and of indexed returns. It con- trasts internal rate of return, which measures wealth accumulation through compound interest, which was Einstein's 'eighth wonder of the world', and time-weighted return, which makes funds with different cash flows comparable in relative performance measurement. Compound interest exposes both the focus on relative rather than absolute return and the dilemma between spending now or growing for the future, considered later in more detail in Chapter 5 'Spending Rules'.

Return may be the most common word in the investment language, but is often the least understood. Whether positive or negative, financial return is an outcome of investment but what does the word 'return' really mean? What is the difference between financial and economic return, real and nominal return, time- or money-weighted return, absolute and relative return, and why do we need to understand these differences to understand investment strategy?

Without understanding the language of investment, we cannot begin to understand invest- ment strategy. This chapter therefore covers the essential vocabulary of return, which is one of the two most important concepts in investment strategy. The other is risk. In this chapter we look at the meaning of return. In the next chapter we look at the elements of return.

2.1 ECONOMIC RETURN

The Nobel prize-winning economist, Sir John Hicks, described income as what someone can spend and expect to be as well-off at the end as at the beginning. The Hicks view is that income is simply the wealth that can be consumed in a year, leaving unchanged the original quantum of wealth to generate the same income in the following year. The amount generated that can be consumed within the year, while remaining as well-off at the end of the year, is *economic return*. Economic return is income plus capital gain less that which must be reinvested in capital for it to generate the same effective return in the following year.

The 'wealth which can, be consumed in a year' can be measured in nominal terms, which is simply counting the dollars and cents gained over the period. This gives a nominal figure of 'well-offness' at the end of the year. But two adjustments may need to be made to nominal return to arrive at the proper level of 'the wealth which can be consumed'.

One adjustment is for revaluation gain. For example, in the UK there are Government bonds which are perpetual or irredeemable fixed income securities. We use them as an example here simply because the arithmetic is easy but the principle applies to all bonds. If a perpetual bond rises in price because yields have fallen, is the capital gain spendable as well as the income if 'well-offness' is to be maintained at the end of the year? Clearly not, in a stable or modestly inflationary period, if the same amount of income is to be generated in the following year. The income hasn't changed, it is fixed. $5 of fixed income is still $5 irrespective of whether the price of the security moves from $100 (implying a yield of 5%) to $200 (implying a yield of 2.5%). The capital gain element of nominal return is 100% but if this is spent then less than $5 of income will be generated in the following year.

The second adjustment is for inflation. The mission of most endowments and foundations is measured in terms of real underlying activity. This means removing from the nominal return the effect of general changes in the price level of a representative basket of goods consumed. The amount that is left to be consumed is real return. Leaving 'unchanged the quantum of wealth', or in other words remaining as well-off, is equivalent to maintaining 'intergenerational equity' – a phrase which refers to the sustainable real value of the underlying capital that generates the return. In a deflationary period the issue is different. The capital value of an irredeemable Government bond continues to rise in real terms as consumer prices fall. There is no requirement to spend out of income to maintain capital and spending power in real terms. The fall in consumer prices simply raises the real value of each year's fixed income payment.

Understanding this basic principle of how much return can be spent, and how much must be reinvested to maintain the same level of spending in future, is one of the key concepts in this book. It is an area which trustees naturally find more difficult to understand comprehensively than almost any other because of centuries of simple belief that income is something that can be spent and capital is something that must be preserved. Reality is different. Not all income can necessarily be spent any more than capital gain all belongs to capital.

2.2   INVESTMENT RETURN

Investment return is the income and capital gain from an investment priced at market value. Investment return pre-dates the coining of money to the extent that it can be measured by what Aristotle first defined as 'value in exchange'. Value in exchange is what someone will pay, a market price denominated in whatever goods, services or units of account one item will be exchanged for another. There is a further distinction in the investment world between market price and intrinsic value which is a measure of what analysts assess the market price would be in a perfect market under normal conditions. To use the words of Benjamin Graham, author of the classic book *The Intelligent Investor*[1]: 'stocks have prices; companies have value.' Most investment analysis is about trying to estimate the intrinsic value and so exploit the difference between value and price.

A theory, known as the Efficient Market Theory, suggests that all known information is immediately reflected in market prices so there is little room for active managers to exploit the difference between value and price. But information is not necessarily disseminated equally and spontaneously and investors' expectations can be volatile. The latest information often includes more noise (reaction to high-frequency economic and financial data) than signal. This arises from unanticipated developments being interpreted as a change of trend. So although markets may be relatively efficient in reflecting in prices the latest information, this information is often too noisy and this can create excess asset price volatility that can be exploited.

What moves prices is the action of demand and supply and this action may not even be rational. Even if it is, action will depend on the objectives of different investors. Classical economics suggests that there is a point of equilibrium between demand and supply, based on rational decision-making in a perfect market with perfect information, but the real world is neither perfect nor static. John Maynard Keynes condemned as 'flimsily based and disastrously mistaken the assumption of classical economists that human nature is reasonable'. Other problems for theory include the reality that transactions are not cost free and markets can be limited by dealing size.

One of the world's most successful investors, George Soros, developed what he called a 'theory of reflexivity'[2] allied to Heisenberg's Uncertainty Principle. The Theory of Reflexivity says first that participants in the economic decision-making process do not have the perfect knowledge assumed in equilibrium theory, nor indeed is there an equilibrium. Also, the thinking of participants in the process of determining market prices affects the situation to which their thinking and actions relate. Soros describes this as a shoe-lace theory that connects facts to perceptions which then in their turn help to determine the facts. He suggests that some events are correctly anticipated and do not provoke a change in perceptions but others change the bias of participants which then determines events. He suggests that historical processes are shaped by the misconceptions of the participants.

Soros is not alone in thinking that the real behavior of investors often contradicts rational and classical economic theory and he has made a lot of money from his beliefs. Despite Keynes's remark more than 50 years ago about human nature, it is only relatively recently that Behavioral Finance, which takes account of human nature in the financial decision-making process, has become an accepted branch of economics. The award of the Nobel prize in economics in 2002 to two economists working in the behavioral field suggests that it is becoming 'less and less like a minor subfield of finance and more and more like a central pillar of serious finance theory'.[3]

Market price may provide a measure of return but prices cannot be eaten. Endowments are ultimately interested in the future stream of consumption that their portfolios provide: the goods and services an endowment can buy with the return on its assets, and equally importantly when, in order to satisfy the endowment's objectives. This implies the translation of investment return into spendable cash to effect that consumption as and when it is required.

Returns based on 'marked-to-market' prices – which is the practice of valuing an investment at the last known price on an exchange irrespective of whether that investment could be sold – will have little value if the investment cannot be realized when it needs to be consumed. But except in times of crisis or panic, the financial markets in publicly traded securities generally provide ample liquidity to permit cash to be raised for spending.

This matter of liquidity is not just an academic consideration. In the real world, financial crises both create and flow from lack of liquidity, not just from falls in market prices. One issue for trustees to understand is the need to ride through financial panics without having to realize assets at distressed prices near the bottom of the price range. Indeed, trustees should look to take such opportunities when they arise to enhance long-term return.

Another issue is not to take for granted a marked-to-market valuation when the underlying market hardly exists. Valuation of assets which are not traded on liquid and public markets, especially private equity or unlisted derivatives such as swaps, is one of the areas which trustees should be prepared to question. Even listed derivatives which are actively traded in public liquid markets may become untradable in a panic. We touch again on this subject in the chapter on risk.

Trustees should also question liquidity protection against extreme scenarios and the high cost of transactions in those conditions. These questions become more urgent in a world where endowments are increasing their commitment to so-called 'low risk' assets such as hedge funds, which usually have limited liquidity. All this will be considered more closely when we look at 'Assets for Strategy' and 'Understanding Risk' but there is a world of difference between low volatility of returns achieved in normal environments and the risk associated with non-normal events.

2.3 'OTHER INCOME' NOT RETURN

Investment is only one way of generating a return. Others include selling goods and services (trading) and gambling. What defines investment return is what is done with an asset that represents the investment. One reason that this definition matters, in the UK at least, is the tax treatment of the return; another reason is regulation of the activity that generates the return. In the UK, for an asset to be regarded as an investment it must have been provided by an investor to someone (an investee) who provides some benefit in return. That benefit, investment return, may come in the form of dividends, rents, interest, a share in profits or capital gain (less capital loss). How the investee uses the asset to generate that benefit does not jeopardize the status as an investment.

What defines an endowment from a financial point of view is the asset base that generates an investment return to help to finance the current and future activities of the entity endowed. And the purest form of endowment is the Foundation, which relies wholly on a gift of assets which represent that capital base.

Many endowed entities have other sources of income. 'Other income' can be a type of financial return, albeit one generated by the activities of the endowed entity or by operating rather than financial assets. Churches may have halls that may be let. Universities have fees. An endowed orchestra will have admission charges to concerts. Some charities even rely almost exclusively on their fund-raising activities to generate operating income and the endowment is regarded as only a short-term reserve. In this case if the fund-raising ceased, the endowment would be consumed rapidly and the activity may have to cease.

Another form of 'other income' is royalties. A chemistry professor who invented 'superglue' gave royalties gained from the patent of fluoride to Trinity College, Hartford. The University of Wisconsin gained from the patent for warfarin, which was first used as a rat poison before its properties as a blood-thinning agent were discovered.

Research[4] by the Commonfund into the growth of educational endowments in the USA over a 10-year period suggested that 75% of their growth over that period came from sources other than investment return. Their annual survey indicated that recent gift income amounted on average to 5.5% per annum for the institutions surveyed.

'Other income', such as gifts, grants, royalties and legacies, can therefore be important to the operating budget of an endowed entity. It is also important to determine whether such other income can be spent within the budget period or treated as an addition to the endowment. One charity in the UK relies almost exclusively on fund-raising to finance its current activities. This means that return on the endowment, which is a fraction of the size of the annual operating budget, is insignificant in the funding of its activities and the endowment simply becomes a reserve to cover any current shortfall in fund-raising.

How 'other income' is factored into the budget clearly has a bearing on investment strategy and so a policy is needed, if not dictated by the donor, on how it is treated. Is a $1 million gift truly 'income' and immediately spendable? Or is it capital to be invested for a return? If the capital is invested to yield 3% does this represent $30,000 per annum of spendable return, or $15,000 spendable now and $15,000 reinvested for the future? Is the gift designed to represent immediate consumption or endowment funding for sustainable giving? Or, if there is inflation, must more be reinvested to preserve the future value of what the endowment can support?

It is also important to determine whether a gift is in fact an asset to the endowed entity or a liability: 'a gift which eats.' An asset given may need other resources to maintain it. In the UK, for example, fine country houses donated to the National Trust must now be endowed to be accepted. Research by the Commonfund indicates that over 90% of gifts to US colleges and universities carry restrictions on their application. The project for which the gift is donated may be a current expense that needs further income to fulfill the obligation because the conditioned gift is insufficient to fund the whole. In such a case, the additional funds required may place an unacceptable demand on the endowed entity's resources encroaching on other current projects or on future projects because the future is being spent in the present.

In the USA many new facilities in the 1990s, such as performing arts or sports centers, were funded by debt. In addition to the liability of maintaining (and depreciating) these facilities is added that of the burden of loan interest and payback of debt principal. The question is then what level of annual outgoing is required to maintain the facility once it is built. Buildings need maintenance and security and they depreciate over time. In addition, new facilities often lead to the establishment of new programs, sometimes with considerable overheads, particularly new staff. These are all part of the liability associated with the asset and spending plans should take these issues into account. In fact one college turned down a gift of $10 million to build an indoor swimming pool after assessing the ongoing costs.

Donations are therefore 'gifts which eat' unless they offer positive net returns or are genuinely financially neutral. Financial neutrality is ensuring that the gift does not generate or maintain a project that will need other income to sustain it. With a capital expense, fiscal neutrality is only ensured by the gift being endowed with other assets, which generate sufficient sustainable income to maintain and depreciate the capital item.

2.4   INCOME, CAPITAL AND 'TOTAL RETURN'

Earlier in the chapter we considered the Hicks concept of income as a definition of economic return. The accounting definition of return is different: income and capital gain or loss. The Hicks and the accounting definitions may be different but they have the same result in a period of zero inflation where gain is generated by spendable real growth rather than simple revaluation which cannot be spent.

The accounting definition of income is interest or dividends provided by a capital asset. This does not include capital gain (or loss), which is the gain (or loss) arising from the sale, exchange or transfer of a capital asset. In the case of a zero coupon bond, however, income is rolled-up in the price of the asset and not paid out, so is received in the form of gain in the price of the bond. For taxable entities this is a gain that is usually treated by tax authorities as income compounded in the price, but this does not of course apply to tax-exempt endowments.

Total return is therefore income return plus capital gains or losses. But, as we have already indicated, it is deceptive to consider total return as necessarily spendable. Any endowment fund trustee must understand fully the concept of total return before considering a strategy both for the investment and the consumption of endowment resources. And during any period when the price of goods and services is not stable, total return cannot be divorced from real return in determining strategy.

Total return was occasionally used as a performance measure in the first half of the twentieth century though it was common practice for only income and not capital appreciation to be spent. In the late 1960s in the USA, the Ford Foundation reports popularized the notion of total return[5] by suggesting that cash could be raised through realizing capital gain as well as income. The concept was subsequently codified in the Uniform Management of Institutional Funds Act, first proposed in 1974 and by now adopted in most States in the USA. In the UK, there are rules on accumulation and spending of total return in respect of endowments that have charitable status. The Charity Commissioners have issued guidance[6] for charitable endowments on consumption of total return and on relevant accounting disclosures.

Total return as a concept can help to avoid underconsumption of the outcome of investment. However, a greater danger to the continued existence of an endowment is failure to maintain a level of capital which is self-generating while continuing to provide a sustainable consumable return, in real terms, for the life of the endowment. Underconsumption is consumption deferred. It is a transfer of real benefit from the present to the future. Overconsumption is a transfer from future generations to the present.

A major cause of overconsumption is 'income illusion', the failure to recognize that a dividend or interest payment may not all be spendable despite being called 'income'. It may be that all of the return from an asset comes in the form of a one-off capital gain and to regard none of that as spendable can be as inappropriate as it is to regard all income as fit to be consumed.

One example of income illusion is part repayment of capital in the income return, even without inflation. Consider an endowment which invests $1 million in a bond which, in turn, provides an income of $50,000 per annum. The bond is priced at $125 and matures at $100 in 10 years' time. In that case, there is a known capital loss of $25 per $100 over the whole period. Just to maintain the initial capital value in nominal terms, $25 per $100 must be taken from income and returned to capital.

Or consider another endowment which buys for $1 million a lease on a property. The lease expires in 10 years' time and in the meantime it yields a rental income of $150,000 per annum. Ten years of $150,000 is $1.5 million but the capital initially invested has gone from $1 million to zero. It is not necessary for the trustee to know how to calculate the annualized return on these investments precisely. It is, however, critical that the trustee understands that the prospective investment return on these two assets is not 5% and 15% respectively. The trustee must understand that part of the 'income return' in both cases represents repayment of capital – capital that generates the sustainable return, and that this amount should not be consumed but reinvested.

A second type of income illusion involves inflation. In this case inflation reduces the real value of the income because some of the income must be reinvested to maintain the capital's ability to fund its activities. To illustrate, consider an investment of $1 million made into a fixed income bond, priced at $100% and maturing at $100% in 10 years' time and yielding $50,000 per annum. In this case there is no nominal gain or loss of capital. If there were no change of consumer prices (i.e. no inflation or deflation) over the 10-year period, then the $50,000 a year could be consumed without in any way consuming the endowment capital and the ability to sustain the 'real' level of consumption. But what if inflation is 3% per annum over that period?

In Year 10 the $50,000 will be worth approximately $37,000 in real terms, that is what it could buy in today's money. The $1 million capital will be worth just less than $750,000. If $50,000 funds five equal grants a year now, it would be funding less than four in 10 years' time. A sustainable consumption strategy would only allow two such grants to be paid out of income today, with the balance of income being reinvested to maintain the value of capital after inflation and therefore the same number of grants in Year 10, ad infinitum.

A third case of illusion is one we touched upon earlier in the chapter. It is rarely considered by trustees and not at all by regulation. It is when total return has been due in whole or part to a change in price owing to a valuation change that may not be sustainable. The valuation shift can create capital gain without enhancing the investment's ability to generate continuing sustainable economic return. A dramatic example of this occurred in the US stock market in the 1990s when the valuation of stocks, as measured by price to earnings, doubled. During the ensuing years valuations returned to more normal levels and returns were negative.

We considered the example of a UK perpetual fixed income security's yield moving from 5% to 2.5% in a year, giving a total rate of return for that year of 105%. Did this meet the Hicksian test of well-offness? Could the whole 105% return be consumed? Is the bond producing any more income, as would be the case if the investment was an equity, not a bond, and the corporate dividend doubled? The answer is no. This is perhaps the most difficult to understand of the income illusions. But the security can be sold and the proceeds made to work in another more sustainable return environment, and that is one objective of asset strategy.

2.5   REAL AND NOMINAL RETURN

'Real income' was a term coined by the classical economists of the nineteenth century to describe what money income would buy. Real returns are therefore nominal returns adjusted for inflation. If an investment of $100 yields $5 after one year during which there is no increase in the general level of prices in the economy, then both the nominal return and the real return on that investment are 5%.

If inflation is 2% – that is, the price of goods and services rises by 2% – then while the nominal return is still 5%, the real return on the investment is only 3%. Nominal monetary values are an accounting convenience which are an economic reality only during a time of general price stability. Price stability, since the ending of the gold standard, has been more the exception than the rule. And risk-free real rates of interest in an economy tend to approximate the structural growth rate of that economy.

The impact of inflation, compounded over the lifetimes of endowments, can be substantial. David Swensen in *Pioneering Investment*[7] cites the case of Yale's oldest surviving endowment fund established in 1822 with a little more than $27,000. Price levels rose more than 21-fold between 1822 and the end of the twentieth century but the endowment value rose to only $200,000. This falls short of the inflation adjusted value by some two-thirds and allows today only a fraction of the real value of the support that was originally intended by the benefactor.

Historic data on inflation and market returns provide some insights into the real returns of the past. A development of the second half of the twentieth century was inflation-linked bonds, and a comparison of inflation-linked and fixed income government securities gives us the market expectation of future inflation and risk-free real returns. The man who is credited with designing the first Government inflation-linked bond to be launched in the UK is Professor

Wilkie. Wilkie submitted a paper to the UK Institute of Actuaries in March 1981[8] which investigated historic inflation and appropriate real yields; there was no precedent at that time for a Government issued bond offering a real yield.

Part of Wilkie's research involved investigating the behavior of UK retail prices, derived from various sources, going back to the year 1661. The year 1661 preceded by two years the introduction of the guinea gold coin (a guinea was 21 shillings) in England and succeeded the great Tudor inflation. Over the end of the fifteenth century, and during the sixteenth, prices had risen 4-fold as coinage was debased, credit instruments such as bills of exchange and borrowing against land became more common, and silver was discovered in the Americas in quantity. There was also a physical demand/supply pressure arising from failed harvests and a growing urban population; cities were making more demands on the supply of food and other commodities.

For the first 250 years following 1661 the price level was reasonably stable, given the influence of the gold and silver standards to which the value of the pound sterling was linked. Professor Wilkie surmised that at the beginning of the First World War one would have concluded that prices had an absolute mean level, perhaps related to gold, with extreme changes over short-term periods as being most unlikely.

The price of gold was the same in 1821 as it was in 1930. The change in purchasing power of gold, however, was a mirror image of the commodity price cycle. Commodity prices fell for 20 years after 1875 then more than tripled between 1900 and 1920. This period included the First World War, and wars tend to be linked to periods of inflation.

While, by 1936, the stability had clearly changed, those changes were still consistent with a belief that even if some disturbance created significant change, there was an inherent 'normal' level and the expected rate of inflation was zero. As Wilkie wrote in his paper, this thinking had become 'institutionalized in many of our business practices, in our legal, accounting, banking, taxation, insurance and pension fund systems'.

In the second half of the twentieth century, however, everything changed and the future level of consumer prices became very unpredictable. The problem with inflation is that the first-order effects are unimportant, even beneficial; it is the second-order effects that cause the trouble: neither incomes nor prices change in equal proportions and the efficient allocation of resources is impeded.

Some of the misallocation of resources is reflected in the different types of index, but earnings inflation has generally outpaced retail price inflation, despite changes to the constituents goods and services, over a long period of recent time. Wilkie pointed out in his paper that the earnings index had risen at 2.3% per annum more than the retail price index between 1946 and 1980. The difference has been maintained. A 2% difference in growth of liabilities relative to the assets that fund them can make a massive difference over 50 years of meeting those liabilities, especially at low rates of interest and inflation.

One of the problems with inflation is measuring it. To ensure comparability most consumer price indices are based on a principle of matching, from one period to another, the prices of the same goods bought from the same outlet. However, there is a number of issues with this methodology. First, there is the relevance of the goods to everyday life for any group of people. In Tudor England, for instance, the prices of many commodities are not known and where they are, they vary from district to district. The only commodity for which there is plenty of price evidence, wheat, was not even a staple food of the bulk of the population.[9]

The UK Cost of Living Index in 1914 consisted of 14 items including candles, corset lacing and mangles. In 1947 it still included unskinned rabbits and tram fares. Today there are over

600 items that are supposed to represent the pockets of 'urban consumers' but this may not be a relevant measure of inflation for a significant percentage of the population.

The Consumer Price Index (CPI) in some countries is also distorted by the extent of government- and quasi-government-related goods and services, including those of government-related monopolies such as utility companies, so private and public sector measures can therefore tell different stories.

Furthermore, the quality of goods, and the nature of transactions in those goods, changes over time. This was first recognized in an agricultural context but it is all the more evident in an era of technological change. The car we buy today is not the same as the one we bought several years ago even if it is the same make and model: there are improvements. This is especially the case with computers and related equipment. Governments have started to adjust for these factors – a process known as hedonics – which may have an impact on the index change by reducing it by as much as 0.25% to 0.5% per annum.

There is also what economists refer to as 'the substitution effect', where consumers trade down in price to meet a given need. The item in the index may continue to rise in price when the inflation experienced by the consumer has a lower order of impact on his lifestyle. The effect is therefore for the CPI to overstate inflation systematically. Another influence on inflation is the outlet through which we buy goods and services. The internet rather than the local store has become a force for optimizing both production and transaction costs.

An endowment established to meet one sort of need may have a liability that is quite different to another that has a different purpose. For example, a Charity for the Relief of Need, where the liability may be related to the price of food and basic services, is different to one that serves educational needs where the rate of inflation has been much higher for a long period of time. In the USA, the index that is used in the educational sphere to measure goods and services bought by colleges and universities is known as 'The Higher Education Price Index' (HEPI). The index covers general operating costs, such as staff salaries and benefits and maintenance of equipment and libraries, and is used by many universities to benchmark costs.

Analysis by the Commonfund indicates a high correlation of HEPI with the CPI index despite a very different basket of goods and services. However, since the index was created in 1961, the CPI has only been greater in 9 out of 43 years. During the 1960s, cost increases per student were 5.8% per annum against a CPI rise of 2.5% per annum. In the 10 years to June 2004 the HEPI has annualized 3.6% against the CPI at 2.5%. One explanation for this is that the economy in general enjoys greater productivity through technology than does higher education, which is still very people-time dependent.

Financial markets adjust to inflation over time, some investments responding more rapidly than others. Yields on cash and bonds adjust rapidly to anticipated inflation; price earnings ratios adjust in due course and while the adjustment is taking place the asset class fails to offer compensation in return for the fall in its real value. The issue is not inflation per se but rising and unanticipated inflation which tends to cause dislocations before the effect of higher prices leads through into earnings.

As we will see in Chapter 6, 'Assets for Strategy', some asset classes clearly offer more protection against inflation than others. Commodities and inflation-linked securities offer higher protection factors than other asset classes, but even where an inflation index-linked security does prove to be a good proxy for real return, it remains important to monitor the underlying drivers of the prices in the index that determine the long-run return of the inflation-indexed security. It is equally important to realize that rises in real yields can still lead to underperformance of inflation by an inflation-indexed security over time periods short of redemption. The inflation guarantee is only effective if the security is held to redemption.

2.6   ABSOLUTE AND RELATIVE RETURN

An absolute return is simply a nominal (or real) rate of return on an investment rather than a return that is relative to a benchmark. It might be argued that every return has some benchmark against which it is measured. If so, the benchmark against which absolute return would be measured is the rate of interest on cash or a hurdle rate based on cash. The measure of success of relative return investment is outperformance of an index, no matter if the index return is negative. If the portfolio is US equities and it falls 10% in value when the Standard & Poor's 500 Index falls 15%, that is success. The measure of success of absolute return investing is compounding return at a rate that exceeds cash or cash plus some margin such as LIBOR (London Inter Bank Offered Rate) plus some percentage.

Return is generally measured in a unit of money in any given currency but most endowments are more concerned with what the money will buy. Real return, as we have seen, is nominal return deflated by an inflation index, so it may be argued that a real return is not absolute because it is nominal return relative to inflation. There is, however, a difference between deflating a nominal return to arrive at a real number and comparing a return against a peer group or unmanaged benchmark index.

In his book *Pioneering Portfolio Management*,[10] David Swensen comments that absolute investing as 'a relatively new asset class, consists of inefficiency-exploiting marketable securities positions exhibiting little or no correlation to traditional stock and bond investments. Absolute return positions provide equity-like returns with powerful diversifying characteristics.' The idea of investing in such a way as not to lose money is of course hardly new but what is relatively new, and to which Swensen is alluding, is the extent to which portfolio managers now can hedge investments using instruments derived from financial assets such as options and futures (therefore called 'derivatives') or using processes such as borrowing stock to be able to sell the stock ('short') to offset other assets held ('long'). When the author started managing institutional money in the mid-1970s there were few if any markets in futures and options on securities outside the USA. Today it is possible to buy almost any form of derivative on almost any securitized asset.

The focus on outperformance of an index led to the unsurprising conclusion that the average institutional asset manager underperformed the average index. The conclusion was hardly surprising since the institutions themselves began to manage a significant proportion of the securities in the index universe and bore transaction costs from which the pure index was exempt. The nature of statistics is also such that even if a fund has outperformed an index in each of the last 14 years, as at least one public mutual fund has done, it cannot be incontestably proved that this was not simply due to chance. The result of this evidence led to a massive increase in the amount of institutional money which was 'indexed' on minimal fees. Indexation meant that portfolio managers were required to invest proportionately, either by full replication or by statistical sampling, in the stocks of an index weighted by market capitalization. This ensured, with a 100% level of confidence, that the portfolio would neither outperform nor underperform the index (known in the trade as 'tracking error') to any significant degree.

In 1999, Charles Gave wrote a paper on indexation.[11] He conceded that indexation 'is the lowest cost way to capture the attractive long-term returns offered by the capitalist system . . . '

but went on to argue that 'big bear markets are caused by a structural error in allocating capital (Japan 1989, Asia 1996). We have no doubt that the next bear market will find its source in indexation.' Free capital markets must be considered the least worst way of allocating capital to areas of enterprise which offer the highest marginal rate of return. But the expectation of higher rates of return can drive down the prospective yield on equity by driving up its price to a point where cheap cost of capital then drives poor capital investment decisions. Japan in the 1980s was a classic case in point. When capital spending fuels growth without productivity, the marginal return on capital starts going down well before profits. This phenomenon is exacerbated by the trend of investment management toward indexation.

The investment process in financial markets relies at the macro level on active fund managers screening the market for return on invested capital and investing money accordingly. In this way their marginal investing maintains prices that reflect the marginal return on capital of the underlying companies. But the system of short-term performance measurement weeds out managers who underperform over short periods of time if their active management weightings vary significantly from those in the index, especially where the index is dominated by a few large capitalization stocks.

Charles Gave commented in his research piece in 1999: 'this allocation of capital on the basis of size was tried out before and the last time we checked the Soviet Union was not doing that well.' He also observed that indexation was the ultimate form of momentum investing. As the market rises, marginal money is added to the largest stocks. This maintains their index position. Market capitalization weighting naturally overweights the most overvalued stocks and underweights those that are most undervalued. As Benjamin Graham observed, in the short term the stock market is a voting machine, but in the long term it is a weighing machine. Momentum investing tends to end in tears. This time was no exception.

In January 2000, only three months before the beginning of a major bear market, a number of managers were fired for not holding some large telecom and information technology companies that subsequently suffered major falls in share price. A number of stocks that money managers had been sacked for not holding were later taken out of the index because they were not large enough to stay in it! The dot-com boom of the late 1990s was, like all other bubbles, a classic example of how to make a small fortune by starting with a large one.

This problem with indexation, the natural overweighting of overvalued stocks and vice versa, was also identified in 1999 by George Keane, founder of the Commonfund for endowments in the USA and member of the Investment Advisory Committee of the New York State Common Retirement Fund, which had a majority of its domestic equity indexed to the S&P 500 index.

George Keane identified three factors that had led to the distortion of the S&P 500 index. The first was the growing trend for large pension funds, particularly state retirement schemes, to move away from active toward passive management. Some $1 trillion was indexed by the end of the 1990s. The second factor was the large amount of money flowing into mutual funds, some of which went into index funds and a large amount into funds that focused on the larger market capitalization stocks.

The third factor was the management of the constituents of the index by the S&P 500 Index Committee. To incorporate the growing number of large market capitalization stocks in the technology sector, the Committee even violated its own published standards by including a foreign telecommunications stock and companies that had no earnings.

George Keane became convinced that there was a better index for passive management and asked Rob Arnott to investigate alternative methods as a research project for his new firm, Research Affiliates. Research Affiliates tested a number of options before developing the RA

Fundamental Index (RAFI) 1000. This is an index of 1,000 companies with weights in the index derived from a firm's fundamental factors: total income, book equity value, total sales, gross dividends. Back-testing of this index to 1962 demonstrates at least a two percentage point per annum outperformance of the S&P 500 index.

FTSE, one of the major index providers, adopted this concept and in 2005 launched fundamental indices weighted by an equal combination of sales, book value, cash flow and dividends. This follows earlier indices that are simply equal weighted and others, such as the S&P/Citigroup Style Index Series launched in 1998, which use a multifactor approach to ranking companies by growth and value scores. Other indices focus on characteristics such as industry classifications, high dividend yields, or definitions of growth or value.

Index relative return is a useful benchmark measure of success for specialist parts of an overall portfolio, but it does not of itself provide an indicator for an endowment's ability to meet its objective over time unless the benchmark index is price inflation. Absolute return strategies seek to obtain high levels of return that are independent of market moves. This may mean investing in asset classes that are independent of public listed markets. It may mean investment in public listed markets employing strategies that involve both investing 'long' and 'short'. Absolute return strategies are about investing to make, rather than lose, money. Disaffection with the loss of absolute wealth by the relative return approach has been a major cause of the rapid rise of the hedge fund business, which has a clear absolute return bias.

The mode of relative return investing is completely different from absolute return investing. Active 'bets' in relative return mandates are made by varying the percentage of the portfolio invested in a given security against the percentage in the benchmark index. A 'no bet' in an actively managed relative return portfolio is to match the percentage of the active portfolio invested in a stock to the percentage of that stock in the benchmark index, irrespective of how large or small it may be. A 'no bet' in an absolute return portfolio is no weighting at all.

2.7   ARITHMETIC AND GEOMETRIC RETURN

Returns, whether historic or expected, are nearly always quoted as averages. It was averages that gave rise to the nineteenth-century quote, attributed by Mark Twain to Benjamin Disraeli, which can be just as valid today: 'there are three kinds of lies: lies, damn lies and statistics.'[12]. It is no less important in the twenty-first century to understand the construction of averages used to measure returns to be able to distinguish between the lies and the statistics.

The word 'average' derives from the Latin *havaria*. Havaria described compensation money for loss of cargo at sea averaged over those whose goods were safely delivered. While there are five different methods of calculating an average, the idea behind each method is that it is representative of a group of values. Trustees simply need to know what a particular average return implies and where it might be misleading in not being representative.

The two averages that will concern trustees of endowment funds most of the time are the geometric mean and arithmetic mean. How these are measured is given in the Glossary (see mean, median and mode), but each method of calculating an average has its own purpose and it is important not to confuse them. It is especially important not to compare the geometric average of one series of numbers with the arithmetic average of another.

The arithmetic mean is always larger than the geometric mean. Consider an investment that returns +50% in one year and −50% in the second. What is the average? If $100 less 50% is $50 and $100 +50% is $150 then the arithmetic average is ($150 + $50)/2 = 100. And 100 is where you started isn't it? So your return is zero. Not quite. If you invested $100 at the beginning and gained 50% then you had $150 at the end of Year 1. However, if in Year 2 you lost 50%, the $150 becomes $75. It's the same if you lost $50 in Year 1 and gained 50% in Year 2, it doesn't matter which way round. The geometric average provides the annual percentage change between the 100 and the 75.

So what does the geometric average do for us? The geometric average gives the annual average for compounding a series of returns. In the above example it is the square root of 0.50×1.50, which equals 0.866, i.e. -13.4% per annum ($100 \times (1 - 0.866)$). Multiply 100 by -13.4% (i.e. by 0.866) twice and you get 75. The geometric average equates a beginning and end value: an investment of $100 realized at $200 after 10 years gives a 100% rate of return (over 10 years) but a compounded annual average (geometric) return of 7.18%. This is an Internal Rate of Return (IRR) which can equally be calculated from a series of cash flows such as from a fixed income bond. The IRR is another name for the redemption yield on a fixed income bond, the rate that equates the cash flows received, both from interest received and from capital ultimately redeemed, with the initial cash outlay on that investment. It is the return that the bond will ultimately provide on the critical assumption that coupons during the life of the bond are reinvested at that rate. It is the basis for calculating compound interest.

Compound interest, according to Albert Einstein, is the eighth wonder of the world. He also called it 'the greatest mathematical discovery of all time'. One of the finest examples of compound interest at work is a trust established by Benjamin Franklin on his death in 1790. The idea for the trust came from a French mathematician called Charles-Joseph Mathon who wrote a parody, called 'Fortunate Richard', of Benjamin Franklin's Poor Richard's Almanac. In the parody, Fortunate Richard left a sum of money to be spent only after it had accumulated interest for 500 years.

Franklin wrote a codicil to his will leaving £1,000 each to the cities of Boston and Philadelphia for 200 years, the funds to be loaned for good purposes at 5% interest, the interest received to be reinvested in further loans at the same rate of interest:

> If this plan is executed, and succeeds as projected without interruption for one hundred years, the sum will then be one hundred and thirty-one thousand pounds; of which I would have the managers of the donation to the town of Boston then lay out, at their discretion, one hundred thousand pounds in public works, which may be judged of most general utility to the inhabitants. . . . The remaining thirty-one thousand pounds I would have continued to be let out on interest, in the manner above directed, for another hundred years. . . . At the end of this second term, if no unfortunate accident has prevented the operation, the sum will be four millions and sixty one thousand pounds sterling, of which I leave one million sixty one thousand pounds to the disposition of the inhabitants of the town of Boston, and three millions to the disposition of the government of the state, not presuming to carry my views farther.

The instructions for Philadelphia were in the same vein and by 1990 the Boston Trust had accumulated nearly $5 million but the Philadelphia Trust, for some reason, rather less.

The geometric average therefore provides a single measure of periodic or 'annualized' return. But there is enormous room for error in comparison between geometric means when different time periods or different cash flows are involved and when beginning and end values are carefully selected. The question that must always be asked by a trustee is whether a particular average is truly representative of what it purports to represent and how much difference to the average does one number make? A fund that made a return of 50% five-years ago, and 5% a year in the last four years, shows a five-year average return of 12.7%. But so does one that made 12% five years ago and 13% per annum for the four subsequent years. Which is apparently the more attractive?

Table 2.1 Annual arithmetic and geometric returns

Year	Arithmetic (%)	Geometric [1+ (%/100)]
1	−6	0.94
2	28	1.28
3	17	1.17
4	−9	0.91
5	27	1.27
6	31	1.31
7	−11	0.89
8	24	1.24
9	22	1.22
10	−23	0.77
Annual average:	**10%**	**1.083**
Std deviation:	**20%**	

This is a trap into which many investors fall. They are attracted by high returns at the very point when such returns are about to reverse. In January 2000 close to $90 billion was invested in 401K plans in one month on the basis of extrapolating high equity returns. The compound average return since then has been poor. Participants in one particularly successful mutual fund at the time are still underwater on their investment. Concerns to avoid such traps are behind the investment strategy rebalancing which we will consider later in the book.

Another feature of geometric and arithmetic averages is the more volatile the series of returns, the larger will be the difference between them. Volatility is measured by a statistic called *standard deviation*. Consider the numbers in Table 2.1.

The arithmetic average of the series of numbers in Table 2.1 is 10. The geometric average, however, is only 8 (8.3 to be precise). The volatility (standard deviation) of this series is 20 – that is, the variation either side of the arithmetic average of 10 is 20. One can say, therefore, that in two years out of three the return is within 10% plus or minus 20%. The nominal return will be somewhere between +30% and −10% in two years out of three. Incidentally, two years out of three is not the same as two years out of *every* three years – another common misunderstanding of a standard statistic. There could be several consecutive years of a number outside these parameters before a longer period occurs within them.

Now consider Table 2.2, which shows the annual average 10-year return of seven investments that have increasing volatility. The arithmetic mean for all seven investments is the same, that

Table 2.2 Impact of volatility on geometric means (10 year returns)

Investment	Arithmetic average return (%)	Geometric average return (%)	Standard deviation (volatility) (%)
A	10	10	10
B	10	9	15
C	10	8	20
D	10	7	25
E	10	6	30
F	10	5	35
G	10	4	40

is 10%, as in Table 2.1, but the volatility of returns around that average is different for all seven investments.

As the volatility increases, even though the arithmetic average stays the same at 10%, the geometric average declines. But didn't we say that it is the geometric average used for compounding returns that determines the accumulation of wealth over time? And indeed it is. This explains, as we will investigate later, the benefit of volatility reduction through portfolio diversification. Even then, however, one must be careful. Two funds may have the same compounded return over a period with different volatilities, but if funds are extracted or added then the wealth ratios – the amount of money you have at the end relative with the amount you started with – will differ.

Volatility is often equated with risk. We will look at risk when defined as volatility, and volatility as it relates to strategy in a later chapter. But if a diversified portfolio can provide a 10% return every year with low volatility, compared to one that achieves the same result but with more volatility of annual returns, then it becomes obvious which one an endowment should invest in to enjoy the magic of compound interest in accumulating wealth.

While the geometric mean gives you the annual average compound return, and the accumulated amount of wealth at the end of the period, the arithmetic return is the most appropriate when measuring the variation of one year's return with the next. It is this average that is used to calculate the excess return, known as premium, which is required for the risks we will investigate in Chapter 3, 'Elements of Return'.

The difference between arithmetic and geometric returns also features in the measurement of relative performance. If one portfolio returns 40% and its benchmark returns 30%, the relative return on an arithmetic basis is $40\% - 30\% = +10\%$. On a geometric basis it is $1.40/1.30 = 1.0769$ or $+7.69\%$. If another portfolio return was 19% and the benchmark was 10%, the arithmetic difference would be $19\% - 10\% = 9\%$. The geometric ratio would be: $1.19/1.10 = 1.0818 = +8.18\%$. So, if you measured relative performance on an arithmetic basis, the first portfolio manager performed better than the second ($+10\%$ against $+9\%$), but if you measured on a geometric basis the second manager performed better: $+8.18\%$ against $+7.69\%$.

It's important therefore to *understand* that there are differences between averages. Both methods of calculating averages are definitions to be applied appropriately in the right circumstances. One is absolute, the other is proportional. Arithmetic may be more intuitive because it measures differences. Geometric measures a ratio but demonstrates that outperforming by a fixed amount in a down market is more difficult than in an up market. But, most important of all, when geometric averages are applied to wealth, the impact of compounding that wealth grows dramatically with time.

2.8   TIME-WEIGHTED RETURN AND MONEY-WEIGHTED RETURN

As institutional investment of high cash flow pension funds developed in the 1960s and 1970s, the question arose as to how you measure and compare the return of managers and funds that had different cash flow profiles. The traditional internal rate of return (IRR) calculation, which is an annualized compounded total return and the basis for measuring bond redemption yields, could not provide the answer needed by plan sponsors. The impact of new cash flows made IRR measurements not comparable between managers.

The problem was solved by the Bank Administration Institute in the USA in 1968. The Institute developed the concept of *time*-weighted return (TWR) rather than *money*-weighted return (MWR). (MWR is also known as dollar-weighted return). The process was quite simply to value a fund every time there was a cash inflow or outflow, to calculate the return for the period between those dates and compound the periodic numbers. These numbers were now comparable to the returns of other funds, irrespective of cash flows, and to indices.

Mutual funds, which are valued and receive subscriptions and pay out redemptions daily, are a perfect example of time-weighted return. Large cash flows into and out of such funds may affect the manager's ability to invest properly but technically the returns are all directly comparable. Time-weighted return therefore solves the technical issue of comparability between funds but the practical problems of immediately investing high levels of cash flow remains. In today's world this can be solved using derivatives and 'program trades' (the purchase and sale of whole baskets of securities) to gain the necessary overall market exposures. As the manager subsequently buys individual securities with the new money, the market exposure represented by the derivative is systematically unwound. This process, not readily available to fund managers in the 1970s, at least ensures that the fund is effectively fully invested at all times.

For funds that do not permit the use of derivatives and program trades, or are invested in markets where such instruments are not available, the problem remains. If an investment manager receives cash in a fast-rising market, then unless that person commits the funds to securities immediately there is a risk of underperformance of both peer group and index benchmark. This can lead to ever shorter timescales for asset shift decisions, even for longer term asset classes. And without precisely timed calls on market tops and bottoms, tactical asset allocation in a multi-asset fund usually fails to add value.

While market timing may be panning for fools gold, asset shifts over cycles can add value where the concern is loss of real money and not relative underperformance. Moving gradually out of manias or into panics may lead to 'time-weighted' underperformance in the shorter term but higher 'money-weighted' return over time. Figure 2.1 illustrates the point.

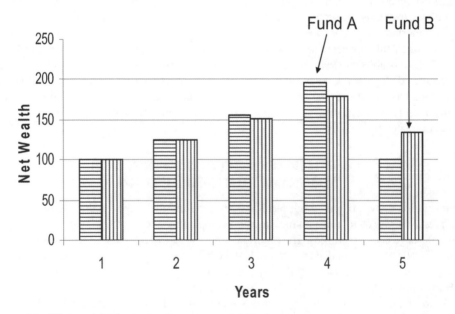

Figure 2.1   Time-weighted returns versus money-weighted returns

The example in Figure 2.1 is of two funds, A and B, which have no cash flows into or out of the funds and are measured over five years. The benchmark for both funds is the same equity market index and the mandate of both funds allows movement into cash at the discretion of the manager. At the end of Year 1, Funds A and B were each worth exactly $100. Both funds had been fully invested in the same equity market index for a number of years and had enjoyed many years of good performance. The index continued to rise in the following years: 25% per annum in Years 2, 3 and 4. The annual return on cash was 5% .

The bull market ended in Year 5 with a 49% fall.

The manager of Fund A did not believe in 'market timing' and stayed fully invested through-out. By the end of Year 4 this looked good and in three years the fund's value had nearly doubled to $195. Fund A had significantly outperformed Fund B as Fund B had begun to move from equities into cash. In fact, by the end of Year 4 the Trustees were considering giving the whole of Fund B to Manager A.

The manager of Fund B had become nervous of equities, even by the end of Year 2. Manager B also did not believe in market timing, in the ability to identify precisely the tops and bottoms of markets. Instead this manager believed in identifying domains of relative value between asset classes – in this case between equities and cash – on a longer term view. These domains are areas of extreme value relative to other asset classes and the relationships tend to regress to a mean. As equities began to reach extreme valuation, the manager began to move into cash.

So Manager B decided as a matter of policy to keep just $100 in equities and transfer any additional positive returns into cash at the end of each year to reduce portfolio exposure gradually. By the end of Year 4, Fund B had significantly underperformed Fund A. It was only $179 in size and now had 44% in cash. After the fall in equities in Year 5 Fund B still had total assets of $133 against $100 in the hands of Manager A. The internal rate of return (IRR) – the compounded annual average return – over the four years from the end of Year 1 for Fund B was 7.4%, an annual return that had comfortably beaten cash. The IRR of Fund A was zero.

This is not a carefully selected set of numbers to make an academic point. It reflects precisely the real experience of many pre-crash markets, whether gold in the 1970s, Japan in the 1980s or 'tech stocks' in the 1990s. Three or four years is the life cycle of many fund managers' mandates. On this time horizon even the great Warren Buffett may have been deserted by his limited partners in his early years if relative performance had been the measure of his success. Long-term horizon investors may not be able to pick tops and bottoms of financial markets. That is not the issue if building net wealth is the objective. The caveat about ability to time market movements remains. The message from Figure 2.1 is that the main value-added in strategy arises from occasional and gradual moves at relative value extremes that capture major scenario changes. These should be the key areas of trustee focus.

The next chapter moves on from the vocabulary of return to look at the elements of return. Elements make up the numbers that constitute financial returns and how they relate to each other. They are the drivers of return – the underlying factors that create those numbers, whether positive or negative. These drivers are essential ingredients to determining strategy and the key areas on which trustees should question their investment advisers.

Elements of Return

Life can only be understood backwards, but it must be lived forwards.

If 'Language of Return' was the vocabulary of return, then this chapter is the grammar. Return is created through economic activity and financial intermediation. The Central Bank sets the price at which money is lent to the government and this establishes the risk-free rate of interest from which other rates are derived. Time is money and the future is uncertain, creating a premium for risk which is amplified in the case of non-government assets by the economic cycle. Guesstimating the future effectively requires analysis of the sources and drivers of return and of the validity of past relationships; it is not simply about extrapolating past returns. It is also about recognizing future uncertainty through scenario analysis rather than a single point estimate being the weighted average of most likely outcomes. As Keynes also wrote in The General Theory: *'The assumption of arithmetically equal probabilities based on a state of ignorance leads to absurdities.'*

3.1 DERIVING RETURN

Financial return implies saving from income employed in capital for investment. But aggregate wealth is created by the implementation of new ideas. GaveKal describes the money-go-round as follows. Entrepreneurs create economic growth and are rewarded by profit. Entrepreneurs need money, which is obtained from rentiers, who take little or no risk, through the medium of financial intermediaries (banks, financial markets, usurers). Financial intermediaries guarantee the return both of and from capital and take a margin for risking their capital. The return of the rentier is the 'rente' which amounts to short interest rates compounded.

The main duty of the Central Bank is to fix the remuneration of the lender, the rentier. When central banks increase the supply of liquidity to intermediaries, those intermediaries seek to lend on the funds for the acquisition of goods, services and financial assets and the funds find their way back in the form of deposits. This flow of funds between borrowers and lenders creates the demand for and supply of deposits and credit. The price at which demand meets supply is the rate of interest, and it is this rate of interest, driven by the underlying flows, that is a prime force in the movement of asset prices. At its simplest, an increase in supply of liquidity causes a fall in the price (interest rate) of money and a fall in the yield of fixed interest bonds: their prices rise. This happens at the short end of the bond maturity structure, the end that is closest to cash, and creates a steepening of the yield curve, which has traditionally been a reliable precursor to stronger growth.

If short rates of interest are maintained below the growth rate of the economy, those taking risk are rewarded and the economy grows according to its long-term potential. If short rates are maintained below the sustainable level of economic growth, it leads to financial bubbles. To quote Alan Greenspan, Chairman of the US Federal Reserve (July 2005): 'History cautions that long periods of relative stability often engender unrealistic expectations of its permanence and, at times, may lead to financial excess and economic stress.' If short rates move above the growth rate of the economy then there is no reward for taking risk and profits collapse. Short rates must then fall too, in order to preserve economic growth.

The net present value of financial assets is derived from discounting future cash flows. In the case of equities these cash flows are profit, whether earnings or ultimately as some form of dividend, from business. If short rates are below the growth rate of the economy then profits on average should grow at least in line with general economic growth. A fall in the rate of discount (interest rate) also raises the present value (current market price) of those flows. So equity assets benefit from two influences: economic stimulus and a lower rate of discount of future cash flows.

For financial return to be consumable it must be realizable. Realizable return depends on an element which we touched on in Chapter 2, which is liquidity. Investment liquidity is the ability to realize an asset for cash when needed and is measured by the time it takes to convert the asset to cash. If the annual daily turnover of a share listed on a Stock Exchange is 10,000 shares and an endowment holds 100,000, then that is 10 days of daily turnover. A holding of $100,000 of a Government bond is a fraction of a minute of turnover in Government bond markets.

Investment liquidity is partly a function of economic liquidity and partly a function of the particular market. What is liquid one day can be illiquid the next. In periods of panic, highly liquid assets can become unsellable; there are simply no buyers. And in periods of boom even illiquid assets can be sold – and at most surprising prices. In the late 1980s Japan had the second largest and one of the most highly liquid equity markets in the world. Yet in early 1999 there was one day on which the volume of trade on the New York Stock Exchange in one stock, Dell Computer, was greater than the turnover on the whole of the Tokyo Stock Exchange.

When an asset has fallen in value there is a tendency to want to sell. This is frequently the wrong reaction but one of the most fatal errors a trustee can make is to be forced into a position of realizing an illiquid asset near the bottom of a market to provide for an endowment's needs. The longer the life of the endowment, the more negligent that error. Long-term endowment institutions should have the luxury of buying illiquid assets when values are depressed below their true worth and selling when such assets are in great demand. But an equally fatal error can be to maintain a pool of liquid assets for a period during which liquidity is simply not a need for the endowment, to satisfy either operating or investment needs. This is the case where future expense, or intergenerational equity, demands higher returns than those achievable on short-term assets.

There is a long debate about the economic need for liquidity in investment markets. In the 1930s John Maynard Keynes considered that the 'fetish for liquidity' provided by exchange markets simply encouraged a form of speculation which added no economic value. He commented famously: 'Speculators may do no harm as bubbles on a steady stream of enterprise. But the position is serious when enterprise becomes the bubble on a whirlpool of speculation. When the capital development of a country becomes a by-product of the activities of a casino, the job is likely to be ill done.'

Keynes discounted the view that speculators helped to counteract short and long period differences in demand and supply because he thought they were unlikely to be better informed on average than producers and consumers. But he did argue that speculators had a role, for which excess profit was their due, in taking on risk which either producers or consumers were unwilling to bear themselves, and that has become conventional financial wisdom. Speculation provides liquidity that improves the efficiency of capital. That has clearly been one of the functions of hedge funds in the contemporary world.

Keynes observed that 'the spectacle of modern investment markets has sometimes moved me toward the conclusion that to make the purchase of an investment permanent and indissoluble, like marriage, might be a reasonable remedy for our contemporary evils.' This was reflected over 60 years later by David Swensen, Chief Investment Officer of Yale University.

Swensen[1] remarked, 'Illiquidity induces appropriate long-term behavior. Rather than relying on liquid markets to trade out of mistakes, investors in illiquid securities enter into long-term contracts, purchasing part ownership in a business with which they have to live.' He showed a close correlation between market capitalization of listed equity and public scrutiny and he commented that less liquid securities are not profitable for sell-side houses to follow closely, which provides greater potential pricing anomalies. Swensen argued that this was what opened the door to superior long-term returns.

3.2   RISK-FREE RETURN

The safest financial return is called the 'risk-free rate of interest'. The risk-free rate of interest is represented by the discount rate on a three-month Government Treasury Bill, converted into a rate of interest. The Treasury Bill is deemed 'risk free' because it provides the closest thing to certainty that you *will* be paid when you lend money for reward.

That, of course, assumes a stable government that will not renege on its obligations. Government bonds are considered to be 'risk free' but history tells us that governments are not above defaulting on their obligations, as holders of Russian Government bond certificates, with coupons still attached for dividend dates after 1917, will testify. Governments that do not have independent central banks also have the power to change the value of money, thereby devaluing their obligations in nominal terms. For this reason Government bonds have been described in the past as 'certificates of confiscation'.

An interest rate derived from a Treasury Bill is certain because such a bill is bought at a known discount today and it matures at 100 in three months' time. This gives what is known as the spot rate of interest, the rate of interest for money today. What the market today believes will be the risk-free rate of interest in three months' time for the ensuing three months, or for a future longer period, can be determined from the futures market for interest rate contracts, and this is known as the forward rate of interest.

The Treasury Bill yield is a nominal rate of interest. From that must be deducted inflation to find a real risk-free rate. The risk-free rate of interest on short-term money is influenced by factors that include the demand for and supply of money and notions of a natural rate of interest, a function of population and productivity growth, which balances demand and supply of real goods and services in the economy.

Analysis by Dimson, Marsh and Staunton[2] shows that the nominal return on Treasury Bills in the USA over the 100 years of the twentieth century was 4.3% and the rate of inflation was 3.2%, giving an average risk-free real interest rate of 1.1%. The nominal rate in the UK over the twentieth century was 5.1% and the rate of inflation was 4.1% so the risk-free real return was 1%. Over the first 50 years of the century the nominal and real returns were 2.6% and 0.6% respectively. This means of course that an endowment invested in risk-free assets over the twentieth century could have spent only 1% per annum of the value of the capital if it were to have preserved the capital in real terms.

The real risk-free rate and the expected rate of inflation are therefore prime elements of the cost of money in the system. Markets today are efficient in pricing inflation into yields to compensate for the fall in the real value of fixed income capital. These rates in turn influence

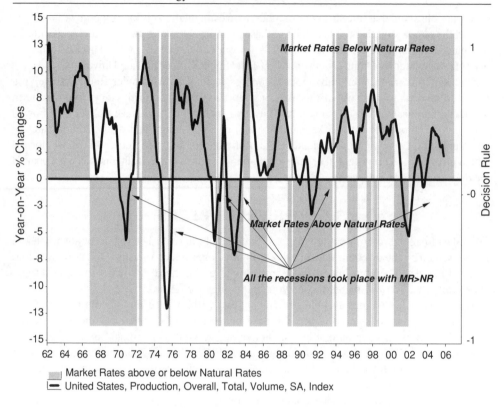

Figure 3.1 US industrial production variations and market versus natural interest rates
Source: GaveKal from EcoWin data.

the level of economic activity. If entrepreneurs cannot invest to achieve the cost of money, they may as well leave the funds in the bank. And if interest rates capitalized grow faster than profits or GDP over the long term, the system implodes.

Figure 3.1 shows that every recession in the USA after 1968 followed a rise in real rates of interest above the 3% level. When market rates were below this 'natural' 3% level, the economy grew normally.

Finally, while this rate of interest is called 'risk free', we will see in Chapter 4 that this does not mean that a Treasury Bill is necessarily a risk-free investment for what an endowment may need to achieve. If the need is long-term real growth in assets, an endowment that is wholly invested in the 'safest' asset, i.e. Treasury Bills, is almost certain to fail to meet its objective, especially when holding large amounts of cash near the bottom of markets. That is not prudent investment by a trustee, quite the reverse.

3.3   PREMIUM FOR RISK

A safe return is worth more than a risky one, so an investor must be paid more to accept a riskier return. If one invests a dollar for a year with an 80% chance of receiving back the dollar plus 10 cents, and a 20% chance of receiving back only 90 cents, the expected return from that investment is 1 dollar and 6 cents ($1.10 \times 0.8 + 0.90 \times 0.2$). If the risk-free rate of interest provides a certain payback of 3 cents at the end of the year (1.03×1.0), then the risk premium with this investment is 3 cents: 6 cents of expected return minus 3 cents of risk-free, Treasury Bill interest. The extra 3 cents is the encouragement to invest in a situation that is not risk free.

Bonds are loans that pay interest (coupons) and are due for repayment on their maturity dates. The longer the maturity date the less certain one can predict the likely interest rate at intervals during the life of the bond. Longer term bond yields therefore include a premium for the risk of an adverse change in the interest rate during the life of the bond. In a normal environment yields therefore tend to rise along the range of maturities to reflect the increasing risk of changes in both inflation and real interest rates over time. This is known as a positive or upward-sloping yield curve and the difference in yield between a Treasury Bill and a longer dated Government bond is known as the 'maturity premium'.

The yield curve can become inverted from time to time, which means that rates of interest are higher at the short end than at the long end. The yield curve reflects the market's view of a future which is shaped by policy-makers who create an inversion by raising short-term rates aimed at controlling inflation and depressing economic activity. This implies lower future real and nominal rates of interest than in the present, more buoyant, economic environment. An inverted yield curve has for long been a reliable precursor of a slowing economy and declining stockmarket.

The yield curve can also be skewed by anomalous market factors such as high demand for long-dated bonds by pension funds. However, various studies have shown that the yield curve has, in the past, still provided an accurate forecast of economic conditions some 12 months in advance. Whether this will continue to be the case to the same degree is even a matter of debate in the Federal Reserve. When Banks were the sole source of intermediation between lenders and borrowers, yield curve inversion implied pressure on bank profitability because of the longer maturity of their assets than their liabilities. This meant that banks reigned in the lending, which helps finance economic activity. But today the many ways in which savings can move into investment other than through banks can weaken the effect of monetary policy.

As always, it is important to understand the underlying conditions that create the curve rather than simply rely on its shape. A disinflationary environment with unused capacity, where short rates are reduced to raise demand, is different from one where short rates are low because inflation is low but demand is strong and capacity well-utilized, and long-term bondholders are beginning to become concerned about inflation.

A yield curve can flatten because short rates rise in response to policy moves to restrain economic activity. The curve can also flatten because long rates fall in response to investor belief that inflation (or real rates) will be lower in the future as a result of policy moves already made. Cause, not just effect, and the next likely policy move is what matters.

Longer periods of time tend to be associated with greater risk and reward. In 1938, Frederick Macaulay[3] outlined a useful concept called 'duration'. This measures the sensitivity of the present value of future cash flows from an investment to a change in the rate at which those cash flows are discounted. It measures the amount of time in years which it takes for an investor to receive half the present value of all cash flows from an investment using the investment's own yield to maturity as the discount rate.

Duration is not 'maturity', which is the date on which capital is finally repaid and any obligation expires. Duration is the average maturity of the cash flows involved. For example, a bond that matures in three years' time and pays a coupon of 10% per annum for three years but is currently priced at a discount such that the yield to maturity is 20% (20% being the discount rate which equates the three coupon payments and the gain on maturity to the present value of the bond) has a duration of 2.68 years. The same bond with the same maturity date and the same yield to maturity but pays no coupon during those three years and simply returns the capital at the end of Year 3, has a duration of three years. If there is only one cash flow, and it occurs on the date at which the investment matures, then duration and maturity will be the same.

Duration is useful in fixed income security analysis as a measure of sensitivity of bond prices to a change in interest rates. The longer the duration, assuming the same coupon rate, the more sensitive is the bond to a 1% change in rates, so the more volatile becomes the price.

Duration is also useful in helping to match assets to liabilities and as a guide to the classification of assets. Duration has a number of useful features as a broad method for categorizing assets classes for endowment funds. First, it encapsulates time and cash flow return, which are both crucial components of endowment fund thinking. Like net present value, duration values the closer cash flows more highly, and the more so the higher the value of money (the interest rate).

Duration also encapsulates volatility risk. The sooner the cash flow, the lower the duration and the lower the volatility risk. The longer the duration, the greater is the sensitivity of the present value of the asset to changes in yield. A long-dated zero coupon bond will change more in value in response to a change in interest rates than a bond, with the same maturity, that carries a coupon. If three zero coupon bonds yield 10% to maturity and one matures in three years, another in five and the last in 10, then a 1% change in yield will make, respectively, a 2.7%, a 4.4% and an 8.6% change in the current price of the bond. Duration generally implies greater return over time. If higher risk means higher reward and longer duration equals more risk, more duration should mean more reward, all other things being equal.

When it comes to investments that do not have government backing, investors demand a further premium on top of the risk-free rate for the risk of default for the interest paid and the ultimate redemption of the bond. This default premium is measured as a 'credit spread', which is the difference in redemption yield between a corporate bond and a government stock of the same maturity. Credit spreads are therefore a barometer of investor concerns about the risk of whole classes of asset (such as corporate bonds) or specific securities. The arithmetic of bond yields is as shown in Table 3.1, where one can see that several variables are implied in a bond yield and the key is to understand what the current market price implies about each of these variables. For example, a corporate bond may yield 7.50% but some questions would be: is this a very high-grade bond (Triple A and therefore rated by the market as minimal risk of default) and is the default risk premium only 0.5%? If so, is the risk-free rate just 1.50%

Table 3.1   The elements of bond yield

Bond Yields (some illustrative numbers)	Percentage per annum	Yield %
Risk-free real interest rate	2.50	
= Government Index-Linked Security yield		**2.50**
Add Expected rate of inflation	2.50	
= Yield on Government fixed income security		**5.00**
Add Credit default risk	1.50	
= Yield on Corporate fixed income security		**7.50**

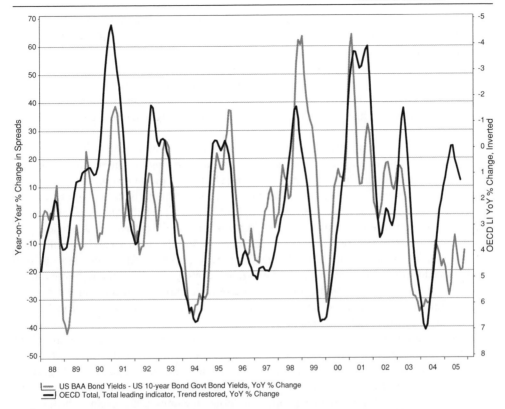

Figure 3.2   Spreads and economic activity are correlated: When spreads widen, activity falls
Source: GaveKal from EcoWin data.

implying an inflation expectation of 4.50%? Or is the real rate of interest 4.50% and inflation premium 2.50%? Or is the credit spread the largest element of the yield?

In an inflationary period, the risk to the bondholder is that the real value of the bond is eroded by inflation, so this risk will be reflected in an inflation risk premium. In a deflationary period the risk is that the bondholder receives nothing because the company files for bankruptcy and the risk will be reflected in a default risk premium.

So, in a deflationary period credit spreads are likely to increase because reduced economic activity makes riskier projects vulnerable. Credit spreads will decrease with economic recovery. The GaveKal chart in Figure 3.2 shows that when leading economic indicators trend upward, the correct investment decision is indeed to sell Government bonds and buy lower grade corporate bonds, and vice versa when they decline.

3.4   EQUITY RISK PREMIUM

The equity risk premium (ERP) is the amount of extra return over Treasury Bills required for holding equity-type assets as a reward for taking risk. Equity-type assets, such as shares or real estate, are those that represent ownership in a business or a property and give entitlement to the income generated by that activity after all the expenses have been paid. The amount of extra return is therefore a function of many things, including the amount of financial and operating leverage and the quality of the underlying earnings which supports the dividends or rent. Common stock is inherently riskier than bonds because if the company fails the bondholders may be paid in full, while those holding equity may lose all their money.

The equity risk premium is only specifically measurable with hindsight by looking at what the total return over a period has been and relating that to the total return on the equivalent Treasury Bill. However, history provides a framework for looking at the future to estimate the expected risk premium.

The equity risk premium, the excess required return, is an important component of the cost of capital. The value of an equity, both a share in a company and an interest in a property, is the present value of all future income, including realization of the investment, discounted by the cost of capital. The value on realization of the asset should be the net present value at the time of realization of subsequent expected dividends or net rents. It therefore follows that the future long-term return on an equity or property is equal to the current dividend yield plus the rate of dividend growth, or the current rental yield plus the growth in net rents, ad infinitum.

Dividends are simply what are paid out of company earnings. The factors that underly dividend yield and growth are therefore the current earnings yield and the rate of earnings growth. If dividends are not paid out but retained in the company they are reinvested at the current rate of return on invested capital. This should create more underlying return which, in turn, is paid out in dividends or is retained.

If the future return on an equity is equal to the current yield plus the long-term rate of growth, it follows that the future equity risk premium is the current yield plus growth minus the risk-free return. The future equity risk premium can therefore be assessed by looking at the expectations embedded in market values. And holders of equity in a company are the last resort, just behind corporate bondholders, on which creditors may draw in the event of bankruptcy of a company. Equity risk premia and corporate credit spreads are therefore naturally related although there have been periods of moves in credit spreads that have not immediately been reflected in equity risk premia.

So, a security that doesn't grow at all but pays a dividend of $5 for every $100 (yields 5%), or earns $5, and is held to infinity, is worth the same as another that pays 3% growing at 2% per annum to infinity, assuming they both embody the same degree of risk. The same is true if the yield is 1% and growth is 4% or the yield is 4% and the growth is 1%. That's the simple mathematics of it. The future equity risk premium is therefore the current dividend yield plus the expected rate of dividend growth minus the yield on Treasury Bills.

In theory, inflation should not affect the valuation of equities, because the same rate of inflation should be incorporated equally in the numerator (earnings or dividend growth) and the denominator (long bond yield) of the equity valuation model. In practice, however, it actually does affect the valuation, and there may be a number of reasons. One reason is that inflation leads to misallocation of resources because of difficulty of judgment of projected returns in capital investment decisions. This might particularly be the case with a changing rate of inflation. Another reason is that stock market investors are subject to 'inflation illusion'. This suggests that investors tend to extrapolate historical nominal growth rates of dividends even in periods of changing inflation. This implies that stock prices are undervalued when inflation is high and may become overvalued when inflation falls.

The Dimson, Marsh and Staunton study found a strong relationship between real dividend growth and stock market performance but dividend growth was below that of GDP growth in 15 of the 16 countries they analyzed over the twentieth century. Furthermore, high GDP growth was not associated with high levels of dividend growth. The correlation, perversely, was negative. This is surprising since the long-term rate of corporate earnings growth will depend on the underlying real growth of the domestic and international economies, subject, in turn, to the company's domestic or international focus.

The explanation for this must lie in the involvement of factors other than just underlying economic growth – including the share of wealth creation going to profits rather than to wages, to taxes and to lenders of capital to the company. The study also argues that GDP estimation is an imprecise science and the three fastest growing economies, Japan, Italy and Spain, had little regard for public-listed shareholder value.

Others have noted that that expected growth was priced into stock markets at the beginning of the period and, in high-growth economies, overly so. But valuations apart, the real growth of profits per share in the USA in the second half of the twentieth century was less than 2% per annum, and dividend growth lower still. This past reality should be recognized in long-term expectations of future return from such assets.

Among other key factors affecting earnings versus GDP growth will be the underlying changes in the economy, reflected in the rise and fall of market capitalization of different sectors of the stock market. If we compare the beginning and end of the twentieth century we find from the Dimson, Marsh and Staunton study that, in the USA, railroads represented nearly two-thirds of the market capitalization of the US equity market in 1900 and just under 50% of that in the UK. One hundred years later they became an insignificant fraction of the US market and zero in the UK. Sectors that were small in 1900 were 62.4% and 52.6% of the USA and UK markets respectively by the year 2000. Chemicals grew from 0.5% of the US market's capitalization in 1900 to 13.9% by 1950 and back to 1.2% by 2000.

3.5   THE EIGHTH WONDER OF THE WORLD

The basic arithmetic of very long-term returns is simple. If future earnings or dividends don't grow at all, then an equity asset is simply a fixed income security. The return will be the same as a fixed income security that is priced at 100% and matures at the same price. The rate of return will simply be the current yield. This will incorporate the market's expectation of the real risk-free rate of interest, the future rate of inflation and the default risk premium of the equity. But if earnings and dividends are to grow, then that rate of growth is in addition to the risk-free rate, the rate of inflation and the rate for default.

In Chapter 2, 'Language of Return', we saw the impact on wealth of compounding interest or return – Albert Einstein's Eighth Wonder of the World. In the Introduction of this book, we also touched on Micawber's Rule, relating growth of an endowment to spending and return. The rule shows the trade-off between current spending of return and future endowment fund (and hence spending) growth. This trade-off is demonstrated graphically in the Dimson, Marsh and Staunton study which shows the difference between dividend income reinvestment and dividend consumption in the case of US and UK equities over the 100-year period of the twentieth century.

Table 3.2 shows what $1 or £1 would have become over the twentieth century: (a) if the $1 and £1 had simply grown in nominal value at the rate of inflation in US dollars or UK pounds sterling, i.e. what happened to the real value of money; (b) if they had been invested in Treasury Bills with the income reinvested; (c) if they had been invested in equities and all dividends had been consumed; and (d) if they had been invested in equities and all dividends had been reinvested in the equity markets.

Table 3.2   Impact on returns of compound interest and inflation

Investment of $1 and £1 in 1900	$ Value in 2000	£ Value in 2000
$1 and £1 growing at the rate of inflation	24	55
$1 and £1 invested in Treasury Bills, income reinvested	67	145
$1 and £1 invested in equities, **all dividends consumed**	198	149
$1 and £1 invested in equities, **all dividends reinvested**	16,797	16,160

Source: Dimson, E., Marsh, P. & Staunton, M. (2002) *Triumph of the Optimists: 101 Years of Global Investment Returns*. Princeton, NJ: Princeton University Press.

The impact of growth and the power of compound interest is clear. Compounding rather than consuming income return from Treasury Bills would have multiplied capital in real terms by three times its original value. Consuming all of the income return from Treasury Bills would have devalued in real terms most of the original $1 and £1 of capital, leaving an endowment powerless to pursue its objectives.

And a substantial part of the long-term superior return on equity investment in the two major equity markets of the twentieth century was due to growth, both inflation and real. Compounding return by reinvestment, rather than consumption of that growth, made an even more dramatic difference to the final total of wealth than simply compounding the income return from a risk-free security.

There is one final and crucial item that affects the arithmetic of return. This is change in yield or, in other words, a change in the basis of valuation. The shorter the time period of measurement, the larger the element of valuation change in the quantum of return. This factor outweighs all others in the short and medium term and can be one of the most difficult aspects of 'income illusion'. It needs special attention.

3.6   VALUATION CHANGE

In Chapter 2 we introduced the idea that part, if not all, of a capital gain element of total return may not be spendable. The 1990s encouraged a belief that long periods of high rates of historic investment return were both sustainable and consumable. Unfortunately this led to some spending rules that could only ensure the gradual erosion in the ability of an endowment to achieve its objectives in the long term. The financial market experience of the 1980s and 1990s was comparable to enjoying the rise in the price of one's home and feeling wealthier by the minute until one appreciates that selling it gives no more actual 'well-offness' if one has to pay just as much to buy another house of a similar type which has also risen in price by the same amount.

It is usually understood that high rates of nominal return due to high, but level, rates of inflation are not all consumable, and that the inflationary portion must be reinvested to maintain the real value of capital. Equally, it is reasonable that high returns due to high levels of real growth are more justifiably consumable. The difficulty with this is that anticipated high real rates of return are reflected in the market and therefore priced in to assets. So the trick is to determine how much of the return is due to underlying real growth and how much is due to valuation change.

The problem is the valuation change. The valuation change on a fixed income security is a function of : (1) the change in inflation; (2) the change in the real rate of interest; or (3) a change in the premium that investors charge for risk on top of the other two factors. In terms of an equity-type asset, such as a share in a company's earnings or a real estate investment, a fourth element embedded in the valuation is any change in the expected rate of future growth of income or gain generated by that security and the risk that investors will accept in different environments.

In order to assess valuation change as an element of return we must go back to Table 3.1, which shows the elements of a bond yield, and add one more component to complete the picture for total return: change in yield. Over the short term, change in yield is generally by far the biggest contributor to total return. It is only over the long term that the compounding effect of the income element of return begins to outweigh the effect of yield change. Because of the power of compound interest, the reinvestment of income is generally the major source of total return in the very long term.

Bond yields gradually rose with the increase in the rate of inflation in the 1960s and 1970s and fell in the last 20 years of the twentieth century as inflation subsided. Consider the corporate fixed income bond in Table 3.1 which paid $7.5 in income for every $100 invested (i.e. yields 7.5%). Assume now that future inflation expectation moves down to 1.00% and all other elements of yield stay the same. The yield on the bond will change from 7.5% to 6.0%. What happens to the price of our irredeemable bond? To yield 6% now when the income received on the bond is $7.5 a year, the price must move from $100 to $125 ($7.5/125 = 6\%$) to give us a 25% capital gain.

The total return on this bond is therefore the income plus capital gain, which is $(7.5 + 25)/100 = 32.5\%$. Is that 32.5% total return spendable? If you take the Hicks view of life which we considered in Chapter 2 it certainly is not. Remember he defined income as being 'the wealth which can be consumed in a year which leaves unchanged the quantum of wealth left to generate the same income in the following year'.

If you apply the Hicks logic to nominal numbers, you need whatever capital is required to produce $7.5 of income. What sum is this? $125. None of the gain is spendable. And if you apply the Hicks logic in real terms, not only is none of the gain spendable, but part of the income is also not spendable. If inflation proves to be 1.0% as expected, then the income you will need in Year 2 to be comparable to $7.5, adjusted for inflation, is $7.575. And the capital sum needed to generate that figure is not $125, but $126.25. So, of the $7.5 of income generated in Year 1, $1.25 should be reinvested in the bond and only $6.25 is spendable.

Equity-type assets are more difficult to assess because they involve elements of income and growth – that is, growth of underlying income and, even with no valuation basis change, of capital gain. This growth of income and capital provides a real increase in Hicksian 'well-offness' and is therefore spendable. But if an equity becomes high growth, the market may change the basis of valuation. It may move the valuation to a higher price earnings ratio because the equity price will rise to reflect the even higher present value of the expected cash flow. Where a stock becomes recognised as a growth stock, the investor gains a double benefit. Underlying growth in income is compounded by positive return from valuation change. The question is: How much of the valuation change is justifiably spendable?

Take an equity that is bought in Year 1 for $150 on a prospective price to earnings ratio of 15 times forecast earnings of $10. In fact it earns $12 rather than $10 over the next 12 months. The higher than anticipated growth in earnings will lead to a higher forecast in Year 2, perhaps

$15, and a higher expectation for the future, so the valuation basis will change. The market might now value the equity on a 17 times prospective earnings basis. 17×15 equals a market price of 225 rather than 150; so, without even any income return, the capital return has been $225/150 = 50\%$ over 12 months. Some of that gain is due to growth, and therefore spendable; some due to valuation gain. Since super-normal growth is not sustainable in the very long term for a portfolio of equities, judgment must be made as to how much of that return due to valuation change is due to rebalancing valuation levels to a more normal basis and how much is due to irrational exuberance.

GaveKal Research has demonstrated that a large part of US equity return in the 1980s and 1990s was due to the secular change in the rate of inflation and a consequent change in valuation basis. Figure 3.3 discounts the return from US equities by the 10-year zero coupon bond in the USA. Earnings growth explained a relatively small percentage of the difference in total return. It is clear that much of the high level of equity market return in the period was due to interest rate change, not real economic growth.

The Dimson, Marsh and Staunton analysis concluded that, of the excess return from equities over Treasury Bills over the whole of the twentieth century, a significant element in the USA

Figure 3.3   US equities discounted by the 10-YEAR ZERO COUPON bond
Source: GaveKal from EcoWin data.

and the UK was due to a substantial change in the valuation basis of equity markets. In the UK, for instance, the yield on equities at the beginning of the twentieth century was 4.3% compared to 2.4% at the end. Dimson, Marsh and Staunton state that valuation change caused 1.4% of the estimated 5.8% excess return of equities over Treasury Bills in the USA and 0.6% of the estimated excess return of 4.8% in the UK. Without the impact of valuation change, the 100-year excess return (equity risk premium) in the USA and the UK would be more like 4.3% and 3.1%, respectively. These are well below both many historic analyses and most expectations of long-term excess return.

But what is the long term? Ever since Edgar Lawrence Smith published his book *Common Stocks as Long Term Investments* in 1924, 'equities for the long run' has been an investment mantra. The Dimson, Marsh and Staunton study shows that only in the USA have equities shown a real return over all the 20-year periods they measured. Investors in other markets, including the UK, were not assured of a real return over that period and in some markets, such as China, Russia and Germany, wealth was confiscated or destroyed. Even in France and Italy there were periods of over half a century without a positive median real return, and in Japan equity investors had to wait nearly as long to be assured of an increase in real wealth.

Valuation change can have a dramatic enough impact on longer term returns, but it has a much more dramatic effect on short-term returns as we saw with our example of an equity which becomes higher growth. As Keynes observed[4]:

> most (professional investors and speculators) are largely concerned, not with making superior long-term forecast of the probable yield of an investment over its whole life, but with forecasting changes in the conventional basis of valuation a short time ahead of the general public. They are concerned, not with what an investment is really worth to a man who buys it 'for keeps', but with what the market will value it at, under the influence of mass psychology, three months to a year hence.

Keynes's words were published in 1936 but, like aphorisms from Shakespeare, will be truisms in every market while human nature is involved. Analysis of equities is all about discovering differences between intrinsic value and market price. But market price can often be driven by irrational optimism or depression. What is remarkable is that generations never learn; there may not be many constants in investment, but fortunately for those with appropriate skills and temperament, one constant is human nature: the fear and greed and herd mentality that drives market extremes and the opportunities for those with level heads.

Manias and panics have been a feature of markets for centuries[5] but it might be thought that increasingly professional asset management in the second half of the twentieth century might have led to some maturity in financial markets. Not so, it seems. The nifty-fifty era of the 1960s was one in which growth in a low-interest environment became valued so highly that prices became increasingly vulnerable to a change in the environment. When the S&P 500 was on an average PE ratio of 19 times, many high-growth stocks reached at least three times that valuation. And several of these stocks continued to grow earnings at a high rate; what changed was a move into a double-digit interest and inflation rate environment. This led to valuation decline and the lowest return from equities for decades, below even that from cash.

Another example of irrational optimism was the equity market in Japan in the 1980s. Some will remember when the land value of the Imperial Palace in Tokyo was greater than the estimated value of the whole of California. The market capitalization of NTT, the Japanese telecommunications company, was greater than that of the whole German stock market. This excess was post-rationalised on the grounds that Japan had found the formula for permanent economic success, as had happened in the USA 60 years earlier, and the exuberance reached its peak at the end of the 1980s before more than a decade of economic stagnation and stock market decline.

The last decade of the twentieth century saw the bull market in US technology stocks. By the peak of the market in 2000, TMT (Technology, Media, Telecoms) stocks represented over 30% of the S&P 500 index, even though these industries never represented more than 10% of GDP. They were an even smaller proportion of total corporate profits – many were making losses. One of the most glaring extremes was AOL which was added to the S&P index in 1999 after reporting a large loss. They stated that they would become profitable, for the first time, at some stage in the next five years.

At an earlier stage, some were warning that the high returns that had been achieved in equity markets – largely on the back of valuation change – were not sustainable. One such was Robert Schiller who testified to the Board of Governors of the Federal Reserve on December 3, 1996, and authored the book *Irrational Exuberance*,[6] which was published with immaculate timing in 2000 just as the bull market came to an end. Schiller demonstrates how valuation, in the form of price–earnings ratios, have forecast subsequent returns: high PEs leading to low returns and vice versa. In his book he commented: 'the recent values of the price–earnings ratios, well over 40, are far outside the historical range of price–earnings ratios.' He further commented:

> according to calculations by Robert Fair, if market expectations for earnings growth are realised, and if US gross domestic product growth is 4% per annum, then after tax corporate profits as a fraction of gross domestic product will be over 12% in 2010, a value almost twice as high as it has been at any time since 1948. It is hard to imagine that so high a fraction of gross domestic product going to corporate profits will be tolerated by the public . . .

Schiller forecast a fall in markets and commented that 'colleges and endowments heavily invested in stocks may find that their ability to pursue their missions has suddenly been curtailed'. He proved to be right, despite the fact that the call was initially made a few years too early. Those who were out of the market two years before the end in Japan in the previous decade were thankful within three months after the end, the timing of which none could predict with any accuracy.

What, therefore, are the answers to the questions: What part of return is consumable? What must become the basis for spending policy? We will find that the key is the source and sustainability of the underlying stream of return and the change and the extent of likely reversion to a long-term trend of valuation. That, in turn, depends on what is driving the long-term trend.

3.7   DRIVERS OF RETURN

Now that we understand the arithmetic that constitutes return – the impact of yield, of growth, of premia for risk and of valuation change – we need to look at the underlying drivers of these factors. Too often the easy option when trying to assess the future is to extrapolate historic returns; the past becomes a simple proxy for the future. But it is the underlying economic, financial and indeed social conditions that created those returns that give us some clue as to what it may be reasonable to expect in future. Different conditions imply different return outcomes.

In the shorter term, unanticipated events are the drivers of changes in the pattern of returns. These are the drivers that change the valuation rates, the current yields and price–earnings ratios, and embody the markets' expectations for the long-term future. But change in expectations can be fickle and create 'noise' rather than reflect true 'signal'. That is where price deviates from value. The evidence shows, however, that the underlying trends in fair value are usually more stable.

A pull toward a value that is determined by given scenarios is not the same as simply 'return to the mean' of long-term returns implied by a fixed asset-weighting approach to portfolio rebalancing, a subject we will consider in Chapter 8, 'Understanding Strategy'. There are elements or return (and types of risk) appropriate to given economic environments and these environments are drivers of value. There are also behavioral and other forces, including momentum investment strategies, which drive price away from this value. Financial gravity will tend to pull price back into line with value even if, in the process, it fluctuates wildly around that value.

Regression to the mean of relationships is different. But, as Peter Bernstein elaborates in his excellent book on risk, *Against the Gods*,[7] even that process 'is a frustrating guide to decision-making. It can be such a slow process that shocks disrupt the trend which is often unstable and subject to wild fluctuations around it.' The mean valuation for an asset class in one environment will not be the same as that in another and these environments can last for decades. For example, the relationship of valuation between bonds and equities whereby the yield on equities historically exceeded that on bonds was rudely broken in the 1960s, one cause being a secular change in inflation that was not thought to be as permanent a fixture as it became. As Bernstein commented: 'although the contours of this new world were visible well before 1959, the old relationships in the capital markets tended to persist as long as people with memories of the old days continued to be the main investors.' Those who are still expecting regression to the mean of 1950 valuations may be closer today than at any time since, but it has been a long wait.

The past as proxy for the future was touched on by Harry Markowitz in an article in the *Journal of Finance* in 1952 which launched the ground rules for contemporary finance known as Modern Portfolio Theory (MPT).[8] Markowitz commented that 'one suggestion as to tentative expected returns and covariances, – covariances are an essential part of risk which we will cover in Chapter 4 – 'is to use the observed returns and covariances of the past.' But he went on to say: 'I believe that better methods, which take into account more information, can be found. I believe what is needed is essentially a "probabilistic" reformulation of security analysis.'

3.8   SCENARIO ANALYSIS

'Probabilistic reformulation' implies scenario analysis. It implies attributing probabilities to different economic and financial outcomes and assessing the implications for risk and return. Understanding the factors that helped to create past returns can shed light on expectations, allowing analysis of the future. Understanding these potential sources of return will help trustees to ask the right questions of their investment managers and avoid 'fighting past wars'. Too often one hears 'equities outperform bonds in the long term so a long-term equity strategy is obvious'. When something is obvious in investment, it's usually wrong. The past must be seen in the context of the scenarios within which past returns evolved before they can be used as a guide for the future.

Scenario analysis should be distinguished from 'black box models' with fixed algorithms that tend to outline one expected outcome and are used as a discipline to prevent emotions muddying the clear waters of rationality. 'Black boxes' are models which incorporate past interrelationships in algorithms that predict future outcomes from given inputs. The problem with models that are rigidly applied, rather than used as a guide, is that they tend, despite their complexity, to oversimplify and fail to recognize trend change.

The efficiency of asset markets in discounting information, and the methods of performance measurement, have encouraged a focus on shorter-term 'noise-driven' tactical asset allocation and stock selection. This has been irrespective of either the timing or quantum of the liabilities of the investor. Bernstein quotes Thaler and Be Bondt in demonstrating that investors over-weight recent, and underweight historic, long-term information. This creates the opportunity for investors with longer-term horizons. They can look through the 'noise' of much short-term information to the signals that determine the long-term asset value direction. And it allows the long-term investor to avoid the major structural misallocations of capital that tend to be the forerunners of major declines in markets.

GaveKal's philosophy of scenario evaluation is based on historical analysis which suggests that investment value is determined by two main variables, economic activity and prices. Economic equilibrium does not exist in the real world and activity follows trends and cycles, as does the movement of prices (inflation and deflation). If this is so then the environment moves through four principal scenarios, shown in Figure 3.4, with very different investment implications for each scenario. Analysis can determine the scenarios with a higher rather than a lower probability of occurring, allowing focus on that set of scenarios that have the highest probability of outcome. And this analysis eliminates low probability scenarios that allow portfolios to exclude assets that protect against a risk that does not exist.

Irving Fisher's classical equation suggests that

$$\text{Economic activity} \times \text{Price} = \text{Money supply} \times \text{Velocity of money.}$$

It postulates a direct relationship between economic activity and prices on the one hand and the supply and the velocity of money (how often the supply is turned over) on the other. So monetary indicators, velocity of money and economic activity are all part of the DNA of return. To quote Charles Gave: 'if there is more money than fools then markets rise, and if there are more fools than money markets fall.'

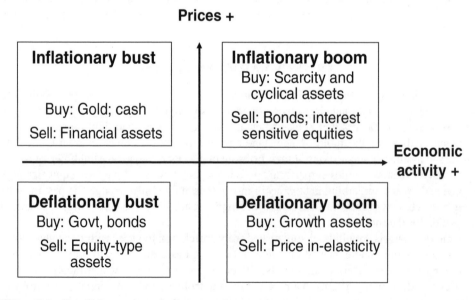

Figure 3.4   GaveKal scenario analysis
Source: GaveKal.

Each of the scenarios has its own implications in terms of asset returns and these are the conditions that drive the major asset strategy decisions. For example, the top two quadrants imply inflation, one with rising and one with falling economic activity. Where current economic and financial developments suggest a high probability of rising prices and rising activity then the portfolio emphasis will be toward real assets, such as commodities and real estate.

If inflation is on an uptrend but economic activity makes equities vulnerable, then bonds are not a good strategic diversifier. Rising inflation expectation will mean rising interest rates and falling bond and equity prices. Where inflation is under control, that means stable or falling, and where economic activity is vulnerable, then fixed income bonds are a good diversification for equities. Government bond yields should fall and prices rise, hence Government bonds become a good risk diversifier for an equity portfolio.

It is not just the rate of inflation but the change in the rate of increase or decrease in inflation or deflation that matters. Financial markets react to changes in the rate of increase because anticipated inflation is priced into interest rates. It is unanticipated inflation change that affects valuations most, along with changes in the real rate of interest arising from the other variable, which is economic activity.

A fixed income redemption yield will reflect the rate of inflation anticipated at that time. If inflation is expected to be 2% in future, the redemption yield might be 5%. But if inflation is expected to be 10% per annum, that yield will become closer to 13%. If inflation is zero, however, then the real element of yield is the driving force of yield change and capital return.

In the late 1940s, those who had placed their life savings in UK Government bonds as a low-risk investment and as a loyal post-war gesture to the national interest found their wealth even more cruelly destroyed by inflation in the 1960s, 1970s and 1980s than a previous generation had found with the redenomination of War Loan in the 1930s. The nominal value of their Government bonds, priced at £100 per cent and yielding 2.5% income in 1949, dropped 85% in money terms by the 1970s. In real terms, the fall was even greater which, together with a 98% maximum marginal rate of personal tax, was a covert government confiscation of wealth comparable to the overt confiscation by communist countries at the time.

Since the early 1980s, after the peak in inflation, there have been inflation-linked Government securities in the UK which many assume to be a risk-free real return. Treasury Inflation Protected Securities were introduced in the USA in 1997. Trustees need to question their professional advisers when this is sold to them as a 'real asset' solution. First, governments are not above changing the goal-posts in terms of the definition of inflation, i.e. changes in the constituents of the inflation indices. Secondly, the inflation-linked 'promise' only applies if the security is held over the life of the asset, which may be 20 or more years. Returns over 10 years or less on longer dated inflation-linked bonds will be much more sensitive in a low-inflation environment to changes in real interest rates than ever they will be to relatively small changes in the rate of inflation.

The bottom two quadrants in Figure 3.4 show falling inflation or even deflation. The fall in inflation in the 1980s and 1990s had the reverse impact of the previous decade on fixed income securities, and fixed income Government securities were therefore one of the best performing assets classes of the last 20 years of the twentieth century. Investing at 17% Government bond yields when inflation falls to 2% and yields to 4% gives the investor not only a massive real and nominal income return during the life of the bond but also a capital gain as the price of the bond rises, albeit not a gain that is necessarily spendable.

We saw in Figure 3.3 that equities enjoyed a comparable element of revaluation due to the fall in inflation in the 1980s and 1990s. The basis for an equally sustained future equity return of a similar magnitude would now be questionable in most markets. Exceptional future return in a low interest rate environment places the onus on real growth. When deflation involves falling prices and levels of economic activity, in a deflationary bust, cash and Government bonds are the only places to hide.

The quadrant scenario analysis is not a panacea. It is, however, a disciplined framework for looking at the world as it is, not as we would have it. Scenario analysis need not be mathematically precise but, to quote Keynes again[9]:

> the object of our analysis is, not to provide a machine, or method of blind manipulation, which will furnish an infallible answer, but to provide ourselves with an organised and orderly method of thinking out particular problems . . . too large a proportion of recent 'mathematical' economics are merely concoctions, as imprecise as the initial assumptions they rest on, which allow the author to lose sight of the complexities and interdependencies of the real world in a maze of pretentious and unhelpful symbols.

Charles Gave reminds us that economists and financial consultants are not like artists who can fall in love with their models. They must take care not to lose sight of the 'complexities and interdependencies of the real world' even if they have access to computing power that Keynes could not even have dreamed of. But models, properly understood, allow that 'what if' analysis that is so important to properly assessing both return and risk. A major input to strategy should therefore be consideration of those scenarios that are priced into markets and those that offer the highest risk of creating a failure of meeting objectives. Strategy should avoid the most risky likely outcomes – where risk is not properly priced – and diversify among the rest.

4
Understanding Risk

What is the sense of a weighted average that adds together a hundred falsehoods and one truth after multiplying each by some irrelevant number?

GEORGE SHACKLE

Risk, like beauty, is in the eye of the beholder. The same set of circumstances and resources can be risky for one endowment and not for another. Risk depends for its source on context and culture and is something to be managed not necessarily minimized. There is a long history in the development of the mathematics of risk which culminated in twentieth-century Modern Portfolio Theory. This changed the nature of thinking about risk. The concept moved from simply averaging risk across a portfolio to assessing the degree of co-movement of investments in determining the level of total fund risk represented by volatility of return. But there are flaws in this simple measure and we define risk for an endowment broadly as 'a measure of the likelihood and the extent to which an endowment's resources fail to meet its financial objectives during its expected life'. This definition accords with the Sortino approach that risk for an endowment is failure to meet a minimum acceptable return. And the definition implicitly assumes that endowment fund risk is more than simply the volatility of return. Risk is benchmarked to the liability demands on the fund over both operational and intergenerational time horizons.

4.1 DESCRIPTION OF RISK

Risk is like an elephant: easy to recognize, less easy to define and measure, capable of being benign yet also of having a big impact. The English word 'risk' derives from the Latin word *riscare* which means to dare. The Shorter Oxford Dictionary defines risk as 'hazard, danger; exposure to mischance or peril'. In the Chinese language there are two characters which, when placed together, mean risk. The first character on its own means danger; the second means opportunity. The two together imply two sides of one coin.

A Security and Exchange Commission's Concept Release in March 1995 on *Improving Descriptions of Risk* brought 3,700 comment letters. Perhaps the most striking observation from the letters was the number of different interpretations of risk. In response to the release, the Investment Company Institute, the US national association of mutual funds, commissioned in 1995 an independent survey of mutual fund shareholders' assessment of risk. Respondents were asked to identify from a list of eight concepts those which they included in their definition of risk and the four most popular were:

1. The chance of losing some of the original investment
2. Investment not keeping pace with inflation
3. Fluctuation in value
4. Not having enough money to achieve investment goals at the end of an investment horizon.

Does risk simply have to do with a potentially perilous outcome? Is it really just the probability of an adverse future event multiplied by its magnitude? Or is the Chinese notion of risk – a combination of danger and opportunity – more appropriate? Is risk like stress or calories which, in the context of health, may in some cases cause damage but equally in others be a necessary condition for above-average achievement? And once defined, is the degree of risk not a function of many things – the situation, the timing, duration and the magnitude of the event in relation to the perspective of the bearer of risk? Is it in some senses like beauty – in the eye of the beholder?

In the words of Lord Kelvin: 'anything that exists, exists in some quantity and can therefore be measured.' That is all very well but what precisely is being measured here? And can risk ever be measured by a single number? Even if it could, would that number be stationary both in magnitude and time? Or does risk not only change with time and conditions but even change according to the vantage point of the measurer, as in Einstein's Theory of Relativity, or in Heisenberg's Uncertainty Principle. Heinsenberg suggested that the act of measuring the location of a particle alters the position of the particle in an unpredictable way – the thoughts that drive Soros's theory of reflexivity.

It is important to realize that while in this chapter we are focusing on understanding risk, the objective of an endowment fund should not be simply to minimize investment risk because such a strategy will not help the endowment to maximize its potential. It should be to manage risk. But at least, in finding a definition of risk for endowments, we are solving for one part of the complicated equation which faces trustees in deciding how best to allocate resources in meeting the mission of the endowment.

This chapter is strictly about investment risk. Trustees of endowments must consider, as part of their fiduciary responsibilities, other types of risk including counterparty, regulatory and operational risk. These risks involve the relationship and controls between a manager delegated to manage the assets, the trustees, the custodian and any other advisers. But they are not risks we consider here in a book that is devoted to the understanding of investment strategy.

We will first of all look at the development of the theories about risk to gain some perspective on the subject before looking at a working definition for endowment funds. We will investigate the ways by which risk may be measured and will look critically at some of the conventional measures of risk used by investment professionals.

4.2   PASCAL'S WAGER

Peter Bernstein, in *Against the Gods – the Remarkable History of Risk*[1] describes a question proposed by Blaise Pascal, a seventeenth-century dissolute turned religious fanatic who was a brilliant mathematician and is regarded as the father of probability theory. Now known as Pascal's Wager, the question was: 'God is, or he is not; which way should we incline?' There may only be two possible outcomes but, as Pascal suggested, there are no experiments that can prove conclusively the existence of God.

Pascal concluded that you either believe, and act as such, or do not and suffer the consequences, and it is the potential consequences that will determine which way you incline: toward salvation or eternal damnation. If God does not exist, whether you live piously or not makes no difference to the outcome. But if God does exist, and you live piously, then eternal damnation can be avoided.

For Pascal the answer was obvious. Disbelief was not worth the risk of damnation given the chances out of two possible outcomes and given the consequences in terms of everlasting regret. And one only has to look at a painting of hell by Heronimus Bosch to understand an early view of the ultimate in 'downside' risk.

Whether or not God plays dice, and Albert Einstein at least was convinced that he does not, man certainly does when making many of life's decisions. All the ingredients of risk lie in Pascal's Wager: cause, including context and culture; chance, confidence, cost and consequence. Herein lie the ingredients of risk. They are not themselves risk but elements of risk and we must discuss these as background before refining them to arrive at a definition of risk for endowment funds.

The risk of one outcome or another will first depend on the context and source of the risk. The sources of financial risk can be many: political, economic, financial and operational to name just a few. Some causes are acts of God, some of human intervention. The human intervention can itself depend on culture (the beliefs people have about their environment and their experience) and the context (the activity to which risk applies).

Culture is a matter of beliefs and depends on the type of person assessing risk. There are clear character types identified by psychology who will view the same probability events quite differently. But even these may change in a crowd, which may develop behavioral patterns peculiar to crowds. Different types of human will assess precisely the same context with quite different perceptions of level of risk. Perceptions will have something to do with consequences, which we look at later, but perceptions will change with experience. It is a documented psychological experiment that the more experience and skill a person has, the less likely is that person to make an error but the more likely, and the more often, will that person take a risk.[2] So, while the skill level diminishes the probability of an adverse outcome, confidence induces a frequency of risk-taking that increases it.

In the Pascal riddle, the proximate causes of the risk of eternal damnation are the inevitability of death and the choice of behavior. Nothing much can change the former but analysis of the conditions that affect that behavior will assist in determining the chance of risk. Pascal himself lived a high rich life before eventually committing himself to a monastery. The likelihood of a greater frequency and duration of good behavior was clearly higher in the latter circumstances than in the former.

Context is the environment that provides the background to the likelihood of risk. In terms of acts of God, the risk of another earthquake in Tokyo is substantially higher than that of an earthquake in London because of the nature of the tectonic structure of the earth. Similarly the coriolis effect of the spinning earth assures that tropical storm formations are spun into hurricanes in tropical latitudes between 10 and 25 degrees but there is insufficient spin at the equator where hurricanes do not therefore occur.

How relevant is physical 'context' to financial risk? Surprisingly, physics has provided theories which adapt well to financial markets. James Montier[3] shows how in physics 'one of the trade marks of a phase transition (for instance when a solid becomes liquid or a liquid becomes gas) is increasing synchronization' and this leads to a pattern of oscillations. The same happens in financial crashes with volatility around crashes like the foreshocks and aftershocks associated with earthquakes.

We have already seen in Chapter 3 that in the financial world there are quite different fundamental environments or scenarios in which different asset classes are subject to quite different risks. For instance, inflation, and potential capital loss on fixed income securities, will be a considerable risk in a background of rising money supply and velocity with strong underlying economic growth. The underlying causes are driven, among other things, by the action of the market and of government policy.

So context provides the background for the investors in aggregate to play out their behavior, which is framed by culture. Behavioral risk, for example, is high in markets where valuations are extreme, that is where economies are booming and individuals are behaving in a confident herd. In 1989, tools based on modern portfolio theory for optimizing portfolios for prospective risk and return had Japanese equities as the highest potential reward-to-risk market in the world when, on other measures, it was the most dangerous exhibiting symptoms of classic crowd behavior. Context is therefore the economic and financial environment underlying the returns that are only the symptoms of risk in an investment portfolio.

4.3 CHANCE

In Pascal's Wager chance has two components, two possible outcomes, which are that God exists or he doesn't. As Bernstein demonstrated, most of the early work on defining risk was driven by considering a game of chance. Indeed it was Pascal and a lawyer in Toulouse called Pierre de Fermat who eventually developed the answer to a question that had been posed over 150 years earlier by Luca Paccioli. The question was how to divide the spoils in an unfinished fair game of balla.

The answer, which 'determined the just distribution of the stakes', established the principles of probability theory which, together with further developments in statistics, led to the development in the twentieth century of a number of risk measures and management techniques. In 1900 a French mathematician called Louis Bachelier applied probability theory to the movement of French Government bond prices and concluded that they fell within a normal pattern around a norm with the bulk of returns being close to the norm. The supposition was that prices move independently of each other and the distribution of returns around the norm (the mean) are symmetrical.[4]

The assumption that returns either side of a mean are normally distributed was used to develop a concept of risk that was formalized in the early 1950s as Modern Portfolio Theory (MPT). For this work, Harry Markowitz and William Sharpe received Nobel prizes in 1990. Modern Portfolio Theory equates risk with the volatility (variance) of return around an average of all the returns. In fact the statistic used to measure that volatility is called the standard deviation. Standard deviation assumes what statisticians call 'a normal distribution', sometimes graphically described as a 'bell curve' because of its shape, as shown in Figure 4.1.

The area of returns above the mean is equal and opposite to that below, and the area represented by one standard deviation is about 68% of the whole. So, 68% of the time, or approximately two years in three, returns will be within the mean plus or minus one standard deviation. In Figure 4.1, if the mean return was 8% and one standard deviation was 9%, in two years out of three returns will be 8% plus or minus 9%, so they will range between -1% and $+17\%$. Two standard deviations, which is plus or minus $2 \times 9\% = 18\%$, gives a range of returns between -10% and $+26\%$ for just over 95% of the time.

From this approach to risk analysis there developed a number of single measures of risk based on historic numbers. Jensen was the first to calculate a return in excess of the market and called this *alpha*. Sharpe developed two measures which are perhaps the most well known and universally used by investment managers. The first is the Sharpe ratio, which measures the return of a portfolio in excess of the risk-free rate per unit of volatility as measured by standard deviation. The second is the information ratio, which is a measure of return in excess of a benchmark.

Standard deviation is fine as far as it goes, all other things being equal; the problem is that all other things rarely are equal in the real world. First, the distribution of returns is not

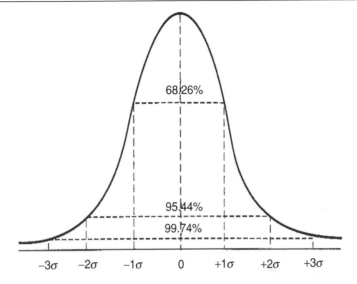

Figure 4.1 The normal distribution: The bell curve
Source: Sortino F. (2001) 'Alpha to omega.' In F. Sortino & S. Satchell, *Managing Downside Risk in Financial Markets*. Oxford: Butterworth Heinemann.

always 'normal' that is not always symmetric around the mean. It is often lopsided, which is technically called skewed or asymmetric.

Secondly, most people would find the notion of exceeding a target – the upside part of volatility – as hardly being a risk, even if it does accord with the Chinese notion of combining danger and opportunity to define risk. Even the father of MPT, Harry Markowitz, questioned the concept of standard deviation from a mean as the principal measure of risk, and suggested that the term 'semi-variance' to represent the bottom half – the downside of risk – would be more appropriate in a normal distribution.

Thirdly, as Figure 4.2 shows, lower volatility about a lower mean can be more of a risk in terms of meeting needs than a higher mean with higher volatility. In Figure 4.2, investment A may be less volatile than investment C but the minimum acceptable return (MAR) is only achieved for a fraction of the time that it is achieved in the case of the more volatile investment C.

The fourth issue with standard deviation as a measure of risk is that there is an assumption that the mean is stationary over time, that it stays at the same level. But evidence shows that this is often not the case. This immediately questions the validity of using a common statistical technique, sample standard deviation, to derive a volatility figure for a larger universe of numbers.

Fifthly, many distributions of stock returns, even if they are symmetric, have extremes known as 'fat tails' which are not predicted by the normal distribution. Mandlebrot explains this as returns following a 'power law' such as is common in nature. Gravity, for instance, weakens by the inverse power of 2 with distance. James Montier points out in *Behavioural Finance* that a loss of 5% on the DJIA in one day has been observed to occur once every two years, but a normal distribution would predict such a loss once every 6,000 years! Montier suggests that risk management tools based on such distributions will be too optimistic about the likely frequency of large downward moves in markets.

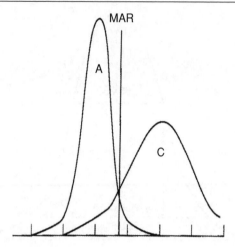

Figure 4.2 Lower volatility may not meet needs
Source: Sortino F. (2001) 'Alpha to omega.' In F. Sortino & S. Satchell, *Managing Downside Risk in Financial Markets*. Oxford: Butterworth Heinemann.

Markowitz may have raised the idea of downside risk but Frank Sortino gives his name to a downside measure, the Sortino Ratio. Sortino credits Robicheck[5] with being the first person who related risk with failure to accomplish an investor's goal, acknowledging that not all investors are simply trying to beat the market. Fishburn took this a stage further by incorporating the effect of magnitude, and defined a measure of risk that probability – weighted the expected deviations from a specified target of return. Sortino refers to that specified target as the 'minimum acceptable return' (MAR) and probability weighted deviations below this MAR represent downside risk.

Downside risk is sometimes thought to be simply the bottom half of a normal distribution, that part which represents returns that are less than the mean. If the distribution of returns is normal and the mean return is the minimum acceptable, this will be true (it is known as semi-variance). But it may not be true if the distribution is skewed or if the minimum acceptable return is not the mean. Even if the distributions are normal, the same investments might be chosen using downside risk as using mean-variance, but the relative risks may be different, as Figure 4.3 shows.

In Figure 4.3 each security happens to have a normal distribution; there is no skew to right or left. Sortino points out that under the MPT approach, an investor would choose C over B and B over A because of a higher expected mean return for the same level of volatility. With a MAR approach the choice of security would be the same, C, but for a different reason, namely that C is the most likely to meet the minimum acceptable return.

4.4   CO-MOVEMENT AND COMMON FACTORS

The article written by Harry Markowitz in 1952 which, according to Charles Ellis 'fired the shot heard round the world starting the intellectual campaign that led to modern portfolio theory', formally introduced the idea of covariance or correlation to determine portfolio diversification. He demonstrated that diversification was not purely a matter of avoiding putting all one's eggs

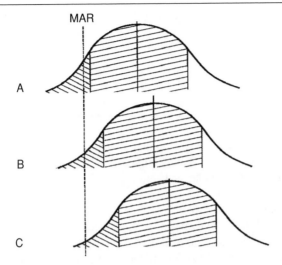

Figure 4.3 Perceptions of relative risk
Source: Sortino F. (2001) 'Alpha to omega.' In F. Sortino & S. Satchell, *Managing Downside Risk in Financial Markets*. Oxford: Butterworth Heinemann.

into the same basket – not just a matter of averaging risk by holding a number of securities rather than just one or two. It is about the pattern of returns of securities within the portfolio.

Covariance, or correlation, is a measure of how returns of different securities in a portfolio of securities move together. Markovitz showed that a portfolio of two securities with the same ultimate average return and the same amount of variation of return around the average return, but moving together in the same direction, offered less diversification than two other identical securities, with the same average and the same amount of variation of return, which did not move together. The first portfolio avoided the 'eggs in one basket' syndrome; the second avoided eggs in one basket and something in addition: an overall portfolio return which was less volatile. This was a very powerful conclusion and Tables 4.1 and 4.2 demonstrate the point.

In Tables 4.1 and 4.2 there are two securities, A and B. They each offer identical returns, identical in the amount of return after two years and in the percentage variation of return. The only difference between the tables is that, in the first case, the returns move together – that is, they are correlated with each other – and, in the second case, they do not. The consequence of this is that if you start with a portfolio that is half invested in each of those two securities, Table 4.2's portfolio return will be the same after two years as that in Table 4.1 but the path would have been smoother. Portfolio volatility will have been less.

When security returns move together and are correlated with a single factor – for example, a high correlation of certain securities to a commodity such as oil, or to interest rates because of

Table 4.1 Correlated portfolio

Security	Year 1 return	Year 2 return	Two year return
A	−10.0%	+20.0%	+8.0%
B	−5.0%	+15.0%	+9.2%
Portfolio A + B	−7.5%	+17.4%	+8.6%

Table 4.2   Uncorrelated portfolio

Security	Year 1 return	Year 2 return	Two year return
A	−10.0%	+20.0%	+8.0%
B	+15.0%	−5.0%	+9.2%
Portfolio A + B	+2.5%	+6.0%	+8.6%

financial leverage – this is referred to as 'common factor risk'. Common factors are therefore what make investments in one asset class similar to others in the same class. It can also make some securities in different asset classes behave more similarly to each other than securities within the same asset class.

To illustrate the point by analogy, if you take all the streets in New York, or at least a representative sample of them, you will find a 'New Yorkness' about them all which in total, and therefore on average, transcends the differences between the streets. However, China town in New York is closer in character to China town in London than to many other areas of New York. And someone once remarked that there are more similarities between 5th Avenue in New York and the Seventh Arondisement in Paris than between 5th Avenue and Harlem in the same city.

Much the same applies with assets classes. A bond may behave more like an equity than like other bonds, for example. A company may have a combination of financial obligations that are all listed on an exchange: short- and long-term debt; debt that is convertible into equity; equity that is preferred; equity that is income shares, capital shares, ordinary shares. All those obligations to investors are ultimately subject to one common factor: the financial health of that one company.

Assuming the company is healthy, and that other things are equal, the prices of those different types of obligation, which involve different elements of risk, will move more closely in line with other similar obligations offered by other companies. That is, other common factors will predominate in their influence on the asset than the health of the company. For instance, the price of the long-term debt of that company will move more closely in line with the equivalent long-term debt in Company B, or indeed of government debt, than with the price of the equity in company A. If the company is not healthy, however, then the common factor risk of that poor health will affect all the securities unduly.

The same idea applies in real estate. Depending on the way in which the interest in real estate is held, the investment can have characteristics that are closer to investments in other asset classes: in private equity (illiquid for a time period; earnings which can be leveraged and are variable); fixed income (where there is a short lease with no rent review); listed equities (where the real estate is securitised and can be as liquid as any traded equity security). It is therefore the characteristics of the investment that matter, not the fact that all these investments are simply classified as 'real estate'.

If a portfolio holds, in due proportion, shares in the equity of all the companies listed on the New York Stock Exchange (NYSE), that portfolio will naturally mirror the asset class called 'US equities listed on the NYSE'. Likewise in Europe, the movement of equities in different countries used to be closely related to the movement of those same national indices because of national economic policies. But with the graduation toward common economic policies between nations in Europe, this degree of co-movement within national indices has reduced in favour of other common factors, such as industrial similarity, across countries in Europe.

Common factors can and do tend to vary, one with each other and each over time. Economic and financial circumstances can produce correlations in the returns of some asset classes under certain conditions but not under others. Clearly the ideal pattern of correlation for investment diversification is one where correlation becomes more negative as values fall and more positive as they rise.

Unfortunately it mostly works the other way. One manager of a hedge fund which selects its investments from more than a hundred different asset classes and sectors within asset classes commented that in 2004 when Greenspan changed the wording of his pronouncements on Fed policy every one of the asset classes moved together.

In periods of financial crisis, many if not most financial asset price movements which have not previously shared a common factor become closely correlated. They all move together as they begin to price risk into their valuations. Montier cites the old market adage that the only thing[6] that goes up in a bear market is correlation. He refers to a study[6] which showed that when the US and German equity markets rose, the correlation was 8.6% but when they fell this rose to 52%. Clearly asymmetric correlations show that many conventional diversification policies will not work as intended in some circumstances when they are most needed. If this is the case, it has some important implications for risk management policies.

One of the most broadly accepted single measures of risk, endorsed indeed by international regulators, is Value at Risk (VaR). VaR is designed to protect against catastrophic loss by looking at the risk of events at the extremes of a normal distribution of returns. But where, as in the case of hedge funds, many market positions are being used by the same funds, their reaction to events will in many cases be complementary. Loss aversion will lead hedge fund managers to act together in response to negative events, and the scene is set for significant asymmetric correlation.

Where investment decisions are made by computers there can be high degrees of correlation between decisions. This applies with VaR limits which may require liquidation of positions to meet margin calls on futures. While VaR represents a cut-off number to set a limit on loss, it does not define the extent of the loss, in the tail of the distribution, once the limit is exceeded.

One other problem is that estimates of covariance are invariably taken from historic numbers without necessarily analyzing the underlying factors. For example, bonds are thought to be a diversification against equities, but, as we have seen, the evidence shows that it depends on the circumstances. In an inflationary environment this has not been the case but deflation is different. The circumstances that lead equities to sell down on lower growth and higher risk are those that lead to flight to the certainty of Government bonds. In the former case there may be averaging of risk and some reduction in correlation. In the latter case, the one has a negative correlation and is therefore a perfect diversification for the other. But the key point is that the correlations are not fixed and they depend on the underlying scenario.

One aspect of common factors is 'Theme management' of investments. This involves selecting investments to represent an idea such as energy exposure, demographic change, social responsibility, or a link with certain economic environments. And the theme can also be an investment style. Value or growth styles of equity management are classic examples where securities are selected on the basis of common factors of investment ratios such as price to book value or growth. We will consider this again in Chapters 6 and 8 but care must be taken in correlation analysis over causation. The movement of securities together may be the result of a third factor, and that factor can be *time*. Where time trends are established and coincide there can be an assumption of cause and effect that may not exist.

4.5 THE GREEK ALPHABET

Modern Portfolio Theory helped create a finance industry. The Capital Asset Pricing Model (CAPM) of William Sharpe developed the idea that you can break down the elements of a portfolio's return into three components. The first is the market return, which is simply the return on an index that represents any given market. The second component is called, in the investment world, one of three words: beta (which was the term representing relative volatility used in the CAPM equation), systematic risk or market risk. It is the market return, leveraged or de-leveraged. If a market goes up or down 10%, but a portfolio goes up or down 12% at the same time, the beta or market risk is 1.20. The theory behind this is that you can diversify away any risk that is specific to a particular security by investing in the whole market.

The third component is called 'alpha'. This was the Greek letter in the CAPM equation representing unexplained excess return. Alpha is that part of a portfolio return that is independent of market moves. It is what is left after a portfolio return has been adjusted for the market return and any beta or leverage. Alpha is also called specific or non-systematic risk and can be positive or negative. Alpha is what you expect to receive from active management of portfolios relative to a benchmark. If a manager cannot add alpha then you might as well buy an unmanaged index and borrow some money to create whatever level of market risk you prefer.

Alpha, the excess return above the risk-adjusted market return, is measured by the 'information ratio'. This ratio measures a manager's value added to a given benchmark. The concept of alpha and beta is at the core of one approach to strategy, which we will cover further in Chapters 6 and 8. The concept is the separation of alpha and beta portfolios, portfolios of pure market exposure and portfolios in which market exposure is hedged out to obtain pure alpha.

Modern Portfolio Theory was also key to the pricing of securities that were derived from underlying assets. In 1973, soon after the Chicago options exchange began, Professors Myron Scholes and Fischer Black published the Black–Scholes option-pricing model based on time, the price of money and historic volatility as a measure of risk. This model became the standard formula for devising the fair price of options, which are rights to buy or sell an underlying security at a fixed price in the future. From this developed an industry based on hedging and 'dynamic hedging', which is a computer-driven process of continuous change in portfolio positions and is also known as 'portfolio insurance'.

Modern Portfolio Theory created a theoretical portfolio that could be regarded as 'efficient' in the trade-off between risk, defined as volatility, and return on the assumption that all markets are 'efficient' in reflecting in prices all information about securities. The theory says that if you want more return you have to accept more volatility risk, but that for every level of volatility risk there is an optimal level of return, and vice versa. So if you draw a line between all the points on a graph that shows the optimal amount of return for every given level of volatility risk, that line will represent an 'efficient frontier'. If you take more volatility risk for the same level of return or receive a smaller return for the same level of risk at any point on that curve, the portfolio is less than optimal.

The problem is that the theories neither predict nor prevent – indeed, in some cases they have helped to create – some momentous losses. Portfolio insurance aggravated the stock market crash in 1987. The theories of Myron Scholes and Robert Merton, who shared a 1997 Nobel prize for their work on option theory, did not account for the practical impact of liquidity risk in markets. Their creation, Long Term Capital Management (LTCM), brought the global financial system to the edge in 1998 when a consortium of financial institutions had to provide US$3.6 bn of support to LTCM.[7] The partners in LTCM lost $1.1 billion. LTCM could not have forecast the debt moratorium declared by Russia in August 1998 which started the widening of spreads that continued, against the odds, to widen and to demand increased collateral to cover the losses. Could they not, however, have predicted some of the lack of liquidity that caused the difficulties, as happened in 1987?

The theory that markets are perfectly efficient at discounting all known information seems to have failed in practice. There are too many unrealistic assumptions, such as there are no transaction costs including market impact from trades, all investors are risk averse, borrowing is at the risk-free rate. And there are too many anomalies. For instance, there are value effects; small company and illiquid market effects; skewness in return distributions. And it is implicit that the future will reflect the past so that return patterns are necessarily measurable in terms of what has happened before, which implies some degree of certainty that the future will mirror the past.

4.6 CONFIDENCE

Frank Knight suggested as long ago as 1921 that if you don't know for sure what will happen, but you know the odds, then that's risk; and if you don't even know the odds, then that's uncertainty. Pure games of chance, like the unfinished game of balla, are based on analysis of past numbers and when it comes to numbers, the more the merrier. The longer the series the greater the confidence irrespective of the cause of the numbers.

Like Frank Knight before him, Keynes[8] made a distinction between uncertainty and improbability. He distinguished uncertain knowledge – which he described as a 'matter about which there is no scientific basis on which to form any calculable probability whatever' – from improbable outcomes, such as to be found in a game of roulette. Keynes went on the suggest:

> the state of long-term expectation, upon which our decisions are based, does not solely depend, therefore, on the most probable forecast we can make. It also depends on the confidence with which we can make this forecast – on how highly we rate the likelihood of our best forecast turning out quite wrong. If we expect large changes but are very uncertain as to what precise form these changes will take, then our confidence will be weak.

Defining a rational process for taking risk had evolved for more than a millennium from the development of a number system to the birth of probability theory and the development of statistical techniques based on a series of historic numbers, which remain part of the process of contemporary risk management. There had therefore been a steady progression away from future expectation being simply based on degrees of belief toward expectation being based on scientific assessment of historic evidence. And here suddenly is a celebrated economist – indeed a mathematician by training, who had even written an important Treatise on Probability – suggesting that financial risk is not just based on probability but on some behavioral notion called the state of confidence.

Keynes wrote that instability depends on human nature and the tendency to 'spontaneous optimism rather than on a mathematical expectation'. He considered it derived from 'animal spirits – a spontaneous urge to action rather than inaction, and not as the outcome of a weighted average of quantitative benefits multiplied by quantitative probabilitites'. 'Our conclusions must mainly depend upon the actual observations of markets and business psychology.'

These words in 1936 recognized that investors will not necessarily take the choice of decision that pure probability would imply for them the greater reward. These words are forerunners of what has developed and is becoming increasingly recognized as a valid discipline for financial market analysis known as 'Behavioral Finance'. Indeed, as a science it has even reached Nobel prize-winning status. And it is largely in the consequences of risk, as in Pascal's Wager, that we begin to find a realistic measure of what many people would recognize, like the elephant, as what they define as risk.

4.7 CONSEQUENCES

While Pascal's Wager demonstrated the ultimate in consequences, it was Daniel Bernoulli who claimed: 'No valid measurement of the value of a risk can be obtained without consideration being given to its utility.' The Utility Theory is associated with Bernoulli but it had earlier been considered, independently, by a Swiss mathematician called Gabriel Cramer. The theory was further developed mathematically such that the 'expected utility' approach came to be 'perhaps the most widely used theoretical framework for human choice under conditions of uncertainty and risk'.

Utility Theory measures the relative degree of usefulness of one extra measure of wealth. It is a subjective measure that relates a probable outcome of a decision to the resources, temperament and objectives of the decision-maker. Most people have diminishing marginal utility. In the words of Gilbert and Sullivan: 'when every blessed thing you hold is made of silver or of gold, you long for simple pewter.' Risk-averse individuals will have an upward-sloping utility curve and vice versa for risk-seekers; a straight line represents risk neutrality. The theory assumes that every extra unit of wealth created decreases utility at a certain level of wealth. It also assumes that the risk appetites of all investors can be aggregated into one function.

That's fine in theory but, as Clarkson[9] observes, even von Neumann and Morgenstern who further developed the theory had some doubts about the validity of some of the axioms behind Utility Theory, deeming one of them to be barely 'plausible and legitimate, unless a much more refined system of psychology is used than the one now available for the purposes of economics'. Clarkson also comments that others had been identifying anomalies in behavior over two centuries ago. Adam Smith in *The Wealth of Nations* wrote: 'the chance of gain is by every man more or less overvalued, and the chance of loss is by most men undervalued' and the French Philosopher Buffon was observing, at much the same time as Adam Smith, that the human mind appears to ignore risk completely when it is below some very small value.

Behavioral finance began to develop in the last quarter of the twentieth century as a 'more refined system of psychology'. It even became recognized formally with the award of a Nobel prize to Daniel Kahneman, based on work with the late Amos Tversky, for what they called (for no particular reason other than that the name should be memorable) Prospect Theory. This is a theory that measures how people actually behave rather than should behave under Utility Theory.

Kahneman and Tversky analyzed how, in practice, people make choices when faced with uncertain outcomes and showed that emotion, and an inability to fully understand the issues, led to irrational judgments. They also observed that we can be risk-seekers in one environment but risk-averse in another, despite having the same choice; we overemphasise low probability but high profile events and underestimate others that happen more routinely. We extrapolate runs of good luck and tend to go for certain gain against a higher, but only probable, gain yet when it comes to a choice between losses, we focus on possible rather than probable outcomes.

Another aspect of Prospect Theory is that change in wealth is more important to people than levels of wealth. This is the difference between Utility Theory and Prospect Theory. Rational man is presumed by Utility Theory to want to maximize the expected utility of wealth, but Prospect Theory suggests that he is more concerned with gains or losses from a current point. Bernstein quotes Tversky: 'it is not so much that people hate uncertainty – but rather, they hate losing.' Thaler and Johnson then observed that losses become even more painful after a prior run of loss than after a series of gains.

One recognized term for this approach to risk, assessing the impact of the consequence rather than the probability of the outcome, is 'Regret'. Regret forms the basis of Dembo and Freeman's approach to risk assessment. They comment[10] that 'regret does not assume either that there is symmetry of outcomes or that we all feel the same whichever outcome occurs'.

Dembo and Freeman liken regret to insurance and suggest that risk is equivalent to the premium we pay for insurance as this is the value we place on the risk it eliminates. Financial people would use an investment equivalent to this insurance analogy: the cost of buying the right to 'put' the risk on someone else. But like the Chinese characters for risk, they regard regret as only one side of the coin. The other side is 'Upside' and they use a financial analogy for this also, being the cost of buying an option to participate only in the upside of a decision.

The difference between these two aspects of a decision amounts to the value of that decision, but Dembo and Freeman recognize the behavioral trait that different people will regard the cost of insuring the downside differently. They recognize that some will be more risk averse than others, depending on the ratio of upside to downside and the importance of the decision in relation to the whole portfolio of decisions being made. This is akin to Keynes's 'state of confidence'. And they recognize that the upside and downside, and the degree of risk aversion, will be dependent on the underlying scenario.

4.8   ENDOWMENT FUND RISK

Our preamble on risk shows that there is a long history of trying to measure what is practically immeasurable to the degree of accuracy that many would like in order to give them confidence in decision-making for the future. But the search for a comprehensive measure of risk has been like the search of the alchemists for the mythical 'philosopher's stone' that would turn cheap metals into gold.

In looking for the 'philosopher's stone' the alchemists developed useful techniques of chemical analysis. Similarly, the search for a single measure of risk has produced what Dembo and Freeman described in relation to their own thinking as 'a structured way of thinking about an otherwise intractable problem'.

A problem clearly stated is half solved because the answer lies in the problem. So if we can start with a simple working definition of risk for endowment funds, then we are half way to solving the problem of what to do about it. The following definition is based on the concept that downside risk measurement is defined by the minimum acceptable level of required spending, not just in any one year but over time. The minimum acceptable return is therefore a stream of liabilities over the life of the endowment. Where the life of the endowment is infinite and the requirements are measurable in real terms, then the definition implies a large element of long-duration risk and a key issue is maintaining a fund that can continue to service required cash flows:

Endowment fund risk is a measure of the likelihood and the extent to which an endowment's resources fail to meet its financial objectives during its expected life.

This definition is similar to the fourth response to the Investment Company Institute's survey on risk, which is mentioned at the beginning of this chapter. It suggests that risk is not therefore purely a matter of nominal loss but a failure to meet objectives. And if this is so, and risk is somehow to be quantified, then the objectives themselves must be clearly defined in terms of quantity, time and duration. So the definition suggests that risk is a matter of falling below the minimum that will need to be available to meet the objectives when they crystallize. Crystallize, incidentally, does not have to mean that assets must be realized; it could mean 'borrowed against' if immediate liquidity is an issue.

What is does mean, however, is meeting cash needs when they fall due. Most endowments equate generating income through dividends, rent or interest with meeting cash needs. But we must be mindful of the Hicks sense of income that we considered in Chapter 2: the amount that we can consume and be at least as well off afterwards. Any quest to generate conventional income to consume as expense may place at risk the ability of the endowment to sustain intergenerational equity. First, this is because income is generally assumed to be spendable. Secondly, income generation is often at the expense of growth. But it is equally crucial to have cash available to meet consumption when needed. It is fatal to have to realize illiquid assets, to have to sell depressed real estate for instance, to meet cash needs when they fall due. For a long-term institution to be a forced seller of a long-term asset could be the most serious mistake that any trustee could make.

This definition of risk for an endowment implies that there is more than one element of minimum acceptable return. One is the minimum needed to run a given level of current programs; another is the minimum needed to keep the endowment in existence by sustaining intergenerational equity.

This definition of risk also suggests that what is risk to one endowment may not be risk to another: risk is not general but particular. This will be the case even though all endowments may be subject to the same external economic and investment environment. This definition of risk is benchmarked to a particular endowment's liabilities, which are the financial expression of its objectives. This definition even calls for care with the concept of the 'risk-free' rate of interest. If an endowment has a need to grow income in real terms over a long period, Treasury Bills might ensure failure to meet the needs over that time, irrespective of how 'risk-free' they may be in nominal terms over three months.

As Sortino says 'the great benefit of "downside risk" is that it is goal-oriented and unique to the target chosen'. If a fund is to be wound up and the capital paid out, then capital preservation with a risk-free return may be the acceptable minimum. But if the objective of an endowment is to beat inflation, then investment in a classic 'risk-free' asset (cash) could almost guarantee failure to achieve the objective, which would not be an acceptable minimum.

The required resources of an endowment are therefore a function of what they can be expected to generate relative to the amount and timing of required outgoings and the consequences, to the beneficiaries, of failure to meet the requirement, whether now or in the future. Trustees today are as answerable as their successors for the outgoings of tomorrow. This means that trustees today must not only consider the budget during their period of office but the preservation of assets that will satisfy the objectives of the future.

A key element to defining the particular risk of any given endowment must therefore lie in the spending rules that are adopted for that particular endowment. This implies that the management of endowment risk must not only be a function of the asset strategy but also the strategy in respect of liabilities. An endowment that has a high level of annual cash need, such as funding an orchestra, will be different from one that has a major outgoing of capital expenditure periodically and at no predefined date, such as buying a major work of art for a museum or maintaining a historic building. The investment strategy that is low risk for one may be higher risk for the other. How many endowments have relied on one of the longest duration assets classes – equities, most highly geared to the economic and financial cycle and most likely to achieve long-term intergenerational equity – to meet short term needs? Equally risky can be meeting long-term real needs with a fund that is committed to short-duration assets unless it is a temporary defence against overvalued markets.

One implication of benchmarking risk to financially quantified objectives is that external sources of income to that received directly from the fund – such as fee income or donations or annual income from other assets not officially deemed part of the endowment itself – must also be considered in the overall risk assessment. Such sources may provide some implicit diversification of cash flow and may allow a less well-diversified portfolio to meet the endowment's overall objectives. They may solve the liquidity risk of a downturn in capital values when immediate needs must be satisfied.

Where the endowment is dependent on its fund as the principal source of cash flow for its activities, liquidity risk in delivery of cash flow in the short term is more of a risk than variation of 'marked to market' (i.e. not realized) value. So an endowment that does not have to satisfy cash need in the near future to meet its obligations has a different risk profile from one that does. Benchmarking to cash flows therefore has a number of implications for strategy, not least because an endowment that has a very long perspective – with any short to medium term commitments adequately covered – can afford to take a contrarian view of short-term moves in values which others may be constrained from doing advantageously.

If an orchestra is funded by an endowment and the cash dries up, the orchestra may have to disband. If repair to the fabric of a monument, or the acquisition of a work of art by a museum, is delayed for a period due to lack of immediate cash, the consequences may be less drastic. However, a museum might argue that a rare addition to the collection may only appear on the market once in a generation, in which case sufficient resources must always be immediately available, hence the need to preserve a larger operational reserve at the expense of a higher return on assets. This may be a small price to pay for a priceless acquisition. If that is the case, the risk is a function of the likely value or price of the piece to be acquired, the opportunity cost of failing to acquire it, and the liquidity of the museum's resources. The museum will have to quantify the trade-off between availability of sufficient resource at all times and the premium lost by not adopting a higher risk strategy.

We have seen that different trustees may each perceive the risk of a given environment differently because of behavioral factors. By benchmarking risk to the projected cash flows of the endowment they can at least share an objective definition of minimum return and the impact of failure in meeting the objective. Cash flow-based benchmarks representing liabilities are clear, measurable and fairly stable financial benchmarks for defining an appropriate investment strategy. But implicit in these financial benchmarks are the non-financial benchmark objectives of the endowment itself.

To say that risk is about the future may seem a rather obvious statement but Dembo and Freeman comment 'very little of existing risk management embraces the basic idea that when we are thinking about risk, we are, by definition, looking forward in time'. There is a tendency to extrapolate past numbers into the future as a measure of risk. But past numbers are relevant only insofar as the underlying factors that helped to create those numbers can be identified and understood.

Timing and duration are implicit in the endowment definition of risk. Cash flows imply a series, not just a single point in time which is so often the basis of risk assessment. One endowment may have one particular large project requiring a specific large sum at a particular point in time. Others will have annual cash requirements of smaller amounts, albeit the same present value as the one project amount.

Even then there may be discretion as to timing. A university, for example, may have flexibility in timing the development of a faculty, both in terms of capital projects and levels of student intake. Furthermore, timing is not only about when something may happen; it is also about the duration of the impact. If an endowment will suffer a lack of cash flow to meet its liabilities in Year 3, how prolonged will this be? Through Years 4, 5 and 6? Can an endowment afford the luxury of looking through a normal financial cycle? An opportunity to one might to another represent unacceptable risk.

The benchmark minimum acceptable return may be real or nominal, may be stationary or vary, may be time dependent or not but expectation of return must be measured against likely long-term available returns and spending plans. The more realistic the expectation of return and the plan of spending, the lower the risk in achieving the objective. The minimum return is what it says. It is not the target return but the base below which a return will not meet the minimum requirements of the endowment.

This all means that the starting point for assessing endowment fund risk must be the cash flow forecast based on a spending rule, which will be the focus of the next chapter. This rule should not just be a single point estimate of what would be nice to be spent over a series of years. It should be a range of possible expenditures: a base minimum cutting all expense to the bone and an upper likely maximum. This forecast may be quite accurate for the first five or even 10 years but thereafter it must necessarily become futuristic. Futuristic does not imply unrealistic, but it does imply that the real and nominal financial implications of the endowment's social objectives must be considered.

Assessing the risk of failing to meet the various cash flow objectives is best achieved through scenario analysis which allows one to pretest the possible impact of probable, improbable and even unlikely, and possibly disastrous, outcomes. Scenario analysis helps to prepare trustees for the future in a way that outlining only one expected outcome never can. It allows a decision to be made on the trade-off between risk and return and the time horizon for both. Indeed it is only within the context of scenario analysis that such risk can be analyzed properly.

Scenario analysis provides a range of possible and probable outcomes rather than a specific forecast. As we have seen in the preamble to this chapter, risk perception is not just about probability and magnitude of outcome but about consequences. Scenario analysis allows trustees to assess likelihood through addressing the causes of financial outcomes, to assess chance and certainty based partly on historic analysis, and to assess the consequence of a range of outcomes. What if this were to occur? How acceptable would that outcome be compared to this one?

Finally, we have focused on one definition of risk and we have related that risk to cash inflows and outflows under different conditions. We must, however, recognize that in practice there are many contributory factors to risk, to potential inability to meet the cash needs when they fall due. We have touched on some of those factors such as volatility and liquidity, interest rate change and credit quality. These are the first-order factors that affect investment risk, but there are many others that must be covered by internal control in a practical assessment underlying these risk factors: counterparty risk; operational risk; and regulatory risk, to name just a few.

As with our look at financial returns in the previous chapter, we can now try to understand the interrelationships of different market returns and the fundamental drivers at work. We can look at the factors that tend to create co-movement of returns, dramatically so in periods of financial meltdown. We can derive from this potential outcomes that may meet or exceed expectations or can mean ruin. And we can then develop judgmentally a strategy that balances reasonably the upside and the downside of potential financial returns.

5

Spending Rules

Annual income twenty pounds, annual expenditure nineteen nineteen six, result happiness. Annual income twenty pounds, annual expenditure twenty pounds ought and six, result misery.

Mr Micawber in *David Copperfield*. CHARLES DICKENS (1812–1870)

Spending Rules determine the percentage of an endowment that can be consumed today at the expense of tomorrow. Intergenerational equity is maintaining sufficient value in the endowment to sustain grant-making in real terms for future generations. This chapter introduces a formula that we call 'Micawber's Rule' after the classic Dickensian figure quoted at the head of this chapter. In Micawber's day, the nineteenth century, capital remained untouched, inflation was not an issue and income was for spending. However, revaluation and inflation tend to create illusory income and capital gain from which amounts should be reinvested, before allocation to consumption, to maintain an endowment's real value. A spending rule, which is purely a percentage of an endowment's net asset value, provides a discipline but not a complete answer. An optimal approach is to set a percentage of the endowment value that is related to the minimum acceptable return and to adjust the value of spending by a price deflator component to account for the change in the value of money. A higher spending percentage maximum limit should also be established to provide some flexibility for the spending rate to rise on a fall in markets. However this upper limit provides a protection for intergenerational equity. These parameters should then be monitored and used as trigger points for spending review.

5.1 THE ENDOWMENT DILEMMA

Large sums of money can mesmerize, and they can even become the target of political interest, especially after a long period of strong markets and high levels of return. This chapter aims to determine the most appropriate approach to spending for any given endowment – a process that has to be an integral part of the whole approach to investment strategy. How much of the investment return is consumed now and how much in the future are policy decisions that are interrelated with generating financial return. These decisions need to be consistent to ensure the fair treatment of current and future generations. Naturally there is a dilemma. Endowments are established to provide money for a given purpose but they are not established to be a savings institution that simply accumulates capital to be expended at some indeterminate time in the future.

But the future is infinitely more uncertain than the present and the latter can usually be budgeted for to a fairly high level of confidence. An endowment can consume all of its return each year, and more, in satisfying the purpose for which it was established. The problem is that the value of the endowment will decline, unless it has alternative sources of income to support it. And the more that purpose is impacted by inflation the greater the decline in real terms. It does not require much inflation: 2% per annum inflation for 40 years more than halves the real value of money.

This ability of an endowment to sustain itself is called 'intergenerational equity' – a term that describes the amount of capital that must be left to maintain the same volume of real level of spending. The tension between current spending and intergenerational equity, between the 'here and now' and the 'here-after', is at the heart of spending and financial strategy. And the impact of that strategy may go beyond the immediate issue at hand, which is balancing the intergenerational interests. If the spend level is set too low in relation to return, it may give a high probability of achieving intergenerational equity but it may also discourage donors who could want to see a higher spend during their lifetime from the assets they donate. If, however, it is too high, then growth in spend suffers and other donors may be dissuaded from trying to support a diminishing endowment.

Too often in endowments the spending and the income parts of the equation are handled independently of each other. In larger entities, one committee may handle operational expenditures, another charitable giving, and another investments. Even in smaller endowments, which may not have the luxury of different committees, investment and spending are usually separate agenda items that are discussed independently. Relating one to the other is so fundamental to the survival of the endowment that both should be considered together as a policy item at the highest level of decision-making.

Other sources of income are also a critical part of the equation. The less the other income, the greater is the reliance on the endowment to finance the purpose of that endowment – usually 100% in the case of most Foundations. And apart from relieving total investment return of the burden of funding all current and future spending, other income can satisfy a critical part of liquidity and duration need, which is the need for predictable funds over specific periods of time without having to realize illiquid investments or hold low return operational reserves.

An endowment with regular fund-raising, where the endowment is small in relation to the annual receipt of gifts and legacies, will clearly need to have a different investment strategy from a Foundation where the whole of its activities are funded from annual realized return on a stable capital sum. And there must be a policy on gifts where this is not mandated by the donor. For example, is $1 million of funds gifted to an endowment simply $1 million to be spent, or is the spendable amount what the gifted $1 million will generate? And what does that mean? If the nominal total return on that $1 million is $70,000 a year, is all of that return consumable? Or should $50,000 a year be consumed and $20,000 reinvested to maintain the real value (assuming 2% inflation)?

And what about future real growth, not just inflation-adjusted consumption? Should only $40,000 be consumed, $20,000 reinvested to maintain the real value and, say, $10,000 reinvested to provide some real growth? And does it make any difference if $35,000 of that $75,000 total return comes in the form of income and $35,000 as capital gain? And what about $1 million gifted for a specific purpose such as an arts or a sports centre? What are the implications for spending then? In that case, of course, the endowment does not generate return, it consumes return. The endowment may be an operational asset but a financial liability: 'a gift that eats.'

A spending strategy needs to answer those sorts of questions as part of the overall financial strategy. The spending strategy, including level and timing, will be driven by the social objective of the endowed entity, subject not only to the financial and other resources but also to what can be reasonably expected by way of return from financial markets. One social objective might, for instance, be a higher spend now, such as on facilities, but a lower pattern of spend subsequently in order to rebuild the endowment to maintain those facilities. Financial markets may enhance or delay the strategy by providing above or below expected returns.

The strategy could be quite the reverse, namely, build the fund now to establish a base for a subsequent real growth of consumption. In the case of an endowment that is more of a reserve than a prime source of funds for annual consumption, the strategy may be simply to build the reserve to a given percentage of the annual budget in order to subsidize spending when the endowed entity is vulnerable to a setback in other income sources. Whatever the spending strategy for an endowment fund, it must be based on economic return as Professor Hicks has defined the word income, and not as accountants and most trustees understand it. Trustees must avoid the 'income illusion' which we covered in Chapter 2, 'Language of Return'.

A simple example of this income illusion as it affects the spending rule is a charity that funds scholarships for education. Currently it has the resources from cash flow on a high income yield portfolio to fund 12 students a year. The income yield is partly achieved through high-yield bonds which stand significantly above par value. It is partly achieved by investment in high-yield equities. The average dividend payout ratio of that equity portfolio is well above average, implying limited potential direct growth from reinvestment of corporate cash flow and a relatively low return on assets employed. The businesses are not those that have automatic pricing power in an inflationary environment.

In sum, the portfolio is in a similar position to a portfolio of real estate being 'over-rented', to use the jargon of that industry. In the real estate world it means that yield is higher today on the current tenancy than would be the case if the property were relet on the open market; the yield is protected until the lease terminates but this will provide no growth on rent review. Likewise, the current income on this portfolio is higher than would be the case if a more balanced portfolio were implemented. Growth of income, endowment and expenditure is likely to be limited, especially as educational spending growth has been well above consumer price growth and is expected to remain so. The consequence of the spending strategy is likely to be a severe reduction in number of scholarships when the bonds mature and a gradual further reduction of number of scholarships, or of scholarship value in real terms, thereafter.

One of the earliest pieces of published research[1] on spending rules, written by Ennis and Williamson as a project for the Commonfund, commented: 'a spending rule allows the institution to *adapt* current spending to unfolding events and continually changing expectations of the future.' They identified a number of desirable features of a spending rule.

1. It should allow flexibility in spending without changing the investment portfolio mix.
2. The rate of growth of the endowment should be subject to control, through the investment mix or the spending rate.
3. The rule should not jeopardize perpetual operation of the endowment such as current over-spending at the expense of the future.
4. The rule should provide for the required degree of spending stability.
5. The rule should be simple and easy to understand.

These precepts remain a sound basis for establishing a formula to guide spending in future.

5.2 MICAWBER'S RULE

Before the twentieth century the spending rules for endowments were simple. Capital generated income that could be spent. Early endowments comprised mostly real estate; spending was constrained by the amount of the income generated by rents after deduction of costs to maintain the property. Growth in rents automatically provided protection from inflation though, as we saw in an earlier chapter, inflation was only an issue for relatively short periods. Currencies were tied to gold or silver standards and this more or less kept a cap on prices, except when Governments debased their coinages to finance wars. Real growth in rents provided real growth in income and therefore real growth in endowment expenditure. Income was deemed expendable and capital became protected by law.

Equities gradually became acceptable as trustee investments in the twentieth century. Initially their dividend yield exceeded the income yield on Government bonds. Equities provided an alternative source of expendable yield to bond or mortgage interest or rents. It was only in the second half of the twentieth century that sustained economic growth and inflation, and the development of equity markets, began to provide a major alternative source of readily realizable return in addition to that from rental, dividend or interest income: capital gain.

Yale University began a policy of spending 'a prudent portion of the appreciation in market value' of their endowment in 1965. Other endowments were prevented from following this policy and raised the percentage of assets in bonds to provide income. The Ford Foundation[2] study concluded that total return, not just income return, was the appropriate basis for assessing the distributable capability of endowments. A second report concluded that unless there were restrictions in the terms of the Foundation it was permissible to distribute capital gains. This thinking became embodied in the USA in the Uniform Management of Institutional Funds Act. This act was approved in 1972 and was gradually enacted in different States. Today there are many investment vehicles, such as some hedge funds, that provide low-risk bond-like returns but no income, so only the capital gain, over and above the capital invested, is available to be spent.

We saw in Chapter 2 that the Hicks's concept of income is one that can be applied to endowments, spendable income or return being 'the wealth which can be consumed in a year which leaves unchanged the quantum of wealth left to generate the same income in the following year'. This fits with the formula outlined by Ennis and Williamson which we call Micawber's Rule because it summarizes the dictum of the Dickensian character quoted at the front of this chapter – underspend return, happiness; overspend return, misery. In Micawber's Rule all the numbers are expressed as a percentage of an endowment's current value:

$$Investment\ return + Other\ income = Spending\ rate + Fund\ growth$$

Investment return is the total return, income and capital gain, real and unrealized, on the endowment's capital assets. Other income is all other income which is not deemed to be endowment capital. The spending rate is the percentage of the endowment capital that is consumed each year. Fund growth is the residual. It is the percentage increase in the endowment capital after all income and gain and all expenses have been accounted for in any given year.

Rearrange Micawber's Rule and we have the following:

$$Spending\ rate = Endowment\ return + Other\ income - Fund\ growth$$

The amount that can be consumed by an endowment each year is therefore a function of investment return, of other income and of the remainder that is necessary to maintain or increase the endowment's capability to sustain itself. At its simplest, assuming no change in the spending rate and that other income is zero, the funding formula then reduces to:

$$Investment\ return - Spending\ rate = Endowment\ growth$$

And it follows from this that if those components remain unchanged, then:

$$Spending\ growth = Endowment\ growth$$

Quite simply, if an endowment has a total return on its assets of 10% over a year and has no other income and no expenditure, it will grow in size by 10%. If it has a total investment return of 10% and 5% of the endowment is spent, it will grow by 5% (10 − 5 = 5) and will be able to spend 5% more in the following year. And if the same happens in the following year – that is, the return is 10% and spending is 5% of the assets – then both spending and endowment will have grown by a further 5%, ad infinitum.

Micawber's Rule is a useful framework for long-term analysis but it makes a number of simple assumptions that we need to look at more closely. The Rule assumes that spending is done on the last day of the year. The numbers change slightly if the funds are removed on Day 1 of the year. The Rule makes no allowance for the pattern of return or the pattern of spending. As we saw in Chapter 2, 10% return achieved with a volatile portfolio gives different numbers from 10% achieved with low volatility. And if the return is a steady annual accumulation, but the outgoing is heavy every five or 10 years, then the spending rule must adequately accumulate income or the asset strategy must adapt to a more risky but higher return strategy.

Micawber's Rule is expressed as a percentage of assets. If the assets vary in value, so do the return and the amount to be spent. A spending rate applied to a percentage of assets that are valued on a rolling three-year basis gives different results again. Taking a fixed rate of spend, but averaging the values of the endowment assets to which it is applied over a number of years, helps to stabilize the pattern of spending. But this has other implications explored below.

Micawber's Rule also makes no explicit assumptions about 'gifts that eat'. The $10 million offer to build a college pool – which was mentioned in Section 2.3 – was not accepted. But had it been accepted, how would the rule have coped? The answer is that the assumptions are implicit. The donation and the capital costs are self-canceling. Money comes in on the left of the formula as a donation and goes out on the right as a capital expense.

But there's more to it than that. The capital expense generates outgo not income which simply increases the spending rate or dislodges some other form of expenditure. If the $10 million was not spent it would translate into fund growth. This in turn would lead to added return on the left side of the equation and translate into either higher spending or fund growth on the right.

Finally, the rule can be expressed in real terms, which addresses the inflation illusion question but takes no account of one of the other issues raised in Chapter 3, 'Elements of Return', namely valuation change. So the rule is a useful long-term framework for integrating spending with investment strategy but we need to develop it further as a practical basis for operational use.

5.3   PATTERN OF FLOWS

Ennis and Williamson appreciated that any formula tends to replicate in static form a process that is essentially dynamic. As spending amounts, other income and investment returns may all vary from year to year, these authors investigated the results of computer simulation of a fund over 25 years using a more realistic pattern of spending and of returns. They simulated different returns to the endowment that replicated the market movements each year, then simulated a 5% spending rule.

In this exercise, which applied differing patterns of market return in separate trials, they isolated the impact of changes in the spending rule on the annual pattern of spending and on the intergenerational equity – that is, the value of the fund at the end of the process. This showed that there are two sources of uncertainty in the intergenerational equity of an endowment fund: one source is change in market values and the other, which amplifies the former, is the stability of spending amounts from one year to the next.

The more that spending is kept at a regular absolute amount, including a steady annual increase rather than a regular percentage of fund value, the greater the variation in intergenerational equity. By contrast, the more that annual spending is linked to endowment fund value, the greater the volatility of spending but the less the intergenerational risk. They concluded, however, that a rule based on endowment values averaged over a number of years dampened volatility and was a simple and effective compromise between relative stablization of spending and relative preservation of intergenerational equity.

The outcome of this thinking was the adoption by many endowments of rules based on values that were averaged over time. A moving average proved to work satisfactorily during the 1980s and 1990s. It provided for current spending and left a healthy amount for reinvestment in intergenerational equity. The average spending rate of educational endowments from the 1990s to date, according to surveys by the National Association of College Business Officers (NACUBO), varied between 4% and 8%. The largest endowments varied between 4% and 5% and the smallest started at 8.0% in 1993 and fell to 5.5% at the end.

The 2005 Commonfund Benchmarks Study[3] showed similar statistics but the proportion of endowment institutions following a 3-year or 12-quarter moving average fell from 80% three years before to 63% in 2004. The funds had been experiencing a side-effect of the averaging policy which the Ennis and Williamson study did warn of, namely a momentum in spending growth, both positive and negative. Growth in spending one year will be succeeded by growth in the next if markets rise and until market values level off or retract. But the same momentum acts in reverse, as endowments discovered in the bear market following 2000.

In December 2003, Verne Sedlacek, President and CEO of the Commonfund, together with Sarah E. Clark, Managing Director and Head of the Commonfund's Strategic Solutions Group, wrote a paper for the Commonfund Institute entitled *Why Do We Feel So Poor?*.[4] The subtitle of the paper sums up the issue: *How the overspending of the 90s has created a crisis in higher education.*

The paper considered the issues that had arisen from this very issue of momentum in a bear market. It likened the spending policy of most educational endowments to the autopilot mechanism of a large aircraft. Set the coordinates and sit back until the aircraft reaches its final destination.

Commonfund research identified that four-fifths of the institutions they surveyed used a formula based on asset values, nearly all of which used a three-year average of those values, and most of which applied a spending rate of 5%. This had led, in the heady 1980s and 1990s, to a spending amount that rose annually well beyond the rate of inflation. So during that period current spending was more than satisfied with plenty to spare for intergenerational equity.

The problems came after the year 2000. An operating budget that suffered continuing inflation of college and university costs was being funded by a fixed 5% of declining market values. As we see from Micawber's Rule, if the spending rate is fixed and there is no other income, and if the total return is negative, then intergenerational equity value sinks.

Averaging the spending rule over a number of years of value may dampen volatility but the other key issue is the rate of spend. There is no magic in 5% as a figure for a spending rate, but that was the figure most often used by endowments in the 1990s. Its origin as a figure probably lies in the work of Ennis and Williamson based on their US return analysis back to 1926. In the case of foundations, the US tax authorities subsequently set 5% as a mandatory proportion of their endowments to be paid out as 'qualifying distributions'. As the Commonfund paper said: 'The objective of this rate, at least from a public policy standpoint, is to assure that large pools of tax-exempt wealth are in fact used for the public good and not hoarded.'

But why 5% and not 4%, or the 6% that the tax authorities first tried as a cut-off rate for Foundations before lobbying had the rate reduced? Or indeed why not any other number? In order to balance current needs and intergenerational equity, each endowment must identify for itself as a spending strategy its own level of spend as a percentage of assets, in view of expected investment return and other income received.

The Commonfund has created a proprietary model that allows endowments to ask the question 'given a specific asset allocation and spending rate, what is the probability of not achieving intergenerational equity or a stated investment objective over a defined period of time?'. The Commonfund used this model to test whether the average asset distribution of funds over $1 billion in size in one of their benchmark studies was likely to achieve intergenerational equity, that is maintaining the value of the endowment in inflation adjusted terms, using a spending rate of 5%.

They concluded from the model that the chances of success were 64.7% over 15 years and a little higher, 68.8%, over 20 years. A 4% spending rate raised the probability of success to 79.4% over 20 years but even a spending rate of zero did not guarantee success: it had a 0.9% chance of failure.

The pattern of expenditure, whether current or future, is a further important consideration in fixing the spending policy. An endowment for an orchestra, for example, will have a regular outflow related to the inflation of musicians' salaries. An orchestra cannot simply decide one year to remove the whole wind section if it is feeling poor that year.

On the other hand, an institution that gives scholarships can add to the number it funds one year and reduce the number another. The pattern of expense may be similar: an annual stable outgo and a commitment to fund each scholarship over a period of years. However, there is more flexibility in the pattern of expense. An endowment for the maintenance of a church may need to fund ongoing small amounts of expenditure and the reroofing of the church every 60 years.

We have seen the trade-off between higher return and volatility. More volatility should mean more return. But if the spending pattern is long duration (that is, the bulk of the payments are far in the distance like reroofing a church), then shorter term volatility of return is not really an issue. These examples imply different spending policies for different needs and more than just consideration of a single rate of spend over a series of years. They also indicate how spending policy must be integrated with investment policy in the development of strategy. Monthly, quarterly or even annual return volatility is less an issue in meeting liabilities in 20 years than in 20 months.

5.4   MORE SCENARIO ANALYSIS

The message, which we have given in Chapter 3, 'Elements of Return', is that we must analyze sources of total return to determine what is and what is not genuinely spendable. The reality is that the 1980s and 1990s were a one-off period of persistent disinflation which created a non-spendable valuation-change element to returns. We must investigate the scenarios that create asset price returns and make reasoned judgments about the future.

We referred above to the Commonfund proprietary model which does just exactly that. It is called the 'Commonfund Allocation Planning Model' (Commonfund APM). The model allows the Commonfund to ask the question: What is the probability of not achieving intergenerational equity over a defined period of time, given a specified asset allocation and spending rate? It defines intergenerational equity as 'the condition in which the nominal market value (after spending) is equal to or greater than the CPI inflation-adjusted market value'.

The model analyzes asset allocations and spending rates under different financial scenarios, as defined by the yield curve. The model uses a statistical technique called Monte Carlo simulation to generate thousands of future economic scenarios and it projects asset class returns in each of those future scenarios. With these distributions of possible outcomes the model can help the user to understand the impact of decisions such as asset allocation, the spending rate and spending policy.

The Commonfund APM uses the relationship between historical returns from, and correlations between, different asset classes. It includes the relationship between those asset classes and the level of inflation, risk-free interest rates, corporate bond spreads and a world market equity premium. The model also incorporates factors that are unique to particular asset classes. The model runs 1,000 different potential yield curves for a period followed by another 1,000 in period 2 and so on in succeeding periods to generate scenarios assuming different levels of spending over periods from 5 to 20 years.

The Commonfund APM model therefore allows an assessment of likely outcomes with differing allocations to assets and differing spending policies. It allows testing of such questions as 'What is the probability of achieving intergenerational equity with a given asset allocation and spending rate?' or 'How much can be spent now with a high probability of maintaining intergenerational equity for the future under different scenarios?' It can help to answer questions such as 'What happens if economic conditions anticipate a deflationary environment?' or 'What happens if inflation rises over time or remains low and stable?'

5.5   DETERMINING AN OPERATING RULE

The starting point for determining a rule must be an assessment of the social objective of the endowed entity, quantified in real or nominal terms, tailored to the endowment's resource. The assessment should be a best estimate cash flow forecast, or series of cash flows, over the expected life of the endowment. This should take account of the significance of other expected sources of funding, whether as annual income or permanent capital gifts. It is also important not to confuse real and nominal concepts when setting the cash flows.

This exercise does not imply forecasting every dollar or cent over the life of the endowment. It does, however, imply making realistic assumptions about likely trends in the future. It implies an accurate budget for the 'operational' years, the foreseeable operational period, and attaching rough numbers, usually in real terms, to the endowment formula for following years. The exercise requires assessment of parameters of expense. What is the absolute minimum required to fund daily needs and what is the minimum reinvestment required to maintain the fund for the future?

Once the preliminary exercise has been completed, a range of spending rates, which provide the amounts required to achieve the social purpose of the endowed entity, can then be expressed as a percentage of the endowment fund. In Chapter 4 we identified 'minimum acceptable return' as the base case for downside risk. A minimum spending rate can be determined on the basis of this minimum acceptable annual amount of spend, adjusted by inflation. A maximum level of current spending can then be based on the minimum acceptable intergenerational equity. Remember Micawber's Rule: if current spending is increased it is at the expense of the future, and vice versa.

The Commonfund paper on overspending in the 1990s used their model to consider how to incorporate inflation into the spending equation subject to bands of spending rate as a percentage of asset value. The Commonfund first tested an example that began with a 4%

spending rate, which set the spending amount in Year 1, and they then escalated the spending amount by the rate of inflation. This approach led to a lower amount of spending than that implied by taking a simple 4% of market value. The reason is that inflation is anticipated over time to grow at a rate that is less than the expected return on long-term assets. The risk of failing to achieve intergenerational equity using a rule of escalation by inflation was no less than that of a policy based on 4% of value, but the potential upside in intergenerational equity was much greater.

The paper then investigated a policy whereby spending was first established as a percent of assets and subsequently varied by inflation within parameters that were a percentage of asset value. The example used an initial 4% of assets for the first year's spend followed by growth in line with inflation. Minimum/maximum spending limits of 3% to 6% of asset value were then set. This implied that when asset returns were high, the excess was effectively reinvested to boost intergenerational equity, and when returns were low or negative, the intergenerational equity effectively funded the present.

The outcome of this model was a slightly higher probability of achieving intergenerational equity than the 4% of spending over shorter time periods but the same probability over 20 years. It led to a more stable pattern of spending than the 4% rule. The 3% band was triggered in 44.9% of the 20,000 annual returns examined over 20 years but only 4% of cases on the upside 6% band. Very few cases led to any drop in spending, compared to the 4% rule which saw a drop in spending in 24% of the cases. And perhaps most significant of all was the greater skew toward upside outcomes of the inflation-adjusted banded approach.

The Commonfund Benchmarks Study in respect of spending rules of educational endowments shows that the largest institutions tend to have higher (5.1%) rates of spending than the smaller institutions (3.5%) apparently because the largest institutions are more dependent on the endowment to fund their activities. The smaller are more dependent on gift flow. The average percentage of operating budget at the larger institutions funded by endowment income has grown to 15%. At the smallest institutions it has fallen to 11%.

At Yale the contribution of the endowment to the operating income of the university rose from 14% to 31% in the 10-year period to 2004, largely due to good investment performance over that period. The spending rule used by Yale, called the University Equation, is ascribed to the late Professor James Tobin by Charles Ellis in the foreword of David Swensen's book *Pioneering Portfolio Management*.[5]

The equation originally worked as follows. To set the current year's spending, the previous year's spending was adjusted by the difference between the long-term (20-year) investment return and the current percentage of the endowment being spent. If the long-term return was higher, then that would be reflected in the spending.

The 1970s saw inflation rising and financial returns falling, which led to an ever-increasing proportion of the endowment being spent on current activities. Ten years after it was introduced, the spending rule was changed. Spending was capped until the spending rate, the percentage of the endowed assets spent, caught up with the expected real return from the endowment. This figure was deemed to be 4.5%, on the basis of historical experience.

In 1982, Yale changed the rule again. This time the spend would be a weighted average of 70% of the previous year's spend, adjusted for inflation, plus 30% of 4.5% of last year's endowment value (4.5% was the expected long-term spend rate). The idea of this was to combine budgetary stability with purchasing power sensitivity. The rule was adjusted another three times between 1982 and 2004, each time raising the long-term spend rate to take account of the improving portfolio characteristics. On the third change, in 2004, the smoothing rule was also adjusted from 70/30 to 80/20. This change was in response to the need for more budgetary stability.

To use a mariner's terminology, a spending rule is a rhumb line, a constant compass course, for endowment fund spending. The 'speed over the ground' will vary with the state of the tide, so in the maelstrom of financial markets the spending rule must be such as to flex to the movement in asset values. An optimal approach to setting the rhumb line is therefore to set a percentage of the endowment value that is related to the minimum acceptable return and contains a price deflator component to account for the change in value of money. As we shall see in Chapter 8, strategy decisions should not be set in stone for time immemorial, but should be able to flex with conditions and be reviewed regularly, but not necessarily frequently.

6

Assets for Strategy

oft expectation fails, and most often there, where it most promises.

WILLIAM SHAKESPEARE, *All's Well that Ends Well*

Until the second half of the twentieth century, few asset classes were available for investment by endowment funds. Modern Portfolio Theory and other financial developments changed the way in which conventional assets were viewed, expanded the financial instruments available and changed the approach to portfolio management. Assets are classified in this chapter first by use and then by characteristics. The classification by use is between operational and intergenerational assets. Operational assets are short-duration investments to cover, with a high degree of certainty, both the daily operating needs of an endowment over the budgeted period and the tactical and risk management needs of an endowment's portfolio managers. Intergenerational assets meet the longer term need to preserve and enhance intergenerational equity. The subclassification by characteristics is based on common factor risk. The asset classes within the operational and intergenerational classifications can behave like chameleons: some fixed income bonds can behave like equities while others will behave like cash or real estate. Some equities behave more like commodities than other equities, or even like bonds. And the behavior of all will vary as scenarios change.

6.1 BACK TO THE FUTURE

Earlier chapters have considered some of the conceptual bones of financial strategy: return, risk and spending rules. This chapter adds flesh by exploring the use and the risk and return characteristics of specific asset classes. Chapter 8, 'Understanding Strategy' and Chapter 9, 'Implementing Strategy' build flesh and bones into a functioning body. Investment strategy can only be implemented through the medium of assets or their derivatives, even if assets are then fine tuned by liabilities such as leverage or hedging. The implementation of strategy is also constrained by the characteristics of those assets.

Early endowments involved few asset classes. As often as not there was only one, land and real estate, which generated rent or tithes as a source of income that provided both cash for consumption as well as protection against inflation. We saw in Chapter 2 that inflation was not the norm of financial conditions in the many centuries during which economies were tied to the gold or silver standards; nevertheless governments have not been above debasing coinage to finance wars and other distractions.

In the nineteenth century bonds and mortgages secured on real estate were deemed to be attractive additional investments for endowments even if equities were still not acceptable until later in the period. In the case of King v. Talbot in 1869, the New York Court of Appeals declared that common stocks investments *always* were imprudent trust investments, regardless of the circumstances.[1] Cary and Bright, in the *Law and Lore of Endowment Funds*,[2] wrote in 1969: 'fifty years ago most trustees would have argued that it was immoral to purchase common stocks with endowment funds.' The pioneers in common stock for endowment funds began between the two World Wars. The years following the Second World War, years of high rates of economic growth and capital market development, followed then by creeping high rates of inflation, were to consolidate and extend the trend.

Initially equities were bought for their greater income yield than Government bonds. They were then held as financial proxies for 'real' assets. The theory was that if equity values are the present value of future dividends then inflation should have no effect on the value of equities. Inflation would increase the earnings flow by the same amount as it would raise the discount rate so they canceled each other out. In practice this did not work over the short term, as we discussed in Chapter 3. Earnings took time to adjust to real values and only when inflation stabilized did equity valuations rise, providing positive real returns.

Until well into the second half of the twentieth century, defining asset classes was relatively simple. There were only four principal types: real estate; listed equity; bonds; cash. Cash could be regarded as an ultra-short-term bond since its principal was protected. These main types of asset were relatively homogeneous. Duration and volatility were linked and there was a long-term average relationship between duration/volatility of each asset class and total return. The more volatility and the greater the duration, the more the return.

Figure 6.1 gives a stylized idea of the relationship between traditional asset classes although, in practice, the trade-off between return and volatility/duration is not a straight line. Furthermore, the line fluctuates with conditions, shifting along the whole spectrum and changing in slope.

The diagram is careful to use the words 'Volatility/duration' on the x axis and not the word 'Risk'. We defined endowment fund risk in the previous chapter and, as we saw, volatility is a component not a total solution to the question of risk in an endowment fund context.

The main conventional asset classes of bonds, equities and cash still dominate the portfolios of most endowments but areas of specialization have developed within these major asset classes. These include: international equities; global regional equities; domestic mid-capitalization

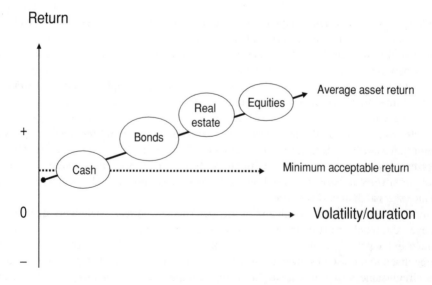

Figure 6.1   Conventional asset class volatility risk and return

and smaller companies; industry sectors; different types of bond portfolio from money funds through to distressed debt. Real estate has its own series of specialization such as industrial, commercial, retail, residential, short-leases.

The last few decades of the twentieth century also saw a substantial development in other forms of investment and in the 'securitization' of assets. Securitized assets may be created to have some or all of the characteristics of the underlying asset classes and the security of the contract is generally a basket of investments in the underlying asset.

Other, 'alternative', forms of investment have developed their own areas of subspecialization. Private equity, for instance, includes venture capital, mezzanine debt and Management Buy-Outs (MBOs). Hedge funds employ many different strategies such as 'global macro', which involves taking positions on macro trends; 'long–short' which is buying one and selling another similar security to arbitrage a common factor; 'convertible arbitrage' which plays off the valuation of a composite security, a convertible, against its constituent parts, to name only a few.

6.2   INVESTMENT APPROACH

The second half of the twentieth century also saw an increase in the types of asset that emerged from styles of investment because of the co-movement of securities or of assets which evidenced style effect. Perhaps the earliest articulated styles of management were of equity portfolios under the headings of 'value' and 'growth'. The distinction between these styles is, at its simplest, based on the accounting ratio of Price to Book Value. High Price to Book Value shares tend to have high Price to Earnings ratios reflecting an expectation of growth. Low Price to Book Value equities represent 'value' rather than 'growth'.

This is the outcome of the thinking we have discussed in Chapter 3, where a low dividend yield with a high rate of growth is comparable in present value terms to a high dividend yield with a low rate of growth. A low dividend yield and low ultimate growth clearly fails in both camps. Many other 'styles', however, are simply specialized management of specific asset classes. Nobel prize-winner William Sharpe pioneered style analysis of portfolios, and consultants have taken the analysis into the marketplace of asset management. Research showed that some 90% of the variation of portfolios could be explained by exposure to a few asset classes which could be replicated by indices.

The emergence of indices and derivatives on indices that represented 'the market' allowed practical application of the theoretical debate between 'active' and 'passive' management. The theory was that market prices reflected all known information and the market could not be outperformed on a sustained basis, especially after active management fees. The lowest cost, lowest risk (in terms of deviation from benchmark) way to achieve market exposure was to buy index funds, eventually in an exchange tradeable form. The main developments in indices were in large, medium or small market capitalization equities, bonds of different types and foreign stocks. As the indices developed, so grew the passive or index management industry in the 1990s. A trillion dollars flowed into market capitalization-weighted indices.

This led to the concept of core and satellite portfolios. The idea was that a large part of return comes simply from market exposure, that this element of return can be obtained cheaply and efficiently by buying an index or a series of indices, and that these become the core portfolio. The satellite portfolios would be investments in less efficient markets where active management was presumed to add value.

The core/satellite approach moved on a stage further in recognition that large markets may not be perfectly efficient. The evidence suggested that some mispricing does exist and that some managers can add value. This value-added could simply come from being 'long' stocks which outperform. It could alternatively come from being 'short' those securities which underperform. Or it could, in a 'long–short' hedge fund, be a combination of long and short positions so placed to exploit mispricing of securities rather than moves in the general market.

This led to the idea that 'alpha' and 'beta' could be unbundled from portfolios, and that market risk could either be added through index funds or derivatives or be removed from a long-only portfolio by hedging from any given actively managed portfolio to leave pure alpha. The traditional approach to strategy has been to analyse and decide asset allocation entirely on prospective market risk and return. The main decision, once asset strategy was decided, was whether an active or a passive approach to managing the asset class should be used. This new approach was to develop a 'risk budget', a total amount of acceptable volatility for the total portfolio, and to decide where to make exposures within the portfolio that exploited opportunity without raising risk.

The 'alpha' approach to identifying asset classes starts with finding managers who can add alpha, then combine them in such a way that it optimizes the risk/return profile of the portfolio of alpha managers. Adding market-related risk on top, where market direction is presumed to add value over any given period of time, is one basis of hedge fund investment and the concept of 'portable alpha'.

'Portable alpha' involves a combination of strategies. When market returns are replicated using derivatives such as futures or swaps, they require only a few out of every hundred dollars as margin. Part of the remaining cash can then be invested in lower volatility-risk, or market-neutral, alpha strategies. Alternatively, a lower volatility-risk strategy can be leveraged and the funds that are made available by this strategy can be invested in a market direction vehicle such as an index fund or exchange-traded fund.

The portable alpha and market-neutral hedge fund approaches to strategy carry both leverage and costs. There are costs of hedging, there are higher costs of management, there are costs of leverage, and liquidity can be an issue. Some markets cannot be hedged at all because the instruments do not exist. Combining portfolios of alpha does not avoid the need for strategy within the portfolio, especially where portable alpha is combined with directional positions. Perhaps the greatest issue is the scarcity of true alpha opportunities, especially given the extent to which money has been moving to specifically targeted asset strategies that can be small universes of opportunity. The amount of money that has now moved into hedge funds is similar to that into indexation and it would not be surprising if subsequent returns were less than expected.

The merits and demerits of portable alpha and of hedge fund strategies may be open to debate, but recognizing different sources of market and non-market risk and return in the assets available for strategy is still important to a proper understanding of investment strategy. We will also see in Chapter 8 that there is a place for both alpha and beta approaches to portfolio management in addressing the operational and intergenerational needs of endowments.

The expansion of asset classes from the traditional classification of real estate, bonds, equities and cash is demonstrated stylistically in Figure 6.2.

6.3   CLASSIFICATION OF ASSETS

So, with a myriad of opportunities, the question arises as to how to classify assets for endowment strategy in the twenty-first century. They can be classified by legal structure or form. They can be classified by their location, by their volatility, by their real or nominal characteristics, by

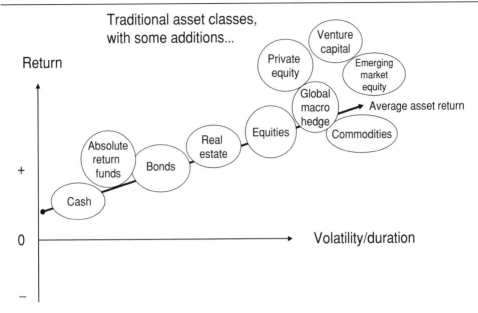

Figure 6.2   Conventional and alternative asset volatility and return

their liquidity, size, or type of return. But it is principally usage and behavior, not nomenclature, that defines categories of assets and their position as assets for strategy for endowments.

In Chapter 2 we considered Aristotle's distinction in respect of assets between their 'value in use' and their 'value in exchange'. The assets with which we are concerned in this chapter are clearly those that have a measurable financial value in exchange. Mostly, but not exclusively, at any point in time these assets have an intrinsic value that is the present value of expected cash flows in the future. Such flows may be from interest income, dividends, rents or terminal values.

Other assets, such as commodities, land, gold or indeed currencies, also have a value in exchange. Their ultimate intrinsic value is derived from their value in use to the end consumer, whether as a capital or a consumption item or a recognized store of real wealth. As with all securitized investment, such assets are generally subject to other and more complex forces. Expectation, as well as the real underlying demand and supply, creates the intermediate market price. Intermediaries have no ultimate 'value in use' other than speculation or a general hedge against inflation. Speculation, however, serves the function of providing liquidity and efficiency to a market to enable genuine end-users to exchange prospective risk and return.

Yet other assets, such as works of art, derive ultimate holding value merely from perceived want, rather than economic need, relative to scarcity. That, too, has an economic rationale. Price is driven by desire and capacity to buy, relative to available supply in a market that can be very inefficient. One major pension fund in the UK in the 1970s turned artwork into an institutional asset class as a store of real value against inflation.

Inefficiencies in markets imply opportunities to exploit. As in financial markets, price in art is driven by patterns of behavior. The difference between art and the assets considered here for strategy is that art does not have a measurable stream of income or an ultimate use to assess an underlying intrinsic value. The only 'stream of income' is the ultimate sale price, which is a function of demand and supply, but a demand that is often fashion based, a fashion that can easily be manipulated.

The anthropologist Arjun Appadurai described art auctions as 'tournaments of value' where status is achieved by bidding wars, rather than tournaments involving arms, between millionaires rather than knights. Tournament of value might be used to describe some company take-overs. The difference is that in company take-overs there is measurable intrinsic value which is not simply based on the last bid price or a vague assumption about art fashion, or any ability to control that fashion, in the distant future.

Finally, in respect of art there is the question of whether it really represents an asset or a liability. Richly endowed institutions may have a wealth of fine and decorative arts, including quantities of silver, but these collections may be more a liability than an asset, even if they could be sold, especially if the cost of keeping the assets (not least the insurance) proves to be high. Art is not therefore considered here as an asset for strategy. In this chapter we focus on those assets that ultimately generate cash flows or have an underlying intrinsic value based on use or as a recognized, realizable store of value. On this basis, one asset can be compared with another asset that is quite different, but as long as it is cash-flow producing, or has a recognized, liquid and tradeable market, relative value comparison can be made. Such assets can then be combined effectively into a comprehensive portfolio strategy.

In this chapter we classify assets for strategy purposes by usage first and behavior second. The prime purpose for which the assets are used defines the first level of classification. There are two principal categories of use: 'operational assets' and 'intergenerational assets'. The second level of categorization is by characteristics of these asset classes within operational and intergenerational asset classes – characteristics in terms of common factor elements.

6.3.1 Operational Assets

Short-term operational needs means obligations over an operating budget period, usually five years, but may be less according to the institution. Operational needs also includes market timing in the management of the portfolio. Operational assets are those that ensure that principal and income are available for consumption with a high degree of certainty over an operating time period. Essentially these are cash or near cash assets. Special projects within the budget period also fall into this category and may need their own specific reserves.

The characteristics of operational assets include low volatility of return, high levels of liquidity and short duration; they imply lower levels of return as well as low volatility and low correlation with intergenerational reserve assets. The shortest duration, highest liquidity and most secure operating reserve assets are Treasury Bills; cash at high-grade banks; high-grade money market instruments and funds; short-dated Government bonds.

Intermediate term operating horizons and reserves for special projects justify investment grade, intermediate-dated bonds. Project needs of a more indeterminate time horizon might also justify the use of carefully selected funds of hedge funds which invest in cautious, non-directional strategies with an objective of achieving returns of a few hundred basis points over the rate of cash with minimal volatility.

Clearly where cash is needed within three months, then reserves must be available to satisfy those claims within the contract time period – that is, they must be in cash or near cash. Where the operating budget will require available reserves in three years' time, but not before that, the reserves do not need to be in three-month instruments rolled over quarterly. The longer duration of operating liability allows more flexibility and more potential reward. It requires less present value of financial resources to be dedicated to meeting those operational obligations.

As we have discussed under the subject of total return in Chapter 2, it makes no difference whether those necessary cash flows are income in the form of dividends and interest or are realized low volatility capital gain. An investment of $100 that accrues $10 of gain in a money market fund which can be realized with certainty at the end of Year 1 is the same, for these purposes, as a bond that pays a dividend of $10 with equal certainty at the same time. Both investments share a common duration, return, risk and liquidity.

Operational assets refer also to the short-term cash reserve needs in the operation of the longer term investment portfolio. These needs may arise for any number of reasons such as new money in to the fund, major switches between asset classes or tactical asset allocation, the process of switching asset classes to gain marginal return. There are economic and market extreme conditions in which higher exposure to cash or near cash can form a key part of deleveraging investment strategy.

A reversal of deleveraging could come at any time, so the same degrees of liquidity and principal protection apply as much to the funds that finance that move back to riskier assets as they do for other operational needs. It is important, however, to distinguish between those funds set aside to meet operational expense needs and those to meet the operation of the investment portfolio. The latter will usually be retained by the custodian as part of the investment manager's portfolio but in larger endowments may be kept in-house.

The amount of operational assets will therefore be a function of two different things. The first is the extent to which expense needs might fail to be met by planned cash flows, whether from intergenerational investments or from other sources of income such as fund raising. The second is the investment decision-making process. The purpose of each is different but the effect of each is the same. It involves the same characteristic of asset and the same impact on the endowment, including the impact on intergenerational equity.

6.3.2   Intergenerational Assets

Intergenerational assets are the endowment itself. Long-term or intergenerational needs are about maintaining in real terms, and growing, the underlying wealth of the endowment, thereby maintaining and growing both the income and the ability to spend in future. The timeframes for intergenerational assets extend well beyond the immediate forecast period for which operational asset reserves are appropriate, hence the concept 'intergeneration'.

Asset classes that are not appropriate as operational assets, because they are illiquid and/or volatile, may be entirely appropriate as reserves for intergenerational equity. Reliance on realization of real estate or private equity, or speculation on equities to meet operational needs over a three-year period, is clearly inappropriate for meeting such a defined (in time and money) need. Real estate and private equity realizations can be impeded by unforecasted events and trustees must never become forced sellers of assets.

It may be the case that a portfolio of equity securities can be bought and sold in a matter of minutes, and equities are therefore technically a liquid asset class, but this does not mean that they should be used to fund short-term needs. There is no forecastable probability of any given equity return over short periods of time. If one takes US equities as an example, Dimson, Marsh and Staunton[3] show that equities provided an arithmetic annual average return of 12% in the last century (against cash of 4.3%). Two years out of three that return varied between −18% and +32% with the worst year being −43.9% in the Great Depression.

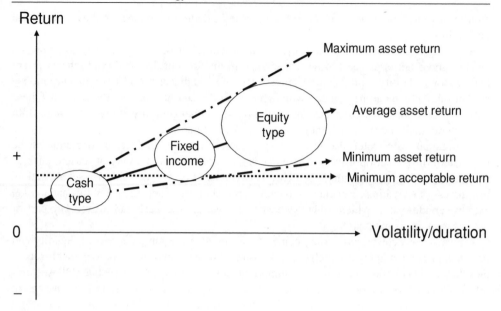

Figure 6.3   Parameters of long-term return

Other academic research in the USA, covering periods beginning with the establishment of the S&P index in 1926, has suggested that the return on US equities was positive at least two-thirds of the time for one year holding periods but nearly 90% of the time for 10-year periods. But what if the need for realization arises after the 43.9% fall?

While operational assets require certainty of short-term realizable return and a low correlation with intergenerational assets, their downside is lower returns and lack of ability to preserve intergenerational equity. Intergenerational assets, however, require patience as well as occasional indifference to potential illiquidity. There may also be uncertainty of correlation with other asset classes designed to provide diversification. The reward for patience, and greater indifference to risk and illiquidity, should be higher potential real return. This, in turn, means higher ultimate spending power since growth of intergenerational equity ultimately equates to growth of spending.

In the long term operational asset classes are unlikely to meet a minimum acceptable return. Figure 6.3 demonstrates that combining operational assets with intergenerational is the only way to achieve this. Long-term returns not only offer a higher likely average but a greater probability of meeting the minimum required return. So where higher long-term return is the aim for intergenerational assets, neither illiquidity nor short/medium-term volatility is an issue.

6.4   ASSET CATEGORIES

Table 6.1 outlines the main types of asset that fall in to the categories we have outlined. It describes the principal characteristics that are common to each of the two main classifications, operational and intergenerational assets.

Each asset class within the operational and intergenerational classifications may have or may combine one or more of the following principal characteristics: fixed return; equity like

Table 6.1   Endowment asset class categories

Category	Asset class	Characteristics
Operational assets	Treasury Bills; cash at high-grade banks; high-grade money market instruments; short-dated Government bonds. Investment grade intermediate-dated bonds; low volatility funds of hedge funds	• Short duration • Low correlation with intergenerational assets • Liquidity • Low but protected return • *Loss of intergenerational equity*
Intergenerational assets	Long-term fixed income, junk bonds and convertible bonds; index-linked bonds. *Equity*: large and small companies and emerging markets; private equity; venture capital; real estate; medium risk single strategy hedge funds and higher volatility funds of funds; commodities and currency funds, swaps and structured products; leveraged funds	• Long duration • Varied common factors for high diversification • Potential or actual low levels of liquidity • Return volatility and potential principal loss. • Potentially high rates of return • *Preservation of intergenerational equity*

return; commodity related. Hedge funds and funds of hedge funds have a section to themselves because they are not, per se, an asset class. The term 'hedge fund' encompasses a broad range of investment assets and styles. Some combinations of cautious styles may be acceptable as medium-term operational assets if they are held in a form that is sufficiently diversified, such as through the medium of a fund of funds. Other hedge fund styles fit only the extreme end of the intergenerational asset category.

Within the two classifications of asset there are asset classes which can be chameleons: they can change within their own asset class and with other assets depending on the scenario. Some fixed income bonds, for example, can behave like equities while others will behave like cash or funds or real estate. There are equities that behave more like commodities than other equities or even like bonds. And even when an equity is behaving differently from a bond in one scenario, it may behave similarly to a bond in another.

6.4.1   Cash

Cash can be represented by deposits in the bank or with other financial intermediaries; money market instruments such as Treasury Bills (TBs) which are 3-month Government securities; money market funds and short-term bond funds. Cash, held in a secure bank or in TBs is the ultimate risk-free (in an absolute return sense at least) asset in a category defined by volatility, liquidity and return.

The main characteristics of cash are liquidity (usually a maturity of less than one year) and access; neglible, if any, volatility risk; significant positive correlation with inflation but low correlation with intergenerational asset classes. The hallmarks of cash are asset protection and flexibility.

Cash is often regarded as risk free because the capital remains unimpaired on any change in interest rates; because it is not influenced by change, especially severe movement, in the market value of other assets; and because it can be realized easily. In extremis banks can be vulnerable to default but the largest would not be allowed by governments to fail because of the impact on the financial system. And where cash is in the form of Treasury Bills, the government has a virtually limitless call on taxpayers to fund the interest and capital repayment.

The capital element of cash is vulnerable to inflation but the average level of the interest rate on cash tends to reflect, with a small premium, the expected rate of inflation. Interest reinvested therefore provides some inflation protection of capital but with little excess return. Interest consumed, on the other hand, ensures loss of intergenerational equity.

Cash has a diversification role to play in a portfolio of assets because of its low correlation, even negative in some cases, with most asset classes and especially emerging market equities and commodities. Cash is often regarded as a dull asset class but it requires attention to detail (the attention that makes Bankers rich) in the proper treasury management of the asset class. This entails constantly checking the market for better rates and selecting the appropriate duration of deposits. Portfolio managers are not generally paid much in fees to manage a low risk asset but the added value to the end investor can make professional management of cash a worthwhile activity.

6.4.2   Short-dated and intermediate-term bonds

Bonds in general are borrowed money. They are loans, divisible into units, usually listed on a recognizable exchange and therefore easily realizable and exchangeable. They carry a coupon (which can be fixed, floating, index-linked or zero) representing interest that is generally payable annually, semi-annually or quarterly. The capital is repayable on a given date or at the issuer's option between two dates, although some UK bonds are practically irredeemable so have a perpetual life. The issuers of tradeable bonds are generally governments, quasi-government domestic or international organizations, municipalities and corporations.

Bonds are generally classified into two groups: investment grade and 'high yield'. The latter term refers to bonds that carry a Standard and Poor's rating of below BBB and/or a Moody's rating of below Baa, and these are also sometimes referred to as 'junk bonds'. These bonds may be domestic or international. International bonds may be issued in a country and denominated in that country's currency or bearer bonds issued and traded outside the jurisdiction of any single country, such as Euro Bonds.

The highest grade bonds are those issued by governments backed by tax-raising powers. Such bonds are generally regarded as credit risk free but not always, as holders of early twentieth-century Chinese and Russian bonds, and those of some current issuers, will testify. Government bonds set the benchmark for interest rates of any maturity, other bonds being described by their yield premia to government issues. Government bonds are generally traded in large and liquid markets in which very fine prices are quoted and the main influences on their price, and therefore yield, are fiscal and monetary policies, government issuance and portfolio flows.

Short-dated bonds are those with maturities of up to two years in the USA and five years in the UK. Intermediate-term bonds are variously defined as having a term to maturity of between short at two years and long at 10 years or, in the UK, between five and 15 years. Most international bonds with a 10-year or greater maturity follow the US classification of long term. The durations of bonds – which is the weighted average time of cash received back from coupons and repayment – may be less than their maturity dates but the longer dated intermediate bonds should only be regarded as operational reserves if the operational needs can be measured in an equivalent timeframe.

Short-dated Government and other investment grade bonds offer stable nominal flows of income and capital repayment to match with operational needs. The shorter the duration, the more predictable the total return but time provides a maturity premium. If the operational need covers two to three years, for instance, and the yield on 3-year paper is 1% higher than 1-year, there is a clear benefit from being sure of the timing of needs. Short-dated bonds also tend to be negatively correlated with equity type assets during stock market declines and during extended periods of poor economic performance. As we shall see in Chapter 8 this provides a useful portfolio diversifier and dampener of volatility and an antidote to negative total return.

Bonds issued by non-government organizations are priced off the nearest equivalent government issue. The pricing depends on their credit rating as determined by one of the major bond rating agencies such as Standard & Poor's and Moody's. Investment grade bonds tend to be issued and traded in sizes that provide liquidity. They tend also to be well researched, and therefore efficiently priced. However, non-government bonds are still subject to credit risk so operational reserves should be confined only to the highest rated investment grade issues.

For operational assets, international bonds should only be used to match an expense cash flow in that currency. Short-term mismatching of asset/liability currencies can lead to large budget variances. Buying short-dated international bonds and hedging the currency, when forward rates of exchange simply reflect interest rate differentials, is defeating the purpose. There must be a good reason, such as matching foreign currency liabilities, for using short-dated international bonds for operational needs.

6.4.3   Long-Dated Bonds

Long-dated bonds are generally those with a term to redemption of 10 years or more although long-dated UK Government bonds are those with a 15-year or longer maturity. The most common issue period is 10 to 20 years. The longest dated maturity, other than 'perpetuals', which are also known as 'irredeemables', is 50 years. Irredeemables are not known in the USA but in the UK they are bonds that were issued with maturity dates on which it was the government's option to redeem and the option was simply never exercised.

Repayment of the bond, and the interest, may be funded from the resources of the issuer or from an underlying pool of other loans or other assets. This type of bond is known as an 'asset-backed security', also called a 'structured product'. The risk (and return) characteristics of this bond will depend crucially on the underlying source of income and capital repayment.

If a long-term bond is not listed or traded on an exchange, it may still be traded 'Over the Counter' (i.e. by dealers) but may be illiquid and more comparable to a real estate fixed rent long leasehold. A bond may carry an option to convert into equity (a 'convertible bond') and its price therefore will vary with equity prices as much as with bond yield changes.

Alternatively a bond's return may be linked to an index of consumer prices (Government Index-Linked bond in the UK; Treasury Inflation Protection Securities or 'TIPs' in the USA) and be an almost perfect hedge against consumer price inflation if held to maturity of the bond. It can equally be a perfectly hopeless hedge against inflation if bought and sold at the wrong times during the term of the bond. A bond may be indexed to gold or other real assets and share similar real-asset characteristics. And a bond or an index of bonds can be used to create a derivative that may be listed and traded on an exchange, replicating the characteristics of the underlying instrument.

Bonds generally offer higher nominal and real returns than cash but lower rates of return than other intergenerational assets, except in disinflationary or deflationary periods. Over the twentieth century bond levels of volatility were significantly less than equities. Both returns and volatility of US and UK Government bonds in the twentieth century were generally half that of their respective domestic equity markets.

Bonds are subject to a number of risks: market risk (prices are a function of yield and longer duration bonds are leveraged to yield change); credit risk (due to a rating change, default or a corporate action involving the issuer); reinvestment risk (reinvestment of interest payments at lower than anticipated yields); prepayment risk (on bonds which may be called in early).

International bonds may be denominated in a foreign country's currency, subject to different regulation, or be denominated in a reserve currency such as dollars. They will be priced off domestic bond yield levels in the country and currency of issue. Their returns may need to be hedged against adverse currency movements, adding a new dimension to the portfolio analysis and management, but unhedged returns have had a larger impact on portfolio diversification because of low correlations with other intergenerational asset classes such as private equity, real estate and high-yield bonds.

International bonds may be less liquid than domestic bonds. They may be subject to tax, regulatory and custodial constraints and costs, and to currency movements that are different from domestic bonds. But they may also be less well researched and offer higher potential returns. The research will need to be of a comprehensive macro-economic nature and, in the case of corporate issues, equally comprehensive at the company level. Currency management will be an integral part of the management of a portfolio of international bonds though it can be managed independently by a separate currency specialist as a currency overlay in the largest portfolios.

6.4.4 High-Yield Bonds

High-yield bonds are those that are rated less than BBB by Standard & Poor's or Baa by Moody's because they involve more volatility and risk. During certain phases of the economy and financial markets, especially periods of monetary easing and steepening positive yield curves, they can provide returns that are competitive with equities but have lower volatility, especially with the better rated issues.

High-yield bonds tend to have maturities in the 7–12 year range but may be callable, which means repayable at the issuer's option, after 3–5 years. The terms of the bonds tend to be varied according to industry and issuer. Such bonds may have split coupons, step-up coupons (carrying an option to raise the coupon rate), carry warrants to buy other securities or carry other derivatives such as default swaps which protect against credit risk. They may be secured or unsecured, senior or subordinated. They may be issued for acquisition or for leveraged buyout of companies or simply the refinancing of existing debt.

High-yield bonds are an asset class for the professional investor as the structures can be complicated and difficult to model. When conditions turn against them, they tend to lose rapidly both value and liquidity, suffer a widening of the bid–offer spread in the buying and selling price and the volume of new issues dries up. Bonds issued by less well-financed companies, which may also be more susceptible to a downturn in the economic cycle, are especially vulnerable. In these conditions even investment grade bonds can become junk and subject to being sold out of portfolios because they no longer meet rating criteria specified in a portfolio manager's mandate, exacerbating the loss of liquidity and value. The default rate on outstanding issues in the USA has reached at least 10% in a poor year.

The converse is that high-yield bonds that have been acquired at an appropriate stage of the economic cycle, and combined in a well-diversified fund or portfolio, can reap risk-adjusted returns that compare favourably with other intergenerational asset classes. Given a less efficient market than investment grade bonds, good analysis can be rewarded by excess return.

The analysis must be deep and specific. It must cover the impact of leverage, corporate earnings, asset quality and covenants, credit availability, management quality and corporate growth prospects. But the asset class is one that can offer excess return, both through income spread over Treasuries and capital gain from yield compression (falling yields through falling risk as prospects improve) at the right point in the cycle.

Bonds form one of the most transparent asset classes for distinguishing between capital and income, and fund managers are constantly being required by trustees to provide, from a portfolio, spendable current income. International and high-yield bonds are often bought solely for this purpose to satisfy this insatiable need, but sometimes without recognition of the intergenerational impact. High-yielding international bonds will almost inevitably carry higher risk, even if they are issued by governments, because the risk in that case will be in the currency of issue. Higher yield will mean higher inflation and this will mean currency depreciation.

6.4.5 Inflation-Indexed Bonds

These bonds are generally known as Index-Linked Bonds or Treasury Inflation Protected Securities (TIPS) and were first issued by the UK government in 1981 and by the USA in 1997. They pay semi-annual coupons, which consist of two elements. The first is a fixed figure representing the real interest rate quoted in the title of the security. The second element is an adjustment factor to the real coupon, and to the capital repaid at maturity, for the change in the inflation index since the time of issue. Maturity dates vary from short to very long term.

There is a time lag in the adjustment figure. In the UK, the coupon payment is adjusted for the change in the Retail Price Index from issue up to eight months before the coupon is paid. This 'indexation lag' is to allow for the full amount of the interest payable to be known before the coupon period begins. In the USA, the time lag is three months and the index is the non-seasonally adjusted Consumer Price Index for All Urban Consumers (CPI-U). If there is deflation during the life of the bond, adjustment is also made for declines in the inflation indices, although the principal amount on the face value of the bond is still guaranteed to be repaid. Other index-linked bonds have been issued in the USA and in over 20 other countries. Some of these are capital-only or interest-only index linked.

The principal characteristic of these bonds is long-term protection of income and capital against the type of inflation that is specified by the index. That involves the change in prices of the specified components of the index and we have touched on this subject in the Chapter 2 'Language of Return'. But in the short term, long-dated TIPs may not provide this protection. Their returns suffer while unanticipated and accelerating inflation become reflected in the price. As prospective inflation looms on the horizon as a result of current government action, real rates will rise and long-dated TIPS are long-duration assets which offer no protection against a rise in real yields.

Governments are also not above changing, from time to time, the constituents of their indices. The constituents tend to be general consumer items but a change in specific components can make a large difference to the numbers involved over longer periods of time. In Chapter 2 we touched on the calculation of inflation and the introduction of hedonics to adjust for improvements in consumer items. This may be designed to keep the constituents current with daily life but it can depress the measurement of inflation experienced in reality.

The consumer price index used for Government Index-Linked securities in the UK is the Retail Price Index, calculation of which is under the control of the Chancellor of the Exchequer who is advised, at the Chancellor's request, by a committee of academics and professionals. If there is a 'fundamental change' to the way the index is calculated that could be 'materially detrimental to the interests of stockholders', then the Chancellor must refer this to the Bank of England, which is responsible for the National Debt. If the Bank judges that a change is significant, then holders must be offered a chance to redeem. The introduction of hedonics has not yet been deemed significant. Investors must make their own judgments and apply a premium for expected risk if this issue is of concern.

Another characteristic of TIPs is their long duration because such a high proportion of their total return is in the inflation-adjusted principal repaid on expiry of the bond. This means an ability to match very long-term liabilities. It can mean a low volatility of return as long as real interest rates remain stable, indeed standard deviations of return have been less than a third of that of equities and similar duration bonds. But it can also mean a high level of price volatility, and of capital loss, with any significant change in real yields especially in a low inflation rate environment.

Even when inflation rates start to decline after a period of high inflation, index-linked securities will not benefit, as other asset classes will, from the secular fall in nominal rates of interest that are linked to inflation. For example, UK index-linked gilts were first issued after a period in the 1970s of very high and persistently rising inflation which pension fund managers had not been able to match in their portfolio returns. Some actuaries at the time were recommending that the new index-linked bond should be bought on real yields as low as zero because even that was better than negative real returns. Needless to say, this was the peak in inflation. Index-linked securities proved to be one of the worst performing asset classes over the ensuing decade as the real interest rate on the index-linked bond rose and other assets, especially long-dated fixed income bonds, gained from the disinflationary fall in nominal rates of interest.

That, however, is one of the key characteristics of inflation index-linked bonds – their relationship, in a portfolio context, with other asset classes. Inflation index-linked bonds have a high positive correlation with unanticipated inflation and therefore a positive correlation with cash. They have a low or negative correlation with equities and with similar duration fixed income bonds. This makes them a good diversifier as an asset class although this does not apply to very short-dated index-linked bonds where there is a closer correlation to fixed income bonds due to co-movement in real and nominal yields.

6.4.6   Convertible bonds

Convertible bonds and convertible preference shares are fixed income securities that are sub-ordinated to other creditors but rank ahead of ordinary shareholders. They can be converted, at the investor's option, into a specified proportion of the equity of a company over a given period at a particular (exercise) price. Such bonds can be both investment and non-investment grade issues and often have complicated additional features.

Such features have included different type of coupon and of terms of conversion or capital repayment. Some, for example, allow the issuer to call the bonds for repayment before maturity;

others call for mandatory conversion or allow investors to 'put' the securities back to the company under certain conditions; others include warrants or conditions for exchange into shares of another company.

The general characteristic of convertibles is an underlying bond with an embedded call option on a specified number of shares in a company at a given conversion price. The main characteristic of convertible bonds is that they move partly like a fixed income bond and partly like an equity. However, the fixed income element reflects both interest rate and credit risk; the equity element includes factors that are relevant to options such as volatility.

The result of this combination is that the combined value of the straight bond and of the option on the equity allows an overall price which ensures a cheaper interest cost of capital to the issuing company and a regular source of income to the investor who retains an interest in the potential growth of the company through the option. Returns on convertibles are more closely allied with equities than with bonds, but with volatility levels 20% to 40% lower than equities.

Some regard convertibles as a poor substitute for either bonds or equities. On a rise in the equity market they participate partially, but seem to participate more fully on a fall. This is especially the case if the conversion element is so far 'out-of-the-money' that there is no option value in the price and there is credit risk to be reflected in the yield. However, with equity-like returns and bond-like income, and with principal protected both by the maturity of the bond and by the prior claim on the assets of the company, convertibles can offer to endowments some relatively high reward-to-risk total returns with a useful element of income. And the portfolio characteristics of convertibles are such that they have a high correlation with equities, modest with bonds, and low or negative correlation with cash.

6.5 EQUITIES

Equities are financial interests in human enterprise which represent ownership of businesses and participation in the profits, assets and distributions of those businesses. The value of equity is, theoretically, the net present value of all expected future cash flows from a business, discounted at a rate of interest that reflects the risk-free rate of interest plus a premium for risk.

The value of a share is the net present value of all future dividends as a proxy for all future profitability of the company. Conventionally shares are valued in the stock market in terms of their dividend yield (dividend per share over the current share price × 100); Price to Earnings (PE) ratio: (earnings per share divided into the current share price); and Price to Book Value (net book assets per share).

Equity investment can represent not only specific exposure to one particular company or industry but, in a portfolio context and with large market capitalization stocks in particular, exposure to an economy as a whole. Where different countries have different areas of specialization, such as technology in one and commodities in another, international equity investment allows the opportunity for both risk diversification and return-enhancement through investment in businesses that may not exist in the home market.

Equities may be held privately or listed on an exchange. They may be held directly or through mutual or other funds that may specialize in areas of the equity markets. They may be held through derivatives such as options and futures and contracts-for-differences. In the developed world, the total market capitalization of listed equity markets tends to be a significant percentage of Gross Domestic Product or other economic measures. This is as much a measure of the development of the financial markets as it is of the growth and size of the underlying businesses.

Within countries, equities are most commonly categorized by market capitalization size, with large, mid, small and micro capitalization being the most common. Size may be judged absolutely, but is most commonly defined by proportion. For instance, the FTSE Global indices defines 'small cap' as the bottom 10% with a screen minimum of US$100 million to ensure that the size of the company is investable by large institutions. To judge by absolute size makes it difficult to classify small, medium and large capitalization across markets which vary in size and over time. The market capitalization of a company may triple but it can still be within the bottom 10% of all companies in that markets.

Conventionally, equities are also divided into 'growth' and 'value' categories. These concepts of 'growth' and 'value' are examples of styles of investment and style indices have been created to track style performance. Styles imply common factors and these form the basis for such methods of investment. The methods can become self-reinforcing. When value or growth investing are in fashion, there is increasing demand for stocks with value or growth characteristics and this encourages another style of investment, which is momentum. Momentum investment is following a trend; its counterpart is 'contrarian' investment, which assumes trend reversal, often based on reversion to a mean.

In the USA investor preference has shifted back and forth between value and growth but there have been substantial periods over which one style or other has provided higher returns. There is some evidence that adherence to a value style can give superior performance over a very long period of time. There can then be merit in diversification by style. Style rotation – which is investment in one style in one period and switching to another style when the underlying economic and financial market variables change – is a valid outcome of scenario analysis, but the switching must justify the transaction costs involved. Switching should be made at times of extreme relative value imbalance.

Equity investment in countries that have not reached the same level of per capita income, consumption and Gross Domestic Product as the developed economies, is known as Emerging Market Equity. The World Bank's IFC index definition of an Emerging Market is a country with a per capita GDP of less than US$1,000. These markets are exposed to less-developed economies which are usually growing fast, where research into companies, many of which are priced inefficiently, can offer opportunities for adding excess return. The markets tend to be volatile and the economies highly leveraged to developed market economic activities, generally because of a high level of exports to the developed world. In many cases these exports are commodity items. Currencies can be unstable and the costs of dealing and custodianship can be high.

Emerging markets offer exposure to an array of countries and cultures in Asia, Africa, Eastern Europe and South America that may have substantial exposure to natural or human resources. Because of the population size and the stage of development of their economy, emerging markets are often seen simply as low-cost sources of manufactured goods. This greatly underestimates the investment potential. Today's emerging market company has proved in many cases to be tomorrow's global leader. In the globalized twenty-first century, capital, technology and productivity move faster than ever before. And the faster these factors move, the quicker the transformation into sophisticated domestic consumption economies.

Emerging market equities tend to be much more positively correlated with developed market equity, hedge funds and high-yield debt than with private equity. They have tended to be negatively correlated with real estate, bonds and cash. Some emerging markets have a high commodity element, so their performance is correlated with the relevant commodity price cycle. While emerging markets have offered high rates of return, levels of risk have tended to be significantly higher. The risks include political, legal, custodial, counterparty and currency and, where applicable, relate to commodity price volatility. The result has been volatile returns and long periods of low absolute return, punctured by periods of substantial outperformance by emerging markets of major market indices.

6.6   PRIVATE EQUITY

Private equity is a generic term that describes two main classes of non-listed equity activity.

The first is venture capital, which is the early stage financing of businesses. These begin as private companies to exploit, with single-minded focus, an entrepreneurial idea. There is generally unanimity of purpose between management and shareholders, though there may be differences of view on the timing of exit. The companies are often simply financed with equity and debt and the capital is supplied typically by venture capital funds, institutions and high net worth individuals.

As these companies develop those ideas and the potential marketplace for their products, a need for more working and other capital can develop before positive cash flow can be generated by the business itself. This leads to further rounds of financing at higher costs of entry to reflect the value brought, and risk taken, by early stage investors in the project. Ultimately, however, the investors will be seeking the route to exit. This may involve listing the business on a stock exchange both to raise further cash from new investors and to provide a listing for current holders to sell. Or it may involve a sale of the business to an interested 'trade buyer' – a larger company that wants to enter the business of the venture capitalist.

The second type of private equity is the buy-out. This either takes the form of a Management Buy-Out (MBO), a Management Buy-In (MBI) or a Leveraged Buy-Out (LBO). MBO is the transfer of ownership of the business to existing management and employees. MBI is transfer of the business to a manager and team who are brought in from outside. LBO is acquisition of one company by another using a substantial amount of debt rather than cash or exchange of shares.

Buy-outs attract a different form of management from entrepreneurial start-ups. The focus of buy-outs is change to the operation to extract profit, and the more leveraged the structure the more urgency for that change and subsequent exit. Again the exit may be by stock exchange listing or sale to another business.

Buy-outs take advantage of a climate in which there is a high level of corporate restructuring, including mergers and acquisitions. They tend to focus on quality of management of the investee business, the market position and potential growth of the business, the cash flow and a clear route to exit. A key feature of private equity is therefore the exit strategy for investments made. Investments are made to be realized not retained and thereby to generate high internal rates of return.

Investment in private equity may be made by investors directly into particular opportunities where there is 'in-house' resource for finding and minding such investments. More usually such investment is made alongside other investors through the medium of a Limited Partnership. The Managing Partner is generally a specialist team who assess the opportunities, arrange the finance and co-invest in the equity of the underlying investments. The difference between such a team managing a portfolio of private rather than listed companies is that the private equity manager must be 'hands-on', especially with early stage venture capital. The managers are rewarded on a fee basis, which is typically 1–2% of capital committed and 20% of the profits made.

One characteristic of private equity is that there is no passive alternative to active management. Another is the low levels of correlation with most other asset classes. It can therefore represent a good portfolio diversifier as well as offering potentially high rates of return for endowments with long-term horizons. However, that comment must be seasoned with a strong note of caution.

First, private equity funds are not valued daily and therefore appear to have low levels of volatility, but that is no indication of less risk of loss. Secondly, rates of return for private equity funds on average have been poor over some significant time periods, especially relative to listed equity, and the dispersion of returns can be very high. The selection of the right manager is therefore critical because paying high levels of fee for low levels of performance is double jeopardy.

Dean Takahashi, director of investments of Yale University, spoke at an AIMR seminar on managing endowment and foundation fund management in 1996.[4] Yale had been very successful in the area of private equity largely, in Takahashi's view, because they had access to good funds. His argument for private equity in endowment funds was that 'the value mechanisms for value creation in private equity are independent of the mechanisms in traditional markets . . . and the long-term cycles of supply and demand in the private equity market provide diversification.'

Takahashi described the drawbacks of private equity as 'overall disappointing returns, difficulty in evaluating money managers, incomplete performance record, oversubscription in the successful funds, costly and lingering mistakes, difficulties of exiting, and the time and effort needed to develop a successful program.'

Takahashi said that one reason for the disappointing returns was high fees. The other was the cyclical nature of the asset class. Yale analysed the amounts raised for venture capital with the subsequent performance and found a negative correlation. He commented: 'unfortunately the increase in capital does not bode well for short-term future returns.' This was 1996, but remember, history rhymes.

6.7   REAL ESTATE

Real estate refers to tangible, fixed (rather than movable) property in the form of land and buildings as well as oil and other mineral rights. The principal categories of real estate for endowment funds are agricultural (farm and timber land), commercial (offices); industrial (warehouses and land for manufacturing businesses); retail (shops and shopping malls); hotel and hospitality; residential (domestic property in the form of houses, apartments, apartment blocks, etc.).

Real estate can be owned in a number of different ways. The most direct is freehold ownership whereby the owner has absolute title in perpetuity. The next most common form of ownership is the 'lease', which is granted by the owner to the lessor for a period of time under contractural terms relating to such items as occupancy, rent and repairs to the property. To enhance return, freehold and long leasehold ownership of real estate is usually leveraged with debt that is secured on the property and funded from the cash flow provided by rent.

Lease structures determine the character of the investment. In the USA, under the 'triple net lease', the investor receives rent without any deduction for operating expenses. The tenant is obliged to pay all costs. In the UK, the full repairing and insuring lease is similar, the tenant bearing all costs, but rent terms are generally 'upward only', typically adjustable every five years.

Single properties and leases, and multiple properties, can be joint owned. One form of common ownership in the USA and a number of other countries is a structure called a Real Estate Investment Trust (REIT). Real estate tends to be a large value item. To have to invest only in one large property with a high specific risk (one type of property situated in one area with one tenant) is relatively high risk. REITs allow an investor the ability to diversify risk across many different types and locations of property with different tenants who, other than in exceptional circumstances, would be unlikely to default on rent all at the same time. REITs are treated for tax purposes as if the investor owned the underlying real estate, as long as 95% of the annual net income is distributed.

Other indirect forms of real estate holding include other forms of open and closed-end fund and property investment and development companies listed on a stock exchange. Mortgages on real estate really come into the category of bonds but they are non-equity ways of capturing part of the cash flow from rent.

Real estate has traditionally had a number of characteristics that are attractive to endowments. The first is a fairly predictable source of cash flow from rents given a good covenant (credit worthy tenant). In recent decades theses cash flows have supported income yields on real estate that have been higher than those on equities, especially in certain types of property. Higher income yields do not necessarily translate into higher total return, but for endowments that cannot trade a donated property asset that is not an issue.

Secondly, rents can enjoy similar characteristics to dividends in terms of potential real growth but have the advantage over dividends, which are distributions of profit, that they must be paid out before dividends and are thus more secure. In a time of inflation rents can be renegotiated or linked to price rises, which provides inflation protection. Where rents are relatively fixed, however, the real estate is a fixed income investment that suffers from compounded diminution of the real value of its rent in a time of inflation until the rents can be reviewed.

Thirdly, there is one factor that makes measurement difficult but is an advantage to finding value. It is the lack of homogeneity within the asset class. While the three most important aspects of any real estate may remain 'location, location and location', within that mantra there is a myriad of factors that affect each property individually and that is what helps to ensure the opportunity to add value in the sector.

A fourth attractive characteristic, if a little misleadingly, is that the volatility of return from property appears to be less than that from equivalent equity-type assets, and property is therefore regarded as less risky. Less volatility, however, has more to do with the infrequency and method of valuation of this type of asset, which is not regularly traded. In a depressed environment there may be no market at all, and in that case, or where there are few if any comparable transactions, the method of valuation is discounted cash flow and replacement cost. Although these are not subject to the noise created by the daily shift in emotions in an active trading market, emotions can run as high in the bidding process for property on sale and purchase as they can on a work of art in a sale room. The volatility of real estate is somewhere between bonds and equities and is perhaps better demonstrated in the market for REITs.

Property prices are driven by specific demand and supply for given properties, and this varies sufficiently to provide low correlation not only with other intergenerational asset classes, such as equity and bonds, but even between classes of real estate. Real estate is a relatively inefficient market offering excess return for knowledgable access and skill. And while the influences on demand and supply are partly the same as macro influences on other asset classes, such as interest rates and economic growth, they can also be very asset specific: zoning laws, land management, government development and conservation policies, especially in specific locations for political and social reasons. As Will Rogers (1879–1935), cowboy humorist, famously said, 'invest in land; they aint makin' it any more' – except perhaps in Hong Kong.

Whatever the merits of real estate in periods of inflation, and even disinflation, the asset class can suffer like other equity type assets from deflation. The income from property rents, depending on lease terms, may lag changes in the economy but lessors can default and rents on average are likely to fall with a general fall in prices. In a serious downturn end-users are forced to rein-back their operations, vacancy rates rise, rental portfolios suffer and risk premia rise. This could even be happening while interest rates rise on the debt, so all these factors can compound the downside into disaster for any who are forced to sell because they rely on the income.

Other less positive characteristics of real estate include potential obsolescence and depreciation; exposure to uninsurable loss; indivisibility and immovability. Transaction costs are usually high and both investment and realization times can be long, during which economic conditions can change radically. Finally, rents must be collected and properties managed.

For endowments that do not plan to trade but to hold real estate, most of these negatives need not be an issue but should simply be part of the overall financial equation. They should not be ignored but incorporated into the assessment and if the numbers still make sense then the investment stands on its merits. Indivisibility can be an issue in terms of diversification but the investment therefore needs to be made in the context of the total portfolio. Obsolescence and depreciation should be annualized and accounted for in the expected return. Transaction costs should be factored into the cost and the initial yield adjusted accordingly. Any proposed sale should be made in good time at an appropriate stage of the cycle and never forced on an unreceptive market.

6.8   COMMODITIES

Straight commodities can fall into that category of asset that has a value in exchange without a cash flow that can be intrinsically valued. The principal categories of commodity are: (1) precious metals (such as gold, silver, platinum, palladium, rhodium); (2) base metals (such as copper, aluminum, lead and zinc); (3) agricultural commodities (such as grains, beverages, livestock, timber); (4) energy commodities (such as crude oil and gas); (5) financials (such as currencies and interest rates).

Straight commodities may be traded in physical form or through futures on one of the commodity exchanges. Commodity Trading Advisors (CTAs) are specialist investment professionals in this field who generally use leveraged, momentum-based high turnover investment strategies. Other forms of gaining commodity exposure, other than physical ownership or trading in futures, include investing in commodity-linked stocks that are listed on stock exchanges and passive investment in commodity indices.

Commodity prices tend to be subject to longer term trends based on underlying end-user demand and supply factors. Shorter term speculative influences take commodities away from trend before reversal, thereby increasing volatility. The impact of this on a portfolio, however, can be diversifying because of the low correlation of commodity prices in general with most other asset classes and even between themselves, given the diversity between commodity types such as agricultural commodities, energy or metals.

One of the characteristics of most commodities, subject to specific demand and supply factors, is a strong correlation with accelerating and unanticipated inflation. Given the negative correlation of financial assets in general with unanticipated and accelerating inflation, this is a clearly positive diversifying characteristic. The Commonfund tested this relationship to see if commodities might provide return enhancement to a portfolio of bonds and equities in an inflationary era and found impressively positive results.[5]

Other forms of commodity-related investment include oil and gas properties, timberland and farmland. Oil and gas investment takes different forms involving different levels of risk.

The safest is clearly producing oil wells and the most risky is speculative drilling. A charity in Texas benefited from a bequest, courtesy of the IRS, of what might euphemistically have been called farmland since it was more like scrub. They discovered oil on this land and, as one of the trustees commented wisely: 'farming is best when minerally supplemented.'

6.9   HEDGE FUNDS

Hedge funds are not an asset class. They are pooled investment vehicles following predefined investment strategies. They may or may not be eligible vehicles for endowment funds because most hedge funds use some form of leverage as well as 'short' strategies (involving selling stock that is not owned) as well as 'long' (simply investing in assets). Federal Reserve Chairman (at the time of writing), Alan Greenspan, in his comments to the Senate Banking Committee on the SEC's plan to increase the regulation of hedge funds said:

> hedge funds have become major contributors to the flexibility of our financial system. They seek out abnormal rates of profit often found where markets are otherwise inefficient. Taking positions in volume as hedge funds do tends to eliminate the abnormal profits and inefficiencies.

The second sentence is as clear a definition of what hedge funds are about as one will find, because the term 'hedge fund' covers a multitude of different styles, structures, managers and asset classes. Even the word 'hedge' can be misleading because while some funds rely on hedging common factor risk (arbitrage funds) – especially hedging market-related risk to gain alpha by exploiting specific investment opportunities – others may simply leverage market risk in different asset categories (macro funds) to exploit directions in markets.

Looking for characteristics that might define the class, one comes to the following conclusions about most hedge funds. These factors are neither definitive nor comprehensive, and they will change with time, but they generally cover the asset class:

- Return targets tend to be absolute rather than relative.
- Objectives tend to be capital preservation (but not always).
- Funds tend to employ leverage.
- Funds can sell short and go long.
- Investment objectives tend to be either very style-focused or completely unconstrained and may not be transparent.
- Good funds tend to be capacity constrained, are privately placed to sophisticated investors and may close early to new entrants.
- Manager rewards are highly incentivized: performance fees on top of a management fee.
- Structures tend to be offshore for tax and for light regulation reasons.
- Funds generally contain a significant percentage of the manager's own net worth.
- The minimum investment in hedge funds is high and exit may be constrained.
- The life of a fund may be limited; the average survivor rate is low.

While most hedge funds may share these various characteristics, they are generally defined in terms of their strategies. And those strategies can generally be included in our classification of operational and intergenerational, based on the same criteria: short duration, low volatility and lower return fund styles can be operational assets; higher return, more volatile funds, are intergenerational assets.

Strategies that might be included in operational assets, through the medium of fund-of-funds or combinations or directly owned hedge funds, are non-directional. They seek to hedge out market risk to isolate and exploit anomalies in order to generate excess returns. The strategies fall into the categories of being (1) of relative value (equity market neutral, bond arbitrage) and (2) event driven (merger arbitrage, distressed debt).

The intergenerational strategies may be directional. They may leverage positions to exploit market movements. These strategies include (1) macro, (2) long–short, (3) other specialist.

Event driven usually describes strategies that depend on some corporate event to drive their returns. These include merger arbitrage (buying stock in the subject of a take-over bid at a discount to the bid price); capital structure arbitrage (a long and short position in two different securities forming the capital structure of the same company to exploit an anomaly in the pricing between them) and distressed debt (bought at discounts to perceived value).

Relative value covers other forms of arbitrage: statistical arbitrage (long and short positions in equities that have similar characteristics); fixed income arbitrage (similar in respect of fixed income securities); volatility (purchase and sale of closely related options) and convertible arbitrage (purchase of a convertible against a short position in the equity and perhaps also a credit hedge); and commodity arbitrage (long and short positions in closely related commodities and derivatives to exploit pricing anomalies).

Directional strategies are 'top-down'. They aim to profit from major market trends such as currency movements, interest rate moves and commodity trends. Such strategies tend to use derivatives and to use leverage extensively. The principal strategies that fall into this category are global macro funds, which use leveraged directional positions in the futures markets.

Long–short funds come in different forms but they all offset securities bought (long) with others which are borrowed and then sold (short). The ratio of long to short will vary according to the view of potential market direction. A market neutral fund will have equal long and short positions. Leverage will vary between long–short funds so it is important to know the gross and net positions.

One example of long–short is 'pair trading', which focuses on securities that have common characteristics, are perhaps in the same industry, and one is expected to outperform the sector while another underperforms. Stock in the first company is bought, and stock in the second is borrowed from the market and then sold.

Funds of hedge funds combine different strategies to diversify risk. They either aim for lower but more stable returns, and so fit into the operational assets category, or they target performance irrespective of volatility and, as such, fit into the intergenerational assets classification. The key questions for hedge funds or funds of hedge funds, as with all asset classes, are: 'What are the characteristics of the different hedge fund strategies?' and 'How do they fit in as an asset class for endowments?'

Many hedge fund performance charts make much of hedge fund return relative to volatility, usually expressed in the Sharpe Ratio. Work by Professors Brooks and Professor Harry Kat[6] show that overdependence on the Sharpe Ratio is misleading because hedge fund returns tend to have different profiles from normal, which make other statistical measures a more realistic gauge of risk. The fact is that hedge fund returns are less dependable and more prone to surprise than simple volatility analysis indicates. And survivor bias in the universe for which indices that track hedge fund performance are created, tends to be high.

The correlation between many hedge fund strategies and against a number of other asset classes seems to be low. But once again care must be taken with a superficial assessment. Low correlation may indeed be the case for most of the time, but if there is extreme volatility in markets, strategies that are usually unrelated can become more closely correlated at the same time as returns suffer. Hedge funds in some strategies, such as merger arbitrage, tend to hold similar instruments and may realize them together.

Many hedge funds depend on leverage to achieve their returns. This may include leverage of low volatility assets to enhance return. In a rising interest rate environment problems can emerge. The cost of debt rises just as yield curves invert, and this reduces the scope for return on higher cost, debt-financed hedge fund strategies. Suddenly low correlated returns become highly correlated risk and some fund strategies become very high risk. Diversification can become 'diworsification' and liquidity can suffer as managers declare *force majeure* to prevent realization of units in the fund. The message of using hedge funds for endowments must be, as with every investment decision, a carefully researched and well-considered policy. This policy can raise the bar of total portfolio return for a modest increase in volatility risk for a large percentage of the time.

Research must include a proper analysis of the fund strategy itself in different economic environments. For example, in a liquidity squeeze, credit spreads widen, relationships between securities and merger terms break down, and arbitrage and leveraged positions are tested. With rising liquidity, carry trade (borrowing short and investing long) and directional strategies tend to be successful. Scenario analysis should test hedge fund strategies in the context of other asset classes when combining the whole in a portfolio of assets.

An alternative example of failing to appreciate the characteristics of a hedge fund in the context of overall strategy was that of one Foundation in the UK which bought a hedge fund denominated in US dollars thinking that the return would offer upside potential with limited downside risk. The hedge fund was in fact a fund-of-funds designed to provide a low-end return with very low volatility. It proved, as designed, a reasonably good US dollar cash-plus proxy. Unfortunately the dollar declined substantially against sterling and the UK Foundation lost money. The hedge fund performed as it was supposed to perform, but the Foundation had unintentionally made more of a currency than a hedge fund decision.

The research must include a convincing analysis of the fund, or of the fund of funds. As important as how the fund fits in with other asset classes is the manager's style within the strategy. This requires in-depth research of the method of generating excess return from any given strategy in different financial environments; consistency over time in identifying and exploiting opportunities; and thoughts on the future, not just explanations of the past. Furthermore, if an endowment must, because of its size, abrogate responsibility for hedge fund manager selection to a fund of funds, then the fund of funds manager must have equally convincing answers to similar questions both in terms of the fund itself and of the underlying component funds.

7

Legal, Social and Ethical

Gain all you can
But not at the expense of your conscience
Not at the expense of our neighbour's wealth
Not at the expense of our neighbour's health.

JOHN WESLEY (1703–1791)

There are matters of law that apply to the establishment, management and monitoring of endowments including trustees' fiduciary responsibilities; there are codes of corporate and trustee governance in relation to the management both of endowments and the businesses in which endowments invest; there are social and political pressures on both 'governance' and 'responsible' investing. These are the issues of this chapter. Corporate Social Responsibility (CSR), which incorporates corporate governance, is how businesses relate to the world in which they operate. Socially Responsible Investment (SRI) is about how institutions invest their money in companies that may have different levels of CSR. External pressures may influence 'socially responsible' parameters to investment, even if this is not outlined in an endowment's original constitution. And since the law today is society's resolution of the social issues of yesterday, we will consider some issues of today's governance best practice that may influence the laws of tomorrow. The chapter ends with a 'reality check' on non-financial issues for endowment funds.

7.1 QUIS CUSTODIET IPSES CUSTODIES?

Who guards the guards? Regulation of businesses in which trustees of endowments invest is one thing, but who or what regulates the trustees of endowments? In the USA and the UK there are both case and codified laws that cover endowment funds and their investment. The laws govern the creation, management and tax position of endowments, but perhaps the most powerful influence on trustees, especially in respect of the focus of this book, is the body of case law that has developed around the notion of fiduciary responsibility.

The law in the USA and the UK is clear on fiduciary responsibility, on powers of investment and on what qualifies for tax relief in the case of charitable entities. In general, private foundations in the USA must make a 'qualifying distribution' of 5% of the net asset value of their investments each year. In particular, Section 501(c)(3) of the Internal Revenue Service Code defines qualifying private organizations. Section 509(a) of the code defines public charities as opposed to private foundations. There are sections on mandatory pay-outs, self-dealing, excess business holdings, excise tax and jeopardy investments to name just a few. There are other rules that are specific to grant-making to charities abroad. Some of these recipients, such as the International Red Cross, automatically qualify as 'public charities'. Others are subject to the 'out of corpus rule', which involves certain procedures and a time limit on expending the grant given.

The Uniform Management of Institutional Funds Act (UMIFA) – promulgated by the National conference of Commissioners on Uniform State Laws in 1972, and since adopted in some form by 46 of the States in the USA – now defines powers of investments, institutional funds, prudent investment and delegation. The act, which is currently undergoing revision, applies to colleges, universities, hospitals, religious organizations and other institutions of an eleemosynary nature. Trustee investment in many States in the USA had previously been guided by 'legal lists' which specified, by statute, permissible investments. Mostly these investments were fixed income securities for the protection of capital.

UMIFA converted the case law 'Prudent Man Rule' into a statutory 'Prudent Investor Rule'. Those responsible for managing endowments and foundations are required to 'exercise ordinary business care and prudence under the facts and circumstances prevailing at the time of the action or decision'. The act also repudiated the rule prohibiting trustees from delegating decisions.

In 1994 the Uniform Prudent Investors Act (UPIA) updated general trust investment law for developments in capital market theory, specifically mentioning in the prefatory note to the act 'Modern Portfolio Theory'. The act changed fiduciary responsibility to 'reasonable care, skill and caution' and to make investments 'not in isolation but in the context of the trust portfolio as a whole ... '. The trade-off between risk and return was identified as a fiduciary's central consideration and restrictions on types of investment were removed to allow any investment that might play a role in achieving the risk/return objectives of the portfolio subject to other requirements of the 'prudent man' rule. UPIA permits a trustee to delegate investment management subject to exercising care, skill and caution in selecting the agent, establishing the scope and terms of the agreement with the agent and monitoring performance.

Laws in the UK covering these areas include the Charities Act 1993, the Trustee Act 2000, the Income Taxes Act and the Financial Services and Markets Act 2000. But the system of law in both the USA and the UK is such that much lies in the interpretation of Statutes through case law.

Section 5 of the Uniform Prudent Investors Act 1994 in the USA is entitled simply 'Loyalty'. It states that a trustee will invest and manage the trust assets solely in the interests of the beneficiaries. The act specifically states that a fiduciary cannot be prudent if it sacrifices the interests of beneficiaries to third parties, not just to the self-interest of trustees. The act also says: 'no form of "social investing" is consistent with the duty of loyalty if the investment activity entails sacrificing the interests of trust beneficiaries – for example, by accepting below-market returns – in favor of the interests of the persons supposedly benefited by pursuing the particular cause.'

One of the most notable cases defining the position of trustees in the UK was that involving the Mineworkers Pension Fund in the early 1980s. In that case (Cowan v. Scargill 1984), Scargill and other National Union of Mineworker appointees who were members of the Committee that was responsible for the pension fund were opposed to investments overseas and in other forms of energy, particularly oil, which they deemed to be competitors to UK coal.

The National Coal Board's lawyer, Mr Cowles, advised that the suitability of investments was to be judged

> almost exclusively by reference to financial criteria rather than their acceptability for political or other extraneous reasons ... what is improper is for the Committee of Management to fetter the way they exercise their discretionary powers as trustees in the future by imposing an embargo on a wide range of investments regardless of the financial consequences.

Judge Megarry's summary was clear:

> The starting point is the duty of the trustees to exercise their powers in the best interests of the present and future beneficiaries of the trust, holding the scales impartially between different classes

of beneficiaries. This duty of the trustees towards their beneficiaries is paramount. They must of course obey the law; but, subject to that, they must put the interests of their beneficiaries first. When the purpose of the trust is to provide financial benefits for the beneficiaries, as is usually the case, the best interests of the beneficiaries are normally their best financial interests. In the case of a power of investment, as in the present case, the power must be exercised so as to yield the best return for the beneficiaries, judged in relation to the risks of the investments in question; and the prospects of the yield of income and capital appreciation both have to be considered in judging the return from the investment.

The second point in the judgment was allied to the first:

In considering what investments to make trustees must put on one side their own personal interests and views. Trustees may have strongly held social or political views. They may be firmly opposed to any investment in South Africa or other countries, or they may object to any form of investment in companies concerned with alcohol, tobacco, armaments or many other things. In the conduct of their own affairs, of course, they are free to abstain from making any such investments. Yet if under a trust, investments of this type would be more beneficial to the beneficiaries than other investments, the trustees must not refrain from making the investments by reason of the views that they hold.

However, Judge Megarry qualified his judgment by saying that the word 'benefit' must be carefully considered. If the beneficiaries are all adults with strict views on alcohol, armaments, tobacco, etc., then the beneficiaries

might well consider that it was far better to receive less than to receive more money from what they consider to be evil and tainted sources. 'Benefit' is a word with a very wide meaning, and there are circumstances in which arrangements which work to the financial disadvantage of a beneficiary might yet be for his benefit. But I would emphasise that such cases are likely to be very rare.

In another case, 'Harries v. Church Commissioners for England', the court also refused to direct an activist approach toward adopting an investment policy compatible with the Christian faith. The court concluded that 'the trustees' choice of investment should be made solely on the basis of well-established investment criteria' but it, too, recognized that there could be a few instances where the investment conflicted with the aim of the charity – tobacco shares in a cancer research charity being an obvious example.

Judge Megarry even went a stage further by saying that 'Trustees may even have to act dishonourably (not illegally) if the interests of their beneficiaries require it', and he particularly referred to a duty to consider a better offer for an asset after a bargain may have been struck but before a legally enforceable contract has been signed.

The 1989 decision of the Maryland Court of Appeal in 'Board of Trustees v. City of Baltimore' gave a different perspective from earlier cases such as Cowan and Harries. This judgment acknowledged that non-financial criteria do not necessarily violate a trustee's duty of prudence and loyalty if there are alternative investments with comparable risk and return characteristics. The Court also established a different standard of prudence from that of simply maximizing return accepting a 'just' or 'reasonable' return achieved without undue risk. This judgment reflected the progress in investment theory away from the idea of risk as it relates to a single investment toward a portfolio approach that does not maximize return *per se* but in relation to the degree of portfolio risk taken.

In the UK, the Charity Commissioners provide guidance on their website on extra-financial issues such as 'ethical' investment for charitable endowments. Trustees may adopt an ethical policy if it avoids investments in businesses that would practically conflict with the aims of the charity, or investments that might hamper the charity's work. If an investment decision is to be made on moral grounds, then the trustees must be clear that the endowment will not suffer significant financial disadvantage – a matter that would probably require professional advice.

7.2   TAX MATTERS

Charity tax relief in the UK began with the first income tax and can be found in the Income Tax Acts of 1799, 1803 and 1842 even though Gladstone tried to repeal the exemption of tax by charities on the grounds that exemption amounted to a grant of public money without public control and that many charities were not beneficial to the community. If an endowment is to enjoy tax advantages, therefore, it must meet given criteria established by law, such as the IRS rules in the USA and the requirements of the Charities Act and the rules of the Charities Commissioner in the UK .

Tax matters. The reliefs now provided by government, both to donors and to recipient charities, encourages both tax-efficient giving and tax-efficient investment both in the USA and the UK. Foundations that may not have access to such tax benefits by not being registered charities should consider, in their strategy, ways to mitigate tax. This is especially so in the building of intergenerational equity where the compounding effect of small annual differences can have a large wealth effect. One percent per annum is an amount easily lost in tax. If a fund returns 8% per annum gross and spends 5%, reinvesting 3% per annum, it will have almost half as much again accumulated capital at the end of 40 years as a fund that could only reinvest 2% per annum.

Each nation, even each nation within the UK, has its own charity law. Accepting the financial benefits of charitable status brings with it public accountability. That is fine in terms of current law on which lawyers can provide clear advice, but what of other social pressures on trustees, and the asset managers they employ, toward non-financial corporate issues? We will look at these non-financial issues below and consider not only the constitutional demands on trustees, but also the subsidiary demands of those trustees on their investment managers.

7.3   EXTRA-FINANCIAL ISSUES

The term 'extra-financial issues' covers a range of topics including Corporate Social Responsibility (CSR), of which Corporate Governance is a part, and Socially Responsible Investment (SRI), a closely allied concept. Also included in the general term SRI is the concept of Program-Related Investment (PRI).

CSR is about how companies conduct themselves in business. SRI is about how institutions invest their funds in businesses which may or may not adopt various levels of CSR. These matters go beyond the immediate financial objectives and responsibilities of endowments but they can affect strategy. Indeed some endowments and foundations have CSR and SRI at the core of their strategy as laid down in their constitution, and we will consider some examples of these in Chapter 9.

In this chapter we address the issues on which trustees need to develop a policy that then guides strategy. First we look at some history to provide context then we look more deeply at both CSR and SRI. Finally, in Section 7.9 we provide some conclusions on a debate that sometimes generates more heat than light.

Motives for endowing assets, whether an altruistic wish to give something of one's good fortune back to the community or a more self-centered desire to insure one's soul against the hereafter, have not changed over the centuries. By their nature, endowment tends to be socially responsible. So why should non-financial issues have reached such a high profile? And how should endowments respond to these issues?

The answer to the first question has something to do with change in the nature of endowment assets and a great deal to do with the change in the climate of general opinion, itself partly a function of increased general wealth. Populations with subsistence economies tend to focus first on survival.

Furthermore, in the early centuries endowments were made for a specific social purpose and were often, if not usually, grants of land that provided a source of income to fund that purpose. The constitutions of a number of early endowments in the UK may have had royal assent, with some commercial privileges allied to the maintenance of standards, but generally they had no fiscal privileges except in the case of tithes on Church land. The universe of available investments was essentially limited to real estate and mortgages, or other loans.

7.4 CORPORATE GOVERNANCE

Corporate governance was the first stage of corporate responsibility. The OECD defines corporate governance, from the Latin word *gubenare* which means to steer, as 'the system by which business corporations are directed and controlled'. Sir Adrian Cadbury used a very similar definition in a book published in 2002[1] but in 2004 used a broader definition:

> Corporate governance is concerned with holding the balance between economic and social goals and between individuals and communal goals. The governance framework is there to encourage the efficient use of resources and equally to require accountability for the stewardship of those resources. The aim is to align as nearly as possible the interests of individuals, corporations and society.

Investment in the equity of businesses, rather than in loans or property or through partnership, was not widespread until the emergence of the Joint Stock Company in the UK in 1844, which required all companies with more than 25 people to be incorporated. The limited liability company, which limited the liability of shareholders to the amount of share capital they had invested in the business, developed a decade or so later. And the picture of external investment in businesses became complete with primary listing on a stock exchange and the subsequent exchange of shares in those businesses through secondary market trading.

These forms of business also emerged in Continental Europe with a more prescriptive and regulatory approach, but it was in the USA that this corporate approach to business, with divorce of ownership and management, reached new levels. The problem was identified early by Adam Smith[2]:

> the directors of such joint stock companies being managers rather of other people's money than their own, it cannot be well expected that they should watch over it with the same anxious vigilance with which the partners in a private copartnery frequently watch over their own.

The case of 'Dodge v. Ford Motor Company' in 1919 was an interesting test of the legal responsibility of directors to their shareholders in the USA at that time. In that case, Henry Ford's ambition was to 'employ more men, spread the benefit of this industrial system to the greatest possible number, to help them build up their lives and homes'. To do this he was 'putting the greatest share of our profits back in the business' and thereby had decided to pay out no dividends other than the regular dividends 'for the present'.

The Michigan Supreme Court drew a distinction between the 'incidental humanitarian expenditure of corporate funds for the benefit of the employees' and 'a general purpose plan to

benefit mankind at the expense of others'. 'Others' referred to minority shareholders represented by John Dodge. The Supreme Court affirmed the lower court's order that the company
declare a dividend, and also reversed the injunction that halted the company's expansion.

In the UK, Lord Evershed made in 1947 a distinction between directors' responsibility to
the company and to its shareholders. The outcome of the case (Short and Another v. Treasury
Commissioners, UK Court of Appeal, 1947) was that shareholders own shares and not the
business; that a long-term investment may have poor short-term consequences for existing
shareholders but long-term favorable impact on the company. As Cadbury says: 'Shareholders
are not a homogeneous group with a common set of interests, as chairmen soon discover.'

But this raises the same question as the Dodge v. Ford case. What should be the balance
between retention of cash for investment to build a business and pay-out as dividends? The
answer is that if the board cannot see their way to reinvesting in projects that offer higher
than average rates of return, then, other factors being equal, including taxation, cash should be
returned to the shareholders.

In 1932 Berle and Means published in New York what has been described[3] as one of the
most influential analyses of the development of corporate governance in the twentieth century:
The Modern Corporation and Private Property.

Berle and Means suggested that the translation of perhaps two-thirds of industrial wealth in
the USA from individual to corporate ownership meant that 'the bulk of American industry
might soon be operated by trustees for the sole benefit of inactive and irresponsible security
owners' and that

> the owners of passive property, by surrendering control and responsibility over the active property,
> have surrendered the right that the corporation should be operated in their sole interests – they
> have released the community from the obligation to protect them to the full extent implied in the
> doctrine of strict property rights.

Adolf Berle commented 30 years later, in 1965[4]: 'large corporations increasingly would
come to be regarded, and to regard themselves, as part of a political-economic system rather
than as classical merchant adventurers.' He did not deny the capitalist origins or maximization of
profit as the prime driving force of large corporations. He simply argued that large corporations
have different dynamics to small-scale firms including, for example, very long-range planning,
sometimes involving massive capital commitment, at the expense of immediate profit. This
would be for a pay-off well beyond the time horizon of smaller scale businesses in recognition
of various factors, not least potential public interference with their strategy through a political
process.

Boards of corporations not only became divorced from their shareholder base with the
development of large listed corporations, they even became separate from the executive management of the company. Cadbury points out that it was high-profile collapses of business, such
as Penn Central, the take-over of underperforming companies and an increasing concentration
of control in the hands of investing institutions that were the wake-up call.

What developed in tandem with the wider debate about the position of companies were
regulations introduced by governments alongside codes of good practice based on the concept of
self-regulation. Common to the codes has been the principle of transparency through disclosure
and guidance rather than prescription. Corporate boards began to change, the old-boy club
began to break down, and non-executive directors were appointed.

As investors became more dependent on free and liquid markets, on a legal infrastructure
that would maintain property rights and on a banking structure that financed transactions,

they also became more dependent on regulations and on the exercise of corporate governance, which maintained those market freedoms and protected their claims. This did not, however, prevent excesses in the USA at the end of the twentieth century leading to public company accounting scandals on a massive scale and the consequent introduction of the Sarbanes–Oxley Act in 2002. This act mandated the construction and operation of boards and committees, of accounting and audit procedures, and it introduced penal personal liability in respect of the future corporate responsibility of directors and officers of companies in the United States, including their overseas subsidiaries.

Clarity of roles, well-constructed membership of boards, active and constructive methods of control, monitoring and reporting of a company's activities, relationship with shareholders, are all part of good corporate governance. And this should be designed to assist and give credibility to the management of a company and assist the process of raising the company's profile and raising capital to meet the company's needs. Ticking of boxes, duplication of effort, increased cost for no visible commercial benefit is not effective corporate governance; it can be quite the reverse.

There has developed a number of organizations to monitor corporate governance. In the USA, the Investor Responsibility Research Center (IRRC) was established in 1972 to provide impartial information on corporate governance and social responsibility. IRRC has now been acquired by an organization that Bob Monks founded in 1985 called Institutional Shareholder Services, Inc. (ISS) which advises shareholders on how to vote their proxies. The first corporate activist shareholder voting advisory organization in the UK was the London-based Pensions and Investment Research Consultants Ltd (PIRC). In the early days some of the issues raised by PIRC seemed radical, such as auditor independence, but the world of corporate governance has moved on. What has not changed is their fundamental belief in the protection of shareholder rights, the minimizing of risk and the enhancement of shareholder value in their companies.

The International Corporate Governance Network is also an influential group of the world's largest investment funds which provides a network for the exchange of views on, and monitors, governance issues. And the World Bank sponsors the Global Corporate Governance Forum, which is designed to 'help countries improve standards of corporate governance for their corporations'. Corporate governance is defined in this Forum as being 'concerned with holding the balance between economic and social goals and between individual and communal goals'.

7.5   CORPORATE SOCIAL RESPONSIBILITY

Corporate Social Responsibility (CSR) is a broader concept than pure corporate governance which it encompasses. It covers the whole nature of how a company conducts its business. CRS is not a twentieth century concept. Many enlightened employers who built large businesses in the nineteenth century, such as Hershey in the USA or Rowntree in the UK, adopted core CSR beliefs in the way they managed their businesses and endowed their Foundations. And CSR became more of an issue for endowments with their increasing investment in businesses, through the medium of listed equities, rather than just in real estate or bonds. This was particularly so for those endowments that were founded on religious or moral principles.

One of the well-known practical examples of CSR at work as far as the location of its businesses was concerned, was the case of Nike, the US sportswear company. Nike's business model is global outsourcing the manufacture of its sports shoes, 'T' shirts and other products. In the early 1990s, corporate activists drew attention to the conditions in the factories of Nike's suppliers.

After an initial period of denial, the company then developed a department for monitoring suppliers' labor practices and external auditors of its 900 or so suppliers. Finally it created a Corporate Responsibility department for managing a process that went beyond simply auditing suppliers for labor law compliance. It became a core part of the business affecting not just labor practices but procurement incentives.

In view of the size and awareness of the business and the brand of Nike, and in order that good practices should not just represent a hit to the bottom line, Nike took SRI a stage further. Nike became involved with other companies, including competitors, in initiatives to develop these principles as standard practice at national and international levels in line with UN labor conventions.

There are perhaps many shades of corporate responsibility from simple governance – abiding by laws, regulations and codes – through to 'social responsibility', which is a moral stance. There is considerable debate on the extent to which businesses, directors and trustees should be responsible for the latter rather than being led by Adam Smith's invisible hand which 'by pursuing his own interest he (the individual) frequently promotes that of the society more effectually than when he really intends to promote it'.

A strong case can be made for the view that free exchange through free markets is simply an inalienable right which a free society should maintain by preventing monopolistic or other 'antisocial' practices, including poor corporate governance, and by requiring transparency. Capitalism encourages entrepreneurs to risk capital to establish companies that create goods, services and employment, all of which are socially valuable. Market exchange of financial interest in these companies determines the value of those interests, and the greater the value that shareholders place on the ways in which business is conducted, the more is that reflected in the share price. The more efficiently the share price reflects true value, and the more efficiently financial institutions intermediate between the investment of entrepreneurs and the 'rente' of the rentiers – taking a margin for risk in between – the less financial cost there is in those goods and services meeting the needs of society.

David Henderson, in a paper called *Misguided Virtue*,[5] draws a distinction between responsible business and corporate social responsibility. He writes:

> CSR raises twin issues that lie at the heart of public policy. One is whether and how far the self-interested actions of individual economic agents in a market economy, including in particular the actions of business enterprises guided by the profit motive, will further the common good. The second concerns what can be done, whether by people and enterprises on their own account or through action by Governments, to ensure that private and public interests are brought more closely in to line and, in particular, to make enterprise profitability a better indicator of social welfare.

This is a distinction between good business practice, which goes beyond just doing what is legal and profitable, and a social responsibility which implies a role for business in the community beyond simply satisfying shareholders' responsibly. Henderson raises two fundamental questions. The first is whether businesses are equipped, or even have a right, to define the goals of CSR, and the second is whether businesses become less efficient by concentrating on issues other than profitability. Milton Friedman maintained in *Capitalism and Freedom* that 'few trends would so thoroughly undermine the very foundations of free society as the acceptance by corporate officials of a social responsibility other than to make as much money for their stockholders as possible.'[6]

Another view is that, in any free society, markets are only free where civil society permits them as part of the process of the generation of wealth. This view suggests that maintenance of this freedom is based on the social contract between members of society who have different backgrounds, beliefs and ways of life and who create forms of government that control degrees of freedom. Where wealth generation leads to inequity, this can lead to extreme forms of government or, at the least, constraints on markets.

This view goes beyond pure corporate governance into the area of corporate social responsibility in identifying the 'stakeholders' in a business other than simply the owners. The World Economic Forum, a community of business and other leaders representing the world's 1,000 leading companies, has committed to 'improving the state of the world'. It has developed a number of initiatives to bring the aims of business and business practice closer to the social and environmental needs of the societies in which they operate.

Whatever the academic debate and moral stance represented by different views of the subject – from one extreme that all judgment should be left to free market forces where profit maximization is the only objective, to the other which suggests that all matters that are considered to influence society negatively must be legislated on – will be decided by politics in a free society. The power of mature free societies today, acting through democratic processes, will ultimately determine the balance between freedom and control on matters such as Socially Responsible Investing (SRI) and Corporate Social Responsibility (CSR).

The outcome of the debate will be left to political processes with the caveat from history that extremes tend to fail. If this means that economic growth suffers to the point where voters lose significant material lifestyle, especially relative to other nations, then the same political processes will move the debate off the moral high ground back to a more mundane level. And if free markets are the best (or the least worst) method of resource allocation, then their preservation requires consideration of these issues to pre-empt what some might regard as excessive control, to the point of significant market distortion, through legislation and regulation.

Where is the middle ground between the extremes of complete freedom and a view that the business community has a responsibility to use its influence to promote human rights and welfare? To the extent that it is not predefined in law, that is an issue on which trustees of an endowment must form a view, develop a policy and factor that policy into their investment strategy. Trustees must decide on a stance, bearing in mind their responsibilities to the beneficiaries, represented by their general fiduciary responsibilities and by the terms of their endowment.

7.6 SOCIALLY RESPONSIBLE INVESTMENT

Socially Responsible Investment (SRI) is closely allied to CSR because it concerns the investment by institutions into companies that evidence CSR. The macro argument is that it is in the long-term interests of all investors to commit to aspects of SRI. Some would go further. They would commit all or at least part of their capital toward promoting social stability and equitable development to ensure that Society provides an environment in which that capital may be retained by its owners and may be permitted to grow for its beneficiaries. Russell Sparkes suggests, for example, that the anti-globalization rallies in Seattle and Prague were a warning to governments to control the impact of the unbridled deregulation of the 1980s and 1990s.

Yale University was one of the first educational endowments to address the question of ethical responsibilities of investors in a seminar in 1969. The New York Times described Yale as 'the first major university to resolve this issue by abandoning the role of passive institutional investor'.[7] Yale adopted 'suggested guidelines for the consideration of factors other than the maximum return in the management of the university's investments'. These factors included voting for propositions that seek to reduce or eliminate social injury caused by a company's activities, and not voting shares that advanced a position on a social or political question unrelated to the company's business.

Socially Responsible Investing is often regarded as being synonymous with 'Ethical Investing' but SRI is really a broader concept. Russell Sparkes[8] suggests that 'ethical' is seen in Anglo-Saxon tradition as being related more to individual, personal values and SRI as more institutional. Sparkes quotes Stephen Timms, UK minister for pension affairs at the end of the 1990s, as suggesting that the term *ethical* tends to 'stifle intelligent debate'. And concern has been expressed that anything that isn't in the universe entitled *ethical* must be unethical, which is a black and white definition of what is sometimes a matter of shades of gray .

The concept of SRI varies from the macro to the micro level, from issues to do with societies globally down to specific companies following policies, or selling products, that are deemed to be in the interests of society. Social investment implies that there are factors other than pure profit motive in committing capital to generate financial return. Russell Sparks quotes Chris Cowton, Professor of Accounting at Huddersfield University in the UK: '. . . ethical investors care not only about the size of their prospective financial return and the risk attached to it, but also its source – the nature of the company's goods and services, the location of its business or the manner in which it conducts its affairs.'

One of the main driving forces of SRI in the USA has been endowments, particularly those of a religious nature. In 1928 temperance groups in the USA started the world's first SRI fund, the Pioneer Fund, which screened out investment in alcohol or tobacco. The 1960s saw shareholder activism by endowments and pension funds in a number of areas: civil rights; the Vietnam War; South Africa; and both human and consumer rights. As Russell Sparkes comments: 'These questions culminated in a major conference at Yale in 1970 where the first sustained debate about SRI took place' and 'concerns about the Vietnam War also led to the establishment of the first "modern" SRI mutual fund on 8th August 1971, the Pax World Fund.' This period saw the establishment of a number of organizations devoted to social research and corporate responsibility.

Another driving force in the development of SRI was the socialization of capital through the development of pension funds. The 1970s saw the commitment of governments to pensions reform to ensure security in old age. Pension legislation forced pension obligations to be prefunded, but with attractive tax concessions. This led to a substantial change in the percentage of listed equity held by individuals toward that held by trustees on behalf of beneficiaries and managed by institutions with inevitable divorce of ownership from beneficial control.

Russell Sparkes quotes the Goode Committee report that led to the UK 1995 Pensions Act:

> As trustees they are perfectly entitled to have a policy on ethical investment and to pursue that policy, as long as they treat the interests of the beneficiaries as paramount and the investment policy is consistent with the standards of care and prudence required by law. This means they are free to avoid certain kinds of prudent investment which they consider the scheme members would consider objectionable, so long as they make equally advantageous investments elsewhere.

In the UK, the 1995 Pension Act required pension funds to publish a Statement of Investment Principles (SIP), but this was subsequently amended with two additional clauses which required trustees to consider:

1. the extent to which social, environmental or ethical considerations are taken into account by trustees in the selection, retention and realization of investments; and
2. the policy directing the exercise of rights attaching to investments.

There have been various practical developments to assist trustees who want to develop and follow a policy of investment that supports CSR. First there are companies that have developed funds based on CSR principles, not just in a western sense, and there are other firms that provide CSR research advice on listed companies. There are Islamic Law Sharia Funds that invest in a way that respects Sharia principles, as advised by Muslim lawyers. And there is an increasing number of SRI funds in Asia.

In July 2001, FTSE launched the FTSE4GOOD series of indices where the constituents are UK companies that meet globally recognized standards of corporate responsibility. The indices are designed to provide a benchmark of 'good practice' companies. The criteria are designed to be transparent and to evolve to reflect changes in globally accepted standards. The criteria are challenging but achievable in order to encourage companies to strive to meet them. The full texts of the principles can be found through the internet on www.ftse.com/ftse4good/index.jsp.

Recently commercial operations have been established by financial institutions to research such matters as environmental performance. European institutional investors have launched the Enhanced Analytics Initiative to encourage investment banks and brokers to provide research on non-financial issues of corporate performance, including environmental issues. And Bob Monks has invested in Trucost, which measures environmental liabilities. He expects environmental stewardship to become a key investment driver and as important an issue as corporate governance over the next 10 years.

7.7   PROGRAM-RELATED INVESTMENT

Program-related investment (PRI) is a term used in the UK when charities pursue their purpose by providing resources to assist beneficiaries, but not necessarily with a financial objective in mind. This assistance may take the form of loans or guarantees (especially below market rate), the provision of land or buildings (again perhaps with concessions on rent) or subscription to shares. PRI is also known as Social Investment. The UK Charity Commissioners are clear in their guidance[9] that social investment is distinct from financial investment because the primary purpose is not a financial but a social return.

As long as it is within the powers of the endowment's constitution, social investment can provide a way of achieving a charitable objective that is at least as effective as financial investment designed to generate a return to satisfy the same objective. Some endowments specialize in this form of assistance to beneficiaries, such as in the case of relief of unemployment or the regeneration of disadvantaged areas. The UK Charity Commissioners also cite as examples the provision of recreational facilities for disabled people or the protection and conservation of the environment.

UK charities can make social investments from the expendable part of an endowment, including income and reserves, but not from permanent endowments that are held on trust for a financial return. So there needs to be a clear distinction between financial and social investment and the resources that are allocated to both forms of pursuing an endowment's objectives.

Social investment requires policies and transparency in reporting, just as much as financial investment. And it may also require independent professional advice just as often as financial investment may require the assistance of investment professionals. There may be a long history and proven resources to support such a policy within an endowment. To another, however, this may be a departure from the usual methods of achieving its objectives.

For instance where loans are made as a social investment, there should be a clear statement of (a) the purpose, (b) the terms including the repayment date, and (c) the methods of monitoring how the endowment's objectives are being fulfilled. If the social investment has fulfilled its purpose and is no longer being used to further the endowment's aims, then there needs, as part of the terms, to be a process for exit.

7.8 GLOBAL VIEW

The corporate debate, which Berle and Means can be credited as having started, has continued to evolve with theories of 'agency', of 'stewardship' and of 'stakeholder', all with the objective of determining the rights, entitlements and obligations of business corporations and their investors. It has been assumed in the West that the world will converge toward a generally accepted Anglo-Saxon model of modern capitalism. However, the Asian approach to life and business is more collegiate and less 'self' dominant. Many Muslim nations regard free-form capitalism as economic imperialism. And in many countries the benefits of economic growth are distributed so unequally that the concept of corporate responsibility is treated with skepticism. The rising tide of economic prosperity does not everywhere lift all boats, in some places it's mostly only the 'gin-palaces'.

The separation of ownership from control first became a corporate governance issue in the UK and the USA where company structures were similar. The legal responses to these issues became enshrined in the laws of those two countries, but these spread to other countries that adopted similar legal systems. As the international movement of capital and savings grew, and the raising, by companies of one country, of capital on the exchanges of another, so the issues of corporate governance and the responses by regulatory authorities began to converge.

The UK/USA model of company development is not, however, universal. Central European companies have tended to reflect the stakeholder mentality of their political systems. German companies have supervisory boards and closer cooperation between unions and management than UK or US companies. The financial model is more bank than securities market dependent.

Japanese and Chinese companies operate within a society that has a different attitude to life: more consensual, group-dependent and less individualistic, recognizing society as a stakeholder. Korean companies, in their conglomerate structure (chaebol), are similar to the Japanese conglomerate model (zaibatsu) where employees are part of a wider family as if they were part of a clan system. In Taiwan the guanxiquiye networks of small family firms are independent of the large banks, unlike in Germany or Japan; the system in Taiwan is more flexible, as it is in Hong Kong.

Muslim countries have clearly a different view to both Anglo-Saxon and North Asian models of finance and business. For example, the Muslim approach to business is dictated by Sharia principles, based on the Koran, the Sunna and older Arabic law systems. Muslims can trade in anything that is accepted (called halal) and not prohibited (haram). Prohibited things are essentially those that are regarded as illegal or immoral. Sharia principles prohibit usury and some Sharia scholars regard all interest as usury. Others consider simple interest as acceptable, but not compound interest.

Diversity of structures has not just been geographic but due also to the level, and change in level, of economic development. Economic development contributes to the growth in size of organizations and to the sophistication of the underlying financial framework: the development of insurance companies and pension funds and other institutional savings vehicles. And as savings institutions grow and begin to take an increasing percentage of public listed shares, they begin to realize that 'voting with their feet' by selling their holdings is increasingly not an option. Large blocks of shares simply cannot be passed through the market, so voting out management or voting to agree a merger or take-over becomes the only realistic way to engineer change or to extract value.

7.9   REALITY CHECK

A session of the World Economic Forum concluded that good corporate governance and corporate citizenship should simply make good business sense. They should balance goals of good citizenship with the traditional obligation of creating profit for shareholders which, by creating wealth, should by itself be good for the community.

There is some academic research that supports the contention that ethical behavior and superior profits are mutually inclusive. Curtis Vershoor of De Paul University compared the financial performance of *Business Ethics* magazine's top 100 'Best Corporate Citizens' and found that they performed better than the average S&P 500 company on a number of corporate metrics. Similar research by the UK's Institute of Business Ethics (IBE) found that a sample of FTSE 350 companies which it deemed ethical also outperformed less ethical companies on a number of metrics, such as market value added, economic value added and P/E.

There is other academic evidence that is more skeptical. Professor Vogel of the Brookings Institute suggests that 'the supply of virtue is both made possible and constrained by the market'. Not all consumers are prepared to pay a premium price for ethical products and while there is a place in the market for ethical companies there is also a place for those that are less responsible.[10] He concludes that 'there is no reason to expect more responsible firms to outperform less responsible ones . . . sometimes investments in CSR make sense and sometimes they do not'.

A study by the United Nations Environment Programme Finance Initiative concluded that there was a threat to share price performance if ethical questions were ignored. But it was also agreed that while corporate leaders have to think beyond just making profits, toward how they affect society, it is not their job to save the planet. Corporate executives are not democratically elected and should not confuse politics with business. They may have obligations to society that affect their prime obligation to their shareholders, but there is then the danger of the tail beginning to wag the dog.

There may be costs associated with CSR, but nor is SRI without financial cost. Screening companies and researching them for specific criteria that are not readily identified can be time consuming – and judgment can be difficult with large globally diversified businesses. Is a company disqualified from the universe if 1% of its turnover is found to be generated in a field that is not regarded as socially acceptable? This might disqualify a large number of companies from the investment universe and significantly impact fiduciary responsibility.

The early part of this chapter made clear the fiduciary responsibility of trustees of endowed assets irrespective, in the words of Judge Megarry, of 'their own personal interests and views'. But as he also pointed out, the trustees must have regards to the 'benefits' or disbenefits to beneficiaries of their actions. What is clear from this brief consideration of extra-financial issues is that an endowment needs to have an explicit policy on such issues. The trustees have a responsibility to their beneficiaries and must weigh costs and benefits in the light of responsibilities to the charter of the endowment.

Ideally, the policy on CSR and SRI in relation to beneficiaries should be part of the constitution of the endowment alongside the mission statement provided by the founders. This will then give Constitutional direction to the Investment Policy Statement which guides the practical implementation of strategy. An endowment's policy on non-financial issues is thereby integrated with the overall investment strategy. Policy should be agreed with the manager of the endowment's investment portfolio and incorporated in the investment management agreement as part of the Statement of Investment Principles.

The endowment policy on non-financial issues should set out broad principles and indicate expected levels of governance intervention. It should also set parameters, where applicable. On governance matters, there should be clarity on items on which to vote; the level of concern that requires attendance at an annual general meeting; and the level of which matters are escalated to the board of the company concerned. The policy should also indicate the briefing that trustees will expect of their managers and custodian banks on corporate governance and other issues, and the process by which the issues are identified, monitored and resolved.

8

Understanding Strategy

Strategy without tactics is the slowest route to victory. Tactics without strategy is the noise before defeat.

SUN TZU. *The Art of War.*

Investment strategy is about assessing resources, quantifying objectives and then marrying those two with a flexible plan. The plan should diversify across opportunities and manage the risk of failure to meet the minimum acceptable return through the most damaging potential financial scenarios. Quantifying objectives involves both a relatively precise budget covering the endowment's operating time horizon, usually a period of one to five years, and a more general long-term, intergenerational objective. The budget will set the level of minimum annual acceptable return required to cover day-to-day operations, including grant-making and administration, and from this will be derived the required core of operational assets. A second element of operational assets will be needed to cover investment management transfers and occasional tactical reduction of portfolio risk out of intergenerational assets at appropriate points of the financial cycle. The allocation to different asset classes within the intergenerational assets, the endowment itself, will be driven by the analysis of valuation criteria and of economic and financial scenarios. The objective with intergenerational asset classes is to 'avoid losers', to diversify among potential winners and to follow an appropriate discipline of rebalancing assets within the portfolio. The recommended route to rebalancing is driven by reversion to a floating mean of scenario valuation relationships rather than a long-term mean of asset class returns. Different scenarios imply different intrinsic valuation relationships between asset classes and when market values reach areas of extreme deviation from mean valuation for a given scenario, there is increasing risk of a powerful reversion to intrinsic value.

Investment is the commitment of resources to achieve a future return. The word 'investment' comes from the Latin for clothing, the notion being that of giving capital another form. The word 'strategy' comes from the Greek word *strategos* referring to command of an army, which implies arranging resources in an optimal way to achieve a future objective, not fighting past wars which seems to be the preoccupation of some generals and not a few asset managers.

Endowment and Foundation strategy is the responsibility of trustees and should have a rolling medium to longer term timeframe, meaning years not quarters. Whether or not components of the decision are delegated to committees, it is ultimately the trustees who must determine the priorities of different spending plans, timeframes for investment, the appropriate proportions of operational to intergenerational reserves, the degrees of acceptable risk, and the balance between liquid and illiquid and between nominal and real assets.

Strategy is about the interaction of all the considerations we have discussed so far in this book: endowment objectives; spending rules; financial resources; likely and unlikely scenarios. It is about setting a framework that guides investment policy decision-making over the short and the long term. And interaction implies an iterative process between the desirable and the possible.

Setting a framework does not imply rigidity; frameworks should be flexible, like houses built in Tokyo, which flex to earth tremors. Endowment strategy should be dynamic, responding to change in endowment objectives and needs as well as pre-empting investment change. The latter implies seeing through the noise of peripheral information and daily market movements to the trends in asset prices that make the real differences in wealth. Wood Struthers & Company wrote in *Trusteeship of American Endowments* in 1932:

> one has only to recall the happenings of the past three years and their effects on permanent funds to appreciate that nothing is so permanent as impermanency, and to acknowledge the importance of giving flexibility to every investment policy.[1]

In the military field there is a distinction between strategy and tactics, even if the latter is part of the implementation of strategy. The same applies in investment. In the investment world, tactics is often described by consultants as Tactical Asset Allocation (TAA). TAA is making short-term judgments, and allocating assets accordingly, within a set of parameters established by strategy to gain a short-term advantage. TAA is considered to be a style of investment management designed to take advantage of short-term opportunities to make relative gain over and above the strategic trend. But, as we saw in the discussion of money versus time-weighted return in Chapter 2, there is more to tactics than short-tem marginal activity.

The development of alpha strategies, touched on in Chapter 6, adds another dimension to asset class strategy. Alpha strategies with additional beta portfolios – pure exposures to different asset classes and markets – can allow both strategy change and TAA to be managed efficiently and cheaply through futures, swaps and options.

It is convenient to be able to place aspects of management into boxes, but a TAA move can become the first stage of a change of direction that can then lead to a fundamental change in long-term strategy. It is a mistake, as we saw in Chapter 2, to regard asset shifts simply as market timing which, on a time-weighted return basis, may not be seen to add value but may still protect or enhance wealth. The skepticism of consultants about TAA is rightly based on how few people can select the timing of tops and bottoms of markets with any precision. Such skill or good fortune is not, however, necessary in order to protect capital from the implosion of occasional irrational exuberance in markets. Nor is precise timing necessary to gain superior return from as yet unrecognized value.

The earlier chapters have given us the foundations on to which we can now build an understanding of investment strategy. We have considered the elements of return and identified a working definition of risk. We have seen the importance, in the chapter on spending rules, of considering the liability side of strategy as much as the management of assets. We have looked at the asset classes and themes that can be combined to make a portfolio. We have seen the importance of scenario analysis, the different behaviors and interaction of asset classes in different environments, including common factors between asset classes. Now we must structure this to a plan to develop investment strategy.

8.1 RESOURCE ASSESSMENT

The first stage is to make an outline of current resources in terms of asset values and types and of other sources, and potential sources, of income. This is an economic 'balance sheet' of what is available now and what is likely to be available in future. It concerns the present and future physical assets and potential streams of income that may be available. It also concerns the covenants there may be on the use of those assets, not only on how the return from them might be spent but on how the funds should be invested. Are some or all of the assets a part of capital that either cannot be spent or must be committed in a certain way to generate, perhaps, a particular activity? Are there operating assets but at the same time financial liabilities? Are there buildings that cannot be sold, or buildings that may even once have generated rent but now consume income through dilapidation?

Resources are not just the endowment assets themselves. If there are other sources of return available to the organization, such as fees and fund-raising, then these sources of income also have a net present value and the endowment funds must be seen in that context. Indeed, the net present value of a stream of fee income can greatly exceed the net present value of the endowment assets themselves, especially in the case of universities and colleges.

So the following questions need to be asked and the answers quantified. What are the other sources of income, if any? What is amount of that income and when does the income arise? If other sources of income or assets can satisfy a high proportion of current outgo, this can allow the endowment assets to be invested for longer duration to the benefit of higher accumulated returns. This higher return is due to investment in higher risk assets and to less of the investment return being consumed, leading to greater potential long-term growth of intergenerational equity.

One major charity in the UK funds its objectives largely from legacies, donations and fund-raising efforts. Were that income to disappear, the endowment would not last long. The 'other income' in this case is indeed a more significant resource than the endowment itself. Does this mean that the endowment funds are simply operational reserves to meet temporary cash flows? Or does this mean that the endowment assets are untouchable intergenerational reserves to be grown to fund future expense? This is a policy decision first and then a strategy decision based on that policy.

Resources can mean infrastructure assistance which reduces the current spend and thereby enhances potential future return. For example, a large sized charity needs an infrastructure for its administration. That is a cost. If the infrastructure is provided free by a well-meaning company, then that is a significant resource that should be counted into the equation as an 'other income' equivalent.

8.2   DEFINING NEEDS

The starting point in defining needs is a clear statement of vision and of non-financial mission. The vision and mission statements are broad and give the endowment an identity. The identity reflects the vision of the founder or the origin of the endowment. The importance of such statements is that they provide fundamental guidance to the governing body in the decision-making process, not only in the distribution of largesse but in the formulation of investment strategy. The statements indicate the intentions in terms of both pattern of spend and long-term survivorship of the organization plus any investment constraints such as socially responsible investing.

Some endowments have very focused missions. The Jim Henson Foundation of New York, for instance, makes grants to artists for the development of new works of contemporary American puppet theater. The MacDonnell foundation supports disadvantaged youth and families around San Francisco. The aim of the Vincentian Endowment Fund is to 'enhance the Catholic and Vincentian identity' of the De Paul University. Many educational endowments are for specific research or programs or facilities.

Other endowments and foundations have broader objectives. A university may be an educational establishment but the endowments may be for a wide range of purposes, from scholarships to research or the building of facilities. The Ford Foundation goals are to strengthen democratic values; reduce poverty and injustice; promote international cooperation; and advance human achievement. The William and Flora Hewlett Foundation was established to 'promote the well-being of mankind by supporting selected activities of a charitable nature, as well as organizations or institutions engaged in such activities'.

The mission, whether broad or narrow, helps to define investment strategy. A Foundation created to support a collection of art to be housed for public viewing will have different strategy implications from one in which growing and changing the art collection is part of the brief. The one requires annual maintenance; the other requires occasional unforecastable needs for large sums of money, as well as the ongoing maintenance; of the home of the collection.

Any foundation or endowment, but especially a museum, clearly needs a specific policy on 'gifts which eat', those gifts that need more resource than the gift itself to maintain. A museum, for example, exists to house a tangible collection. Any museum has finite resources and if a donated collection is substantial enough then its acceptance may depend on funds available to build and staff a new wing to house the collection. Or a college accepting an endowment exclusively to build a facility must find the resource to staff and maintain that facility.

The Getty Museum, for instance, has developed a set of principles that clearly embrace the idea of continually building on the existing collection as a live entity, not simply a memorial to the taste of past collecting members of the family. The principles include direction to secure the greatest remaining works of art; seize the unexpected chance; be prepared to specialize but in doing so concentrate resources on the best in a limited number of areas; fill gaps but with patience to achieve quality more than coverage; and buy whole collections to strengthen existing, or to create new, areas of art.[2]

The vision or mission statement will most likely evolve because circumstances change. Founders' visions may be achieved or their original purposes may become less relevant with time. For example, many of the ancient trade or craft guilds of the City of London, established in another era with endowments for the fellowship and mutual protection of members of the guild, have evolved into broader charitable institutions with a purpose that is different from the original because many of the ancient trades or crafts no longer exist.

Objectives are derived from the overall mission of an endowment. Objectives are more specific than mission or vision statements. They are goals that can be clearly articulated in specific proposals and are to be achieved, measured and monitored. The following are the sorts of questions that define the objectives. What is the purpose of the endowment? What is or is not mandated by the donors? Who is the endowment intended to benefit? How and when, and in what way, is that benefit to be provided? What are the limiting factors? For instance, is timing critical? Is there a minimum, or even a maximum monetary (or other) amount for the benefit to be effective? Are the benefits to be geographically restricted? Are there infrastructure issues in the delivery of that benefit? What is the operating timeframe, the period over which quite definite financial targets can be set (usually up to five years but may be longer)?

Objectives need to be clearly defined. Endowments may be created to fund education, for instance. There is however a big difference in scale, in continuing commitment and in establishment of infrastructure, between funding an ongoing educational establishment and providing scholarships. And the education envisaged may not even be in the country of origin. A UK or US Foundation established to foster Anglo-American relationships, for instance, must consider the potential mismatch between return and expenditure in different currencies. The notion of Purchasing Power Parity, which says that currencies adjust to relative inflation rates over time, may in the long term have some validity. But it is clearly the case that large differential currency movements take place over a substantial number of years in the meantime. Funding UK sterling scholarships out of US dollar assets without any investment strategy adjustment for the currency mismatch could lead to the mission being adversely affected.

An endowment may be designed to satisfy one-off capital expenditures on an occasional basis. Or an endowment may represent funds that are reserves to be drawn on at short notice to fund temporary shortfalls in income relative to expense. The investment strategy for these two different objectives should be equally different. In some charities, centuries old buildings are maintained from endowed funds. These funds can be left to accumulate until there is a crisis, when both accumulated income and capital gain are called upon to meet the need. This is similar to insurance underwriting of long-tailed liabilities which depend on the build up of large reserves, unlike insurance underwriting short-dated risk. Other charities need fund-raising every so often to boost their reserves. All will have time horizons for major commitments such as reroofing or refacing centuries old buildings.

Defining the time horizons of needs is therefore important. Long-term reserves to satisfy long-term objectives, including growth, do not have the same liquidity constraints as short-term obligations. These funds can pay more attention to long-term investment opportunities: longer gestation and illiquid investments, such as real estate developments or private equity. And such funds can play long-term investment cycles by investing contra-cyclically to add value to the endowment fund.

As an instance of this, it is axiomatic that liquidity evaporates in investment markets that are in shock. This is both a cause and an effect of financial market crashes. Endowments with long-term horizons and unaffected intergenerational assets that can be realized, or with accumulated near-cash reserves, are better placed than most to exploit the value opportunities invariably offered in those circumstances of temporarily illiquid (if you are a seller, but not if you are a buyer) and highly depressed assets. Where cash has been accumulated out of increasingly inflated asset values there is a price to pay in short-term return forgone. The longer that assets are held in cash, the longer premium levels of return (and risk) are forgone. But in Chapter 2 we saw the advantage in gradual shifts out of overvalued into other asset areas and this was not market timing. And as Warren Buffet said to Berkshire Hathaway shareholders about sitting on cash: 'it's a painful position to be in but not as painful as doing something stupid.'

Where the endowment resource must do all the work, where there is no other source of income but there is a regular pattern of spending, a reasonable degree of predictability of realized return must be provided. This need not just be satisfied by a secure source of income. The source could be partly income derived from such assets as real estate or equity which have growth potential, and part realizable low volatility gains. Cyclical capital gains, generated by higher volatility assets, could be systematically reinvested in to lower volatility assets. Some trustees believe that predictable return must necessarily be in the form of income such as interest or dividends, leaving capital untouched. Indeed some trusts are established with the principle in mind that capital cannot be expended, and these are known as 'permanent endowments'. But as we have shown in Chapter 2, under 'income illusions' (see p. 22), it is an error to assume simply that all income can be consumed because it is called income. And it's a mistake to assume that capital cannot be spent because it is not called income.

Finally, this stage of developing strategy should incorporate a policy on the governance and the non-financial corporate issues that we investigated in the previous chapter. It is too late to paste a screening mechanism over financial strategy as an afterthought. Non-financial issues may involve fundamental beliefs, as with investment philosophies, and these should imbue and facilitate decision-making. They may well affect the universe of investment opportunity which trustees and their managers will plan for. They may also, subject to the issues of trustee fiduciary responsibility, affect the returns that are available to be consumed.

8.3   QUANTIFYING NEEDS

From stage two comes the third stage, which is a budget for a reasonable operating period. Five years is not too long and provides a road map for the foreseeable future. It determines the minimum acceptable realized return needed to meet intended expenditures over a given timeframe. That timeframe should be rolled forward annually and continually. The numbers should be clear, but to round millions, thousands, tens or digits according to the scale of the endowment. They should be expressed in real or nominal terms and care should be taken over the assumptions used when converting from nominal to real or vice versa. Five years of 3.5% inflation compounds to 19%; that is a significant margin of error for a budget.

This third stage determines the cash flows that are going to be needed, and when, as that is what sets the demand for realized return. This stage has an influence over the balance of operational and intergenerational assets because this is the stage that sets the target spending, even if this must be changed later to meet the reality of likely return from the given resources in the most likely scenarios.

Quantifying needs also includes setting parameters around the budget. 'Budget minus' gives a downside, which is the minimum acceptable return. Below this figure the endowment might not even be viable. 'Budget plus' on the upside is a figure that may incorporate a level of growth in spending that the endowment would be happy to achieve without jeopardizing intergenerational equity.

These may not all be hard-and-fast figures but they give guidance to strategy. For instance, a low 'budget minus' or minimum acceptable return figure leaves room for error, for belt tightening if returns prove to be below expectation, and this leaves scope for risking more investment upside. A high minimum acceptable return puts pressure on the endowed assets. Investing to generate either high income or less volatility implies lower growth in the long term and greater difficulty maintaining intergenerational equity.

The third stage includes determining the amount and the pattern of expenditure beyond the operating period. This involves best estimates of how lumpy, how stable, over what time periods the expenditure will be, and a longer term spending rule. Beyond the operating period is necessarily 'back of the envelope' and depends on futuristic guesses about endowment social strategy and cost escalations. The expenditure may be forecast in real terms only; the periods of major expenditure may be only guesses to the nearest five years. This does not matter, as this stage is an exploration and a basis for long-term planning.

The budget parameters reflect not just the amount but the pattern of needs of an endowment, the timing and the size of the expected cash outflows. The pattern of needs will not be a single point figure for each year but a range of figures from the 'need to have' to the 'nice to have', as well as the minimum acceptable return. A reasonable estimate of the pattern of needs is essential to the process of strategy formulation, not just so that investments are made to produce the necessary cash flows on time. There is a trade-off between time and return as well as between return and volatility. If too much of the endowment is committed to short-term or low volatility reserves, which naturally offer lower returns, then future return is almost inevitably being sacrificed unless the reserve is there for reasons of short-term tactical asset allocation.

Part of the pattern of needs is a judgment on the extent to which return is consumed in the year it is generated. To what extent do the beneficiaries of the endowment rely on there being a continued and perhaps a growing – at least in line with inflation – source of funds? It may be possible, for instance, for an educational endowment to award a given number of scholarships this year but not as many next. An orchestra, on the other hand, cannot just remove the wind section because it is short of funds and still function in the same way; or a hospital cannot open and close and open again depending on the fluctuating stream of endowment return.

Assessment of timing and duration of need, when the need arises and how long for, can enable the endowment to be invested in assets that are more cyclical, and assets that are not forced into realization at the wrong point in the cycle, to gain enhanced return. For instance, a program of building repair is usually cyclical. If the cycles coincide with cycles of positive and negative return then a natural asset rebalancing mechanism is established, withdrawing funds when times are good and restoring funds when they are bad.

This pattern of need is not just a question for investment strategy based on endowment assets. It also bears on the matter of 'other resources', namely fund-raising ability. Not surprisingly, the ability to raise funds tends to be highly correlated with the return on intergenerational assets: when markets are high and rising, people can afford to give more than when they feel poor. One school in the UK coincided fund-raising for a sports center with a high level in financial markets and extracted, in exchange for a glass of wine, a high proportion of the funds required. Two years later, in the middle of a depressed domestic stock market, that would have been unthinkable.

8.4   SPENDING RULE

Chapter 5 focussed on Micawber's Rule. Assuming no other income:

$$\text{Investment return} - \text{Spending rate} = \text{Endowment growth} \qquad (1)$$

and following from (1):

$$\text{Spending growth} = \text{Endowment growth} \qquad (2)$$

Micawber's Rule is useful as a long-term framework and should be monitored as a discipline. For shorter term planning, however, the chapter indicated a number of inadequacies to the Rule. First, it made no allowance for the pattern of return or the pattern of spending. If the return is a steady annual accumulation but the outgo is heavy occasionally, then the spending rule must adequately accumulate income or the asset strategy must adapt to a more risky but higher return strategy.

If the assets vary in value, so does the amount to be spent under Micawber's Rule. A spending rate applied to a percentage of assets that are valued on a rolling three-year basis gives different results again. Taking a fixed rate of spending, but averaging the values of the endowment assets to which it is applied over a number of years, helps to stabilize the pattern of spending. This, however, has other implications.

Finally, Micawber's Rule takes no account of one of the issues raised in Chapter 3, 'Elements of Return': valuation change. Disinflation, for instance, can cause a structural change in interest rates that raises the present value of an investment yielding the same intrinsic return as before.

We suggested in Chapter 5 that a minimum spending rate can be determined on the basis of a minimum acceptable annual amount of spending, adjusted by inflation, and a maximum level can then be set, based on the minimum acceptable intergenerational equity. This minimum can only be set in relation to a conservative estimate of the return that can be achieved from the resources available, escalated by inflation.

An analysis of spending rules by Verne Sedlacek and Sarah Clark of the Common Fund[3] suggested that in the current environment 5% of assets as a spending rule was too high. An initial 4% of assets, escalated by inflation, was considered a reasonable benchmark number as a spending rule with a minimum/maximum parameter of 3% to 6% of assets. It implied that when asset returns were high, the excess was effectively reinvested to boost intergenerational equity, and when returns were low or negative, the intergenerational equity effectively funded the present.

The outcome of this model was a slightly higher probability of achieving intergenerational equity than a straight 4% of spending over shorter time periods, but the same probability over 20 years. It led to a more stable pattern of spending than the pure 4% of assets rule. The 3% band was triggered in 44.9% of the 20,000 annual returns examined over 20 years but only 4% of cases on the upside 6% band. Very few cases led to any drop in spending, compared to the pure 4% rule which saw a drop in spending in 24% of the cases. Perhaps most significant of all was the greater skew toward upside outcomes of the inflation-adjusted banded approach.

The spending rule of an endowment must also be set in relation to the particular pattern of spending need. Some endowments will have a regular flow of expense with a higher multiple for inflation, which might imply the need for a lower starting ratio than 4% of assets. Some endowments will have a policy of accumulating assets for one-off expense at different intervals of time. These then have to be interpolated into annualized return accumulations to arrive at a figure that will satisfy the need when it occurs.

The need that is quantified in the operating budget, such as regular grant-making, upkeep of premises or administrative expenses, will be met partly by a predictable realized element of the total return, such as from regular income. Where the need is exceptional in size, or where a minimum sum is needed to cover short-term operational balances, this must be met by separately identified operational assets. To the extent that the need is well into the future, assets must then be notionally allocated out of the intergenerational reserve asset pool.

8.5   OPERATIONAL ASSETS

Meeting the daily operational needs of an endowment organization with a high degree of confidence, which is essentially asset/liability matching for the budgeted period, follows on from developing the operating budget framework. This part of the operational assets is defined by a multiple of the monthly requirement adjusted by the volatility. A stable $1,000 per month needs a smaller operational reserve base than $0 one month and $2,000 the next. The financial options, and the systems available for funding disbursements and monitoring budgets, should allow a minimum of cash left in checking accounts that pay no interest.

The second element of operational reserves is investment driven and arises from rebalancing or from tactical asset allocation. This type of reserve is part of the investment manager's discretionary portfolio. The manager may be seeking to deleverage the portfolio ahead of an economically and financially hostile environment, or switch between asset classes for which operational reserve assets are simply a temporary residual home for proceeds.

We have seen that there is generally a trade-off between operational and intergenerational assets. Operational assets provide higher degrees of certainty and liquidity at the expense of lower levels of long-term return. Intergenerational assets provide the opposite characteristics. Strategy has to find the balance to optimize total portfolio return. An overestimate of the amount of operational assets required means diminished intergenerational returns other than in adverse financial scenarios. An overestimate of intergenerational assets may mean vulnerability in meeting operational needs.

Determination of asset classes within the operational reserve is therefore dictated first by the known liabilities. Contingent reserves must naturally be invested in high-liquidity, low-volatility assets such as Treasury Bills, money market funds and high-rated-bank deposits. Nominal liabilities of longer maturity, say three years out, have greater latitude to exploit interest rate differentials. Such liabilities could be covered by three-year bonds or even to low-volatility funds of hedge in a benign financial environment.

There is little value, however, in placing a high proportion of three-year operating reserves in one-week cash deposits, yielding little, when the three-year bond yield may offer 50% more return. That said, where the yield curve is inverted there may be no point in taking a three-year risk when one-year money pays a significantly higher rate if the reinvestment risk – the ability to reinvest at the end of Year 1 at comparable rates – is not too high.

The choice of asset classes within the second type of operational assets, the short-term home for tactical moves out of intergenerational assets, is limited. In this case the prospective environment that encourages the move may be one of extreme risk and this would demand investment in asset classes of only the highest security such as Treasury Bills, money market funds and the highest rated banks.

Careful selection of operational assets can raise the endowment return for a very marginal increase in volatility risk. Cash may be the natural operational reserve asset for a tactical move into a more defensive asset class, but other asset classes, including in limited measure appropriate low-volatility funds of hedge funds, may offer significantly higher returns than those provided by cash at the expense of only a marginal increase in volatility. Figure 4.2 in Chapter 4 described the point graphically. Commitment of all the operating assets to low-risk asset category A passes up the opportunity for significantly higher return with marginal risk increase (in an endowment sense of the word) by an appropriate combination of categories A and C.

Longer duration operational assets are where the more liquid low-risk 'alpha' strategies can be employed. Market-neutral strategies can offer returns that exceed cash deposit interest rates by several percentage points with low levels of volatility. They can enhance cash returns while retaining liquidity. This presupposes that the strategy and manager of the fund, or of the fund of funds, are both picked with care such that the strategy is unlikely to suffer on any meltdown in prices that a move out of intergenerational assets was intended to avoid. However, there must be a prudent judgment, based on scenario analysis, as to potential risk in the environment that could cause normally secure investments to suffer loss from outlier events. Investing in CDO hedge funds at a dangerous stage of the credit cycle, with potential for total loss, could be a case in point.

Raising the return significantly for a marginal rise in volatility, subject to other risk assessment, raises the average return of the portfolio along any combination of operational and intergenerational assets. The diagonal line in Figure 8.1 is illustrative of the concept, in very stylized form, showing the trade-off between duration/volatility and return. Line A shows the

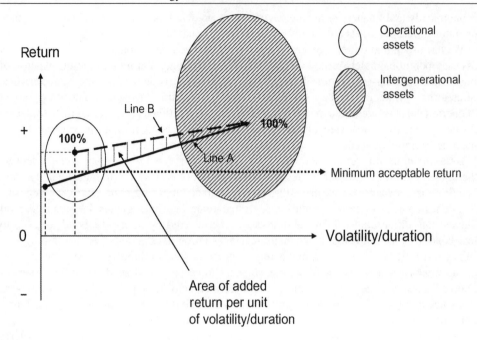

Figure 8.1   Raising the bar

anticipated volatility risk/return profile of operational/intergenerational asset classes within a policy that restricts operational reserves to cash. Line B shows the effect of the introduction of a new asset class, such as low volatility funds of hedge funds, where the strategies are relatively low risk and uncorrelated to long-duration returns.

This move to higher return operational assets demonstrates a total portfolio decision because it is not just a question of what that investment will do in isolation but the contribution it will make to the whole portfolio of assets. The impact of flattening the portfolio return line is to change the risk/reward trade-off along the spectrum of different portfolio combinations.

This changes the dynamics of the strategic and the shorter term tactical decision. A horizontal line implies little value in taking on extra volatility risk because there is little compensation in extra return. This will be so at points in the cycle when long-duration assets are significantly overvalued.

8.6   INTERGENERATIONAL ASSETS

Returns on intergenerational assets are most sensitive to changes in the underlying economic and financial environment. It is this environment, or more accurately the prospective environment, that affects the two main portfolio decisions with intergenerational assets: (1) the duration/volatility exposure (reduced by increasing the ratio of operational to intergenerational assets) and (2) the balance between asset classes within the intergenerational asset category.

The next stage in developing strategy is therefore economic and financial scenario projection. This gives some idea of the limits of likely asset return that can then be compared with the expenditure parameters to develop a sense of what is likely to be achievable. This gives a median position for the range of foreseeable (and to an extent unforeseeable) environments.

It also provides stress testing of outlier scenarios, and helps to answer such questions as 'What if we are entering a long-term deflationary/inflationary period?' or 'What if we had a major shock comparable to the worst bear markets of the last 100 years?' Or, 'What if the twenty-first century proves to be Pacific based with growth of investable opportunity not yet reflected in world market capitalizations?' Classically stock indices represent whole asset classes in these scenario projections even though they reflect history rather than the future.

Scenario analysis is about risk as much as it is about return. It is about assessing the likely downside scenarios and diversifying assets between the others. It is about avoiding 'the stumers' in Keynes's parlance. It is not about striking the home runs but avoiding the losers. It is not just what is likely to happen but the implications of worst case events. Scenario analysis incorporates the common factor effects that drive portfolio – not just individual investment – risk and return. It is assessing the situations when common factors unite in negative (or positive) returns and when they can be assured of providing diversifying characteristics.

The scenario projections must inevitably involve assumptions. We know that the future is unknowable. As J. Pierpont Morgan said when asked if he knew what the market will do: 'Yes, it will fluctuate.' It will indeed, but we can still make rational judgments based on most likely outcomes while insuring against outlier events. Using the framework we have considered in Chapter 3, we can draw some sensible conclusions from 'what if' assessments using experience of the past and thereby set the investment options.

For instance, do we blindly diversify a portfolio of equities with one of bonds without understanding their likely interaction in different environments? There are times, with prospective deflation, when bonds are a perfect hedge for equities and times, such as in an era of rising rates of inflation, when equities and bonds will both fall dramatically together and neither will be a hedge for the other.

The chapter on 'Elements of Return' (Chapter 3) introduced the GaveKal quadrants as a framework for scenario analysis of asset class risks, returns and common factors. The asset classes that are appropriate to the different scenarios are shown again in Figure 8.2.

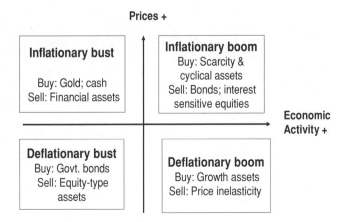

Figure 8.2   GaveKal scenario analysis
Source: GaveKal

Economies follow cycles of rising or falling prices and rising or falling real economic growth with different implications for asset prices. Financial markets tend to discount these implications in advance. It is an old joke that the stock market has predicted 10 of the last seven recessions but governments and central banks use asset prices as leading indicators, so analysis must focus on the emerging factors, and likely policy responses, that markets have not yet discounted. What are the common factors across asset categories that imply risk reduction as well as enhanced return?

These are the elements we considered in Chapter 3. Look again at two intergenerational asset classes, long-term government bonds and equities. Combining these two asset classes in any given portfolio has historically been regarded as prudent diversification. When the price of Government bonds went up, equity prices went down, and in much of the nineteenth century, and during deflationary periods of the twentieth, this was usually true.

The reason for this was that falling long-term Government bond yields through rising Government bond prices in a non-inflationary period was associated with declining economic growth and pressure on company profits. The yield fall was due to a fall in the real rather than any inflation element in yields. This implied low or negative earnings and dividend growth and falling equity prices. As it also implied rising credit spreads, corporate bonds were not a diversifying asset class.

This tidy relationship was disturbed in the inflationary part of the twentieth century when rising nominal yields on the back of rising levels of inflation devalued both bonds and equities. The theory was that equities were real assets, and that adding the rate of inflation to the denominator (interest rates) of the model that priced equities was offset by adding the same figure to the numerator (the inflationary increase in nominal profits).

In theory that should work, but inflation was not stationary and predictable and the problem was unanticipated inflation – an increase that could not be forecast or priced into securities in advance. What became evident was that the proper diversification for equities in a time of rising inflation was not conventional fixed income or zero coupon bonds but real assets such as commodities, real estate, timber land and inflation index-linked Government bonds.

If the portfolio opportunity line in Figure 8.1 becomes flatter, whether as a result of optimizing the selection of operational assets or as a result of lower estimated long-duration returns, there is little point in paying more for long duration/volatility risk. There is little point in shifting the balance of assets toward higher levels of risk because there would be little extra reward. Where intergenerational asset classes are vulnerable to one or more likely scenario, there is no value in taking added risk. In these circumstances the portfolio duration should be shortened, the volatility reduced and the portfolio made defensive.

The opposite is equally true. Where intergenerational asset markets have fallen several standard deviations below normal limits of valuation, or other strong relationships with given economic conditions, potential reversal provides increasingly probable exceptional levels of return. In this case the line can steepen dramatically even if the short term volatility also rises. In this case there is margin in shifting the balance of return and volatility/duration risk significantly to the right. There is the potential both for exceptional return and for volatility reduction to more normal levels.

The diagram in Figure 8.3 illustrates the point. The 'risk button' measures the proportion between operational and intergenerational assets. The button can be shifted along the line depending on the trade-off. With a flatter line there is less need to chase return at higher duration/volatility levels. In fact there is more sense in shifting the balance to the left, as this reduces portfolio risk for the same return.

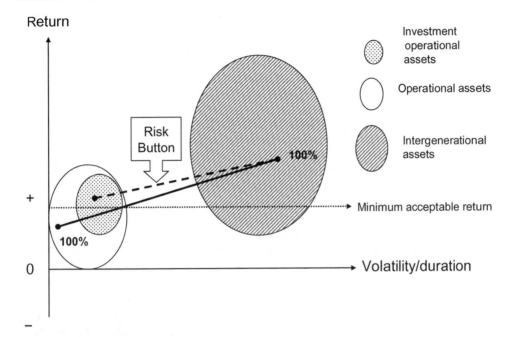

Figure 8.3 Shifting the risk button

The large oval on the left shows the totality of operational assets. The larger oval includes both those assets that meet specific operational needs and, in the small oval, those that are used purely as volatility risk dampeners in investment strategy. The larger universe outside the small oval will not change significantly with changing investment scenarios because the amount of assets is determined by daily operating needs as defined in the budget, not by investment-driven needs. So the total amount of operational assets will likely change more with investment-driven needs.

A long-term strategy should decide the upper and lower limits of potential allocation of intergenerational assets. The actual proportion, within those parameters, is thereafter a function of the slope of the portfolio line. Where there is potentially significantly higher long-term return for intergenerational asset classes, then the risk button is shifted to the right. This means that the proportion in those asset classes is increased and the added risk should be well rewarded.

The boundaries between intergenerational and investment-driven operational assets, and the limits in the underlying asset classes, must be established *ab initio* when the Investment Policy Statement is written, albeit subject to review. Clear responsibility for the guidelines lies with the trustees. There must be equally clear definition of responsibility for the moves between asset classifications and classes.

In theory, the greater the percentage of the prospective total return on intergenerational assets that comes from income, the shorter is their duration and the less their volatility – therefore, the smaller can be the potential proportion of investment-driven operational assets in a financially austere environment. The more that total prospective return relies on growth and volatility, especially in illiquid investments classes, the larger the pool of operational assets that is needed to dampen risk and take advantage of the downside of volatile asset classes.

In practice, there can be a tendency for trustees of endowment funds simply to seek those intergenerational assets that provide sufficient income to cover current and prospective needs, where expenditure is regular and easily forecast, and to give less attention to the potential growth aspect of return. Growth is, after all, not a given and if 7% yield plus 3% growth gives the same long-term total return as 3% yield and 7% growth, why not go for the income certainty now? This approach seems to provide a continuing flow of working income, thereby minimizing the need for a high level of low-return operational assets. It also seems to solve the problem of taking an asset strategy view because it helps income to meet expenditure. There is no need to worry about the fluctuation of capital values and especially realization of losses at an inappropriate time.

Apart from the implications for intergenerational equity, one problem of this approach is the potential for the income illusion we described in Chapter 2. The income generated to allow trustees to avoid making any difficult asset allocation decisions may be gained from long-term bonds and may lack growth or inflation protection. This may be less of an issue in a period of deflation when it is the assurance of that income that matters most. In other conditions, however, the income and the underlying asset value may both be especially vulnerable to some adverse scenarios (such as rising inflation). The tendency for all income to be considered spendable often means that insufficient is reinvested for the future.

While intergenerational assets can provide relatively secure liquidity in the form of cash flows (such as rents from property), it is not an optimal solution to seek income over total return other than for immunized portfolios, especially if intergenerational assets are simply being held to generate cash flows at the expense of higher total return numbers. A classic example of this is holding a fixed rent piece of real estate in a low rental growth environment – effectively a fixed income security – over a long period of time when other significant growth opportunities are being ignored. If the rent is fixed and the costs of the endowed entity are escalating with inflation, or if, within a foreseeable period, there will be a need for a large capital sum that cannot be financed by a loan secured on that property, then the endowment has a looming problem with an inappropriate investment strategy. There is even a risk of an outcome that would require the endowment to curtail its activities substantially or make a fire-sale of the property. Curtailment of actvities might be necessary any way but this can be done in an orderly fashion with a little impact now compared to a rather greater impact later.

Another potential issue with higher income is that it can be associated with higher absolute risk and the latter may not be properly structured into the overall portfolio. The last and perhaps most practically damaging aspect of forced income generation in the long-term, however, is foregoing growth simply because growth assets do not yield income. Asset strategy should be driven by prospective total return, not by income as a by-product.

If the income stream must be deemed a determinant of asset strategy, let it then be a subset of the risk button approach above and a proactive choice of 'value' as a style of investing in securities. In that case, buy yield as a value strategy when value is appropriate to the economic and financial market environment. When the yield curve becomes inverted – that is, short rates exceed long rates and inversion predicts economic downturn – switch long into short-duration assets to maintain yield and avoid loss from economically sensitive intergenerational assets.

The assessment of asset sector and investment style prospective return, and of common factor risk for portfolio construction, is part of the same scenario analysis involved in changing the duration-risk profile between operational and intergenerational assets. Rebalancing on the basis of scenario analysis presumes one or two things, which amount to the same. It presumes a shift out of (a) those asset classes that have become vulnerable to external risk or (b) those assets that have discounted most of what is anticipated from the expected scenario. If high rates of growth are already factored into high Price to Earning Ratios, the likelihood of disappointment is beginning to outweigh the probability of growth being sustained or exceeded, other than in exceptional circumstances.

In an environment in which prospective change in inflation is not yet discounted and remains a risk, diversification would involve commodity-type investments, including commodity futures, farmland and timber as well as precious and other metals, together with inflation protected securities (TIPS), cash, and directly owned real estate. Equity-type financial assets, including REITS, tend to have poorer inflation protection characteristics in the short term.

Long term, the returns of equity-type financial assets tend to adjust because inflation impacts earnings and rents. But long-term fixed income bond returns provide no inflation protection; their adjustment is by yield change, which may protect new investors against anticipated inflation, but crucifies those already committed to bonds. Prices fall in nominal terms and this is exacerbated by real loss of value.

An alternative approach to selecting asset classes to meet specific economic scenarios is to average across all asset sectors and styles, make no market directional bets and aim to find managers who add value in each asset category. This approach combines economy-sensitive classes of intergenerational asset such as growth equities, smaller companies and cyclical stocks at one end of the spectrum of volatility and illiquidity, with defensive value stocks at the other.

The same decision would be made for hedge fund styles. Global Macro, and Emerging Market funds employing leverage are at the aggressive end of the spectrum, while Equity Market Neutral, Fixed Income or Convertible Bond Arbitrage are more defensive. This decision implies style underperformance at different points in the cycle, with an emphasis on manager selection to achieve selection outperformance. It implies no ability to preempt cycles.

Once assets are selected, the issue is rebalancing the distribution of the asset portfolio because, as asset classes perform against each other, they change their relative weighting. There are three different approaches to rebalancing assets. One is to do nothing. This is a momentum approach based on 'the trend is my friend'. Momentum involves letting winners increasingly dominate the portfolio or selling laggard performers to buy winners until the winners start to be losers. Passive or index management is an example of momentum rebalancing as well as being the least-cost method of pure market exposure. As a company or an asset class in a market capitalization-weighted index grows in size relative to its peer group, more must be invested in that asset class or company out of the proceeds of sale of portions of the remaining constituents of the index. An index fund must continually rebalance in favor of market capitalization.

The danger with momentum strategy comes when an asset class or company becomes a substantial part of the index, dominates its performance and is valuation vulnerable. There have been numerous examples of this in the past and, as discussed under indexation in Chapter 2 (see page 26), the process whereby indexation drives investment funds into assets irrespective of the marginal efficiency of capital is intrinsically flawed.

The second strategy is to rebalance by weight. If assets A and B start at 50/50 in a portfolio and this ratio becomes 55/45 simply through market movement, rebalancing by weight means selling 5 from A to invest in B. Rebalancing can take place at predetermined percentages, predetermined index levels, or periods of time. This contrarian approach is based on expecting return to a mean of relative returns; it involves selling rising asset classes to invest in laggards. However, in the introduction we saw one problem with this method in the experience of the early Yale plan. In that case rebalancing equity to fixed income took place during a secular decline in the fixed income market. A 20-year period of equity price growth relative to bonds in the middle two decades of the last century clearly favored a momentum rebalancing strategy. The contrarian strategy added to an underperforming asset class, fixed income, from one that continued to outperform, equities, and the balance was not restored in the rest of the century.

A more recent and more dramatic example was that of a Japanese Equity and Warrant Fund established in the late 1990s. The fund invested 70/30 in equities/warrants and maintained those proportions. As the value of warrants fell to zero on falling prices (the reverse of the intended shift from warrants to equities), the fund sold equities to fill the black hole in the hope of a geared recovery. The fund eventually had to be liquidated.

This form of rebalancing is a discipline that can help to prevent overconcentration in any one asset, as a result of continued outperformance to a point that makes that asset class vulnerable to sharp correction. However, it can also be counter-productive when conducted with a frequency that adds more transaction cost than value, or where there is a seismic change in trend beyond previously understood parameters such as in the examples above. This is where low-cost derivatives can add value to the process.

Relationship rebalancing is the third strategy. It is also contrarian and mean-reverting. This rebalances assets not just in line with asset return differentials of one asset class outperforming another, but by differential valuation relationships, rather than simply returns, which tend to revert to a mean. The effect of this was demonstrated by the time-weighted return versus money-weighted return example in Chapter 2. As valuation relationships became stretched by market movement and a deteriorating financial scenario, portfolio manager B began to reduce systematically the exposure to equities and underperformed over the short term, but more than made up the difference when market valuations reached extremes and the correction began. Returns do not invariably revert to a mean but valuation metrics tend to come back to those average valuations that reflect given economic and financial environments. That is the difference between simply rebalancing asset percentages that move out of line through market movements, and adjusting for valuation relationships that tend to revert to scenario means.

Relationship rebalancing is therefore shifting asset weights away from classes that are at extreme levels of relationship for a given scenario. The scenario is, however, important: the relationships between bond and equity valuations in an inflationary boom is very different from the relationship in a deflationary bust. The chart of long bond yields (Figure 8.4) shows the movement, during a secular period of inflation then disinflation, that took place in the nominal yield of the US 10-year bond over the second half of the twentieth century. Whatever happened to nominal yields, real yields tended to remain in a band between 2% and 4%. Deviations outside those parameters, during periods of inflation and disinflation, triggered extreme warning signals for equity assets. And where endowments spent excess nominal bond return due to secular valuation change during the period, they destroyed potential endowment earnings power.

Relationship rebalancing is also about learning to avoid the behavioral tendencies toward the 'moral epidemics' described by Charles MacKay in *Extraordinary Popular Delusions and the Madness of Crowds*.[4] This book was first published in 1841 but describes the continuing tendency of human nature to follow trends irrationally beyond limits. It helps to explain the psychology behind the reasons why asset managers can only sell product to investors at the top of markets when prospective returns are at their lowest, not near the bottom when prospective returns are at their highest.

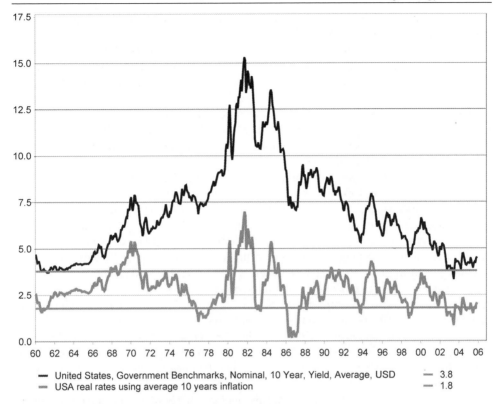

Figure 8.4 US twentieth-century bond yields: nominal and real
Source: GaveKal from Ecowin data.

Every decade seems to bring its excesses, whether gold, oil, real estate, Asia or technology. Boom tends to lead to bust. The higher the rise the greater and quicker the fall or the longer it takes for values to readjust. Time or distance in markets is the message. Either markets go nowhere for a long period of time and value catches up with price, or markets move a distance and price catches up with value. When the fall comes quickly, liquidity dries and exit can become impossible.

We have already alluded to one or two classic examples of the distortions created by funds flowing into excess valuation through commitment to the concept of indexation by market capitalization. It is, however, illustrative to look in greater depth at one example: the Japanese stock market. In 1989, the Japanese stock market capitalization, helped by a strong yen, became over 60% of the Europe, Australasia and Far East (EAFE) Index – an index representing the market capitalization of mature markets excluding the USA. It was the benchmark index for international investment by US institutions.

The Japanese stock market capitalization became, at one point, larger than that of the USA even though the Japanese economy was a fraction of the size of that of the US. Value investors began to underweight the Japanese market from the middle of the 1980s. By the beginning of 1988 the valuation of Japanese equities had reached a price to cash flow ratio of 27.6 times. This compared to a world ex-Japan ratio at that time of 6.1 times and even less if you excluded the USA. As a result, value investors underperformed the benchmark index substantially.

Entities that employed international managers began to wonder why they were paying active management fees for index underperformance.

If $100 had been placed in the EAFE index and another $100 invested in one international value-oriented mutual fund at the beginning of 1984, it would have accumulated by the end of 1987 to EAFE, $361; the Fund $241. Despite this massive disparity in performance, it was possible to show that underweighting Japan could still be proven right. If one was to assume that the Price to Cash Flow ratio of Japanese equity was to decline to twice the world average, i.e. 12.2 times (not even as far as the P/CF of Germany at 3.9, France 3.7, UK 6.9) then, assuming other market valuations remained the same, those dollar amounts would have retracted to: EAFE $234; Fund $214. These numbers implied that the stocks held by that fund, on below-average PEs, would have fallen in line with the highly overvalued financials (the Japanese banks were on 100 times PE ratios) on any Japanese equity underperformance.

If you then assumed that an overvalued yen was to decline to its purchasing power parity – an unlikely assumption in the short term but well justified by the history of long-term movements – then the numbers became: EAFE $202; Fund $207. If it could be accepted that Japanese valuations could even fall in due course (as, with hindsight, they eventually did) to the longer term average of world levels, then the numbers would be: EAFE $167; Fund $200.

The storm broke early in 1990. Neither the economy nor the market made any sustainable recovery for the rest of the century and beyond. Managers who had underweighted Japan consistently since 1987 became vindicated within months in 1990 in terms of preservation of portfolio value. They had made a wrong decision for a number of years, dramatically wrong in the short term, as it was for those who left the US dot-com party early toward the end of the 1990s. It should not be forgotten, however, that the power of compound interest works viciously in reverse on a large number.

Dr Allan Bufferd, Treasurer of MIT, in a presentation to the NMS Forum in 2003[5] compared endowment asset allocations between 1992 and 2002. In 1992, the word 'alternative' referred to any asset that was not a conventional fixed income or equity security. The median allocation to alternatives by endowments was 9%. Real estate was the largest component of alternatives, followed by venture capital and buy-outs. By 2002 the median allocation to alternatives was 48% and the largest component of that was in hedge funds. With the rise of domestic equities there was a shift into other asset classes. When the end of 'irrational exuberance' hit the equity markets, those endowments and foundations that had leaned against the wind with more diversified exposure found their downside largely protected.

We cannot know the future but we surely know one thing. All this will happen again. History rhymes. It is never the same but is always the same. The key is to recognize the behavioral signs and the levels of relationships at which to begin to leave the party. This does not mean market timing because no one rings the bell at the top of exuberant markets any more than they do at the bottom. But risk can be managed by shifting between asset classes at levels of deviation from the parameters expected for any given scenario.

8.7   REVIEW

Strategy is a dynamic process even if the time horizon is longer term. It needs to be flexible and it needs to be forward looking. Review is not about analyzing the past other than as a guide to the future, however much monitoring of managers may be a relevant part of the tactical aspect of implementation of strategy. The facts can change on all sides of the strategy equation. The very mission of the endowment can change, especially if the original purpose for which it was established becomes obsolete. The spending needs can change; indeed they often do and most often upward. The time horizon for satisfying a given need may change, which can imply a very different investment strategy.

Most often the economic and financial scenario will change, implying a different set of prospective risks and returns. The biggest impact this is likely to have in the short term is on Tactical Asset Allocation between relatively liquid asset classes within strategic parameters, such as a move at the margin from listed equity to bonds and then to cash. It is only a major prospective change in trend of asset returns that would trigger a large-scale strategy review of investment class parameters. Commitments to less liquid asset classes, such as real estate and private equity, need to change more slowly. In such cases, even if the facts change, it might simply be impossible to do anything about the investment despite a change of mind.

Strategy review is therefore a perpetual reconsideration of future scenarios and has both a tactical and a strategic element. It involves rolling budgets and rolling scenario analysis. It means constantly considering the potential impact of shocks, especially when conditions have been benign. 'What if?' is the watchword of review. Review does not necessarily mean change, however; it may simply mean confirmation of current course. More often it means modest adjustment to budgets or investment parameters, but not on a quarterly basis.

Perhaps the most frequent interval for strategic review, rather than the shorter term tactical or policy review, is annual because this is a normal reporting period. But this need not be the case; it may be longer, and it may be different for different aspects of strategy. The fundamental vision and mission statements will not change on a regular basis, but the operational budget will. What is appropriate for monitoring operations, of investment as well as other performance, may not be an appropriate time interval for strategy review. Equally, review might be driven by change of circumstances, not by time periods, and a distinction must be made between tactical review – that is, of change of asset allocation within given parameters – and fundamental strategy review.

Strategy review should start with a reminder of the vision and mission statements. It should then go through resource assessment followed by budgets. Resource assessment should be all-embracing, covering other income and existing assets. It is at the fundamental review stage, for instance, that an endowment may realize that its existing endowment funds cannot meet the expectations of expense and that a whole new fund-raising effort may need to be established. If a potential new source of recurrent income can be established, this would then change the dynamics of the investment policy.

Tactical or policy review, which may be monthly, quarterly or half yearly, is part of the process of implementing strategy. Implementing strategy in larger endowments will often be through the medium of specialist asset managers. These managers, however, may not have an overview, their task after all is at the micro level. They may select their specialist stocks purely on corporate information and valuations, so tactical or policy review may only require them to account for their security selection and provide a general view on the status of their specific asset class in the context of historical returns and valuations of that asset class.

Where an investment manager is hired to make both asset allocation and stock selection decisions for an endowment, the review focus should be different from that involving specialist managers. It should be primarily about the future prospects for, and interaction of, the different asset classes. Only secondarily should it consider the selection of individual stocks because tactical asset allocation will determine the greater element of performance.

The manager's report is very often mostly about history. It is about economic and financial developments in the reporting (historic) period. It is about returns achieved and the asset class areas from which they came. It is about changes made to a portfolio of assets and the reasons for them. All this is a proper and reasonable part of the governance of an endowment. It is not, however, about future policy review. The future review of immediate policy is usually squeezed in at the end of a manager's presentation to trustees when some 'what if' scenarios may be described, albeit heavily conditioned by future uncertainty. But that should be the key part of the presentation.

Any manager's current portfolio reads like a book to another investment professional. It describes perfectly what the manager is really thinking and therefore his committed position on the future, because portfolios are by definition anticipatory. So what the portfolio distribution is saying should be spelled out to the governing body. The manager should be reviewing the future scenarios, including outlier events, and explaining how he has arrived at his conclusion about the most likely scenario. This is what he will already have incorporated implicitly in the structure of the portfolio at the time of the meeting. The manager cannot know the future but can be expected to present a structure based on his best estimate of what may happen, also bearing in mind the less likely outcomes. This gives the trustees a sense of what is expected, but equally importantly a sense of the implications of the unexpected and the ability to express a view before rather than after the event.

Like the distinction between strategic and tactical asset allocation, that between policy and strategic review can become blurred. Laffer Associates has described macro investing not as a style but as an argument waiting to happen. Where the argument is fundamental to the future operation of the endowed entity, it is strategy. Where it isn't, it is tactics. This is where process can help to determine the distinction between the two and the people who need to be involved in the discussion: trustees, investment and other committees; consultants; managers.

9
Implementing Strategy

When you're adding up committees there's a useful rule of thumb: that talents make a difference but follies make a sum.

PIET HEIN. *More Grooks*

Implementing strategy for an endowment fund requires principles and philosophy, structure and process, and people. Principles and philosophy are usually established by the initial bequest and this defines the mission and the character of the endowment. These, and the structure and process, are then defined in the Investment Policy Statement (IPS). Key to implementation is people, people involved on the board of trustees, on the investment committee, in the staffing of endowments and in service provision such as investment management, legal counsel and other consultancy. Implementation involves deciding, and then rebalancing, allocation between and within operational and intergenerational assets to meet current and future spending needs. It involves determining the investment management model appropriate to the size and sophistication of the endowment, assessing styles of asset management and parameters of risk, selecting advisers and custodial relationships, and identifying costs – especially remuneration of asset managers. It includes monitoring the achievement of objectives and measuring results after setting benchmarks that inevitably drive investment behavior. Performance measurement is accountability for the outcomes in the broadest sense and at all levels: of the trustees, the investment committee and the service providers.

9.1   INVESTMENT POLICY STATEMENT

The Investment Policy Statement (IPS) of an endowment fund clarifies investment goals and provides a framework for structure and process in the management and monitoring of an endowment. It provides for all the components involved in the implementation of strategy and is a dynamic rather than an immutable statement.

Investment Policy Statements are the blueprint for the management of the endowment assets. They may be the product of the Board of Governors, or of the Investment Committee, but IPSs must still be approved by the former even if designed by the latter. In the case of the San Diego Foundation, for instance, the statement is clearly articulated by the Board of Governors. One of the items in the statement then concerns the establishment of an investment committee to which is delegated other clauses in the statement.

The statement will outline the various responsibilities of all those involved with the investments such as managers, consultants, custodians and counsel. It will outline spending policies to help to place asset strategy into context of the Foundation's needs. It will cover investment philosophy, processes, people and performance. It will authorize investments and policy asset class ranges. It will articulate time horizons, targets and attitudes to risk.

The statement also helps to set the scene for the type of culture of an endowment. Culture is something that is not tangible but is represented in the behavior of the organization through the medium of its people. Trustees of an endowment have a responsibility to respect the wishes of the donor. In the case of foundations, the IPS should outline the social aspects that are important to the founder. These may involve key principles of social responsibility in investing as well as in grant-making.

In the previous chapter we touched on such questions as alcohol and tobacco stock investment by foundations and endowments, and there was a time when avoidance of investment in South Africa was high on many institutional agendas. The charter should incorporate any deeply held beliefs that the founder wishes to incorporate into the process of investment.

Joseph Rowntree in the UK, who spoke more by action than through words of his quaker religious beliefs, set up three Charitable Trusts in 1904 with about one half of his wealth. The Joseph Rowntree Charitable Trust today specifies[1] its aim to invest in companies that are of 'benefit to mankind with minimal harmful impacts and with an emphasis on meeting basic needs rather than luxuries'. The statement specifies industries to be avoided and company profiles to be considered for inclusion in the portfolio.

The Jessie Smith Noyes Foundation, established in 1947 by Charles Noyes as a memorial to his wife, is very clear about its beliefs and how these should be reflected in the management of the foundation. Their statement of fiduciary responsibility begins with the words:

> We recognize that our fiduciary responsibility does not end with maximizing return and minimizing risk. We also recognize that economic growth can come at considerable cost to communities and the environment. We believe that efforts to mitigate environmental degradation, address issues of social justice and promote healthy communities should be incorporated as part of business and investment decision making. We believe that management, directors, employees and investors should consider these social issues in the pursuit of financial objectives.[2]

The Jessie Smith Noyes Foundation derives its investment policy from these beliefs, namely to invest in companies 'which provide commercial solutions to major social and environmental problems and/or build corporate culture with concerns for environmental impact, equity and community'. Like the Rowntree Foundation, the investment policy goes on to define clearly the types of companies in which the foundation will invest. And the Noyes Foundation investment guidelines give specific 20-year investment horizons.

Culture also defines investment beliefs that are fundamental to the selection of managers in ways other than social criteria for investment. Is the culture of the endowment or the foundation one of genuinely long-term thinking like the Noyes Foundation? Is it inclined to a contrarian approach? Does it believe in active versus passive management? Does it eschew a 'top-down' process (choose asset classes, markets and sectors then select securities consistent with the macro-overview) in favour of 'bottom-up' security selection (portfolio weights in sectors or countries are driven by selection of underlying securities)?

If the culture inclines toward contrarian, active and 'bottom-up' selection of securities, it would then be totally inconsistent to select a manager of assets who has a philosophy of short-term momentum utilizing index funds to implement market directional policies however good the past investment record. Equally, if the fundamental belief is that active management of large and public listed companies does not add value, then it would be consistent for a core element of the portfolio to be indexed and smaller companies to be actively managed.

Dr Allan Bufferd, who, after more than 10 years working with his predecessor assumed primary responsibility for the investments of MIT's endowment fund in 1987, describes periodic developments within MIT over the past 30 years which reflected that endowment's beliefs. MIT regularly came across individuals and organizations whose ideas did not fit the standard asset class definitions. These individuals and groups had well-enunciated approaches to making productive investments. The commitment was to people even more than to some 'asset class'. This focus on the individuals was especially important in the consideration of private equity managers when the field was quite young and there were no long-term investment histories.

Over time the MIT Investment Committee delegated manager selection and related decisions, especially in the alternatives area, to the staff. The staff operated within proscribed guidelines but with a general understanding that 'a turtle doesn't move forward unless it sticks its head out of the shell'. To facilitate some innovative investments, there was an allocation of about 2% of total assets to 'opportunities'. Dr Bufferd described this allocation as providing a 'hunting license' to search out and consider individuals and organizations with money-making ideas. Dr Bufferd, an engineer himself with a legal training, suggests that this was all about backing people, not running numbers or looking to consultants to evaluate and suggest managers. To quote the final slide of a presentation he made in 2003[3]: 'It is not optimizers; it is not asset classes; it is about good investors . . . with good ideas . . . '.

The terms of a bequest can be framed as an Investment Policy Statement. In the codicil of his Will, Benjamin Franklin made clear both the grant-making and investment objectives of his Trust for the City of Boston (ands likewise for Philadelphia). Benjamin Franklin had been grateful for the opportunity to establish a business in Philadelphia that had been afforded him by loans from friends. He was also intrigued by the idea of accumulating capital through compound interest to create a fund that could be used for grant-making purposes in future.

In a codicil to his Will, he brought his objectives of grant-making and investment together:

> The said sum of one thousand pounds sterling, if accepted by the inhabitants of the town of Boston, shall be managed under the direction of the selectmen, united with the ministers of the oldest Episcopalians, Congregational, and Presbyterian churches in that town, who are to let out the sum upon interest, at five per cent, per annum, to such young married artificers, under the age of twenty-five years, as have served an apprenticeship in the said town, and faithfully fulfilled the duties required in their indentures, so as to obtain a good moral character from at least two respectable citizens, who are willing to become their sureties, in a bond with the applicants, for the repayment of the moneys so lent, with interest, according to the terms hereinafter prescribed . . . to assist young married artificers in setting up their business.

The Will went on to determine what investment of the given sum at 5% per annum reinvested in the endowment should achieve:

> If this plan is executed, and succeeds as projected without interruption for one hundred years, the sum will then be one hundred and thirty-one thousand pounds; of which I would have the managers of the donation to the town of Boston then lay out, at their discretion, one hundred thousand pounds in public works. . . . The remaining thirty-one thousand pounds I would have continued to be let out on interest, in the manner above directed, for another hundred years. . . . At the end of this second term, if no unfortunate accident has prevented the operation, the sum will be four millions and sixty one thousand pounds sterling, of which I leave one million sixty one thousand pounds to the disposition of the inhabitants of the town of Boston, and three millions to the disposition of the government of the state, not presuming to carry my views farther.

9.2   TRUSTEES OF AN ENDOWMENT

Not only did Franklin have a clear idea about both investment and grant-making. He also had beliefs, articulated in the codicil, about the type of person he wanted to oversee the trust.

The first trustees of an endowment or foundation will set the tone of the organization but there are characteristics that can be helpful in a board with the task of implementing the charter. Russell Olson[4] quotes Ambachsteer and Ezra:

> Competent boards have a preponderance of people of character who are comfortable doing their organizational thinking in multi-year time frames. These people understand ambiguity and uncertainty, and are still prepared to go ahead and make the required judgments and decisions.

Franklin's trust also had something to say on the remuneration of trustees, 'having long been a fixed political opinion of mine that in a democratical state there ought to be no offices of profit.' The codicil comments: 'it is presumed that there will always be found in Boston virtuous and benevolent citizens, willing to bestow a part of their time in doing good to the rising generation, by superintending and managing this institution gratis.' A distinction has long existed between 'philanthropic trustees' who are not paid, and 'commercial trustees' who make a business of trusteeship under a corporate umbrella. Corporate trustees tend to be rewarded by fixed, transactional or *ad valorem* fees, not fees that are related to performance.

And many charters clearly indicate the position in respect of fees. In the Code of Conduct of the Packard Foundation,[5] for instance, it states: 'The Packard Foundation does not compensate Trustees for their service as Trustees.' The same code goes on, however, to say that it does pay travel and other expenses incurred on behalf of the foundation and has a matching program of grant-making for trustees.

It may be in future, however, that fees have to be paid to obtain the professionalism that trusteeship is increasingly demanding. And this raises the whole governance matter of 'agency issues,' which is the term used to cover questions surrounding the alignment of interest between decision-makers and beneficiaries. David Swensen raises agency issues in *Pioneering Portfolio Management*[6] in relation to management where he suggests that 'the wedge between principal goals and agent actions causes problems at the highest governance level, causing some fiduciary decisions to fail to serve the interest of a perpetual life endowment fund.' He cites fiduciaries who wish to see immediate pay-offs at the expense of the future and others who prefer uncontroversial and safe decisions at the expense of return. He covers the conflicts of managers who place business interest before investment excellence and underlying investments run for management rather than shareholders.

Harry Turner, who worked as part of Rodney Adams's team at Stanford University, and cofounded the Stanford Management Company, suggests that 'successful management requires structural alignments of incentives of the trustees with the fund's investment success, and motivations to discipline the fund's management staff, who usually have an agency conflict.' This is a controversial suggestion but he suggests that David Swensen may have the answer in co-investment.

David Swensen's point was made in relation to managers of assets of an endowment, rather than trustees, when he suggested that:

> although agency issues pervade the relationship between investors and external advisors, co-investment provides a powerful means of aligning fiduciary and fund manager interests. To the extent that a manager becomes a principal, issues regarding agency behavior diminish.

Fees for trustees takes us back to Chapter 7. *Quis custodiet ipses custodies?* Who guards the guards? The managers of an endowment, including in-house managers, may be substantially incentivized by required co-investment with the endowment's own fund. But who supervises this involvement except the trustees? Who decides, and how, whether the incentivization should be to grow in the long term or the short and the level of risk that is taken to achieve the endowment's objective? If trustees themselves are incentivized in some way, do they not lose objectivity? At least directors of companies, who may vote themselves substantial packages, are ultimately subject to shareholder vote.

Benjamin Franklin, in *Dangers of a Salaried Bureaucracy*, argued strongly as long ago as 1787 against payment for prestigious appointments on the grounds that 'It will not be the wise and moderate, the lovers of peace and good order, the men fittest for the trust. It will be the bold and the violent, the men of strong passions and indefatigable activity in their selfish pursuits' who take the posts. He went on: 'Besides these evils, sir, though we may set out in the beginning with moderate salaries, we shall find that such will not be of long continuance. Reasons will never be wanting for proposed augmentations. . . . '

9.3   INVESTMENT COMMITTEE

The endowment bequest may outline the governing body's authorization to delegate investment to an investment committee without framing any terms for investment. Where this is the case, the investment committee will be expected to draft, for the governing body's approval, the investment policy statement. In some endowments investment might both start and end with the trustee governing body, supported by professional staff.

As an endowment asset size grows there can be increasing need for a more sophisticated structure to cope with more complex strategies and this might require delegation to a committee. Such strategies may involve a greater number of investment products and managers to achieve appropriate levels of diversification. A trustee governing body will have responsibilities other than purely the investment of the endowment. A medical endowment, for instance, may need medical professionals on the board to assess the direction of effective grant-making in that profession. An art-related foundation will need art skills and experience on the board. Both may need board members who are skilled in fund-raising. These other responsibilities will take up an increasing amount of board time and increase the need for a committee to be focused entirely on investment.

In some foundations and endowments the investment function will be delegated to the finance committee. However, the finance committee may be too preoccupied with operational issues such as fund-raising, grant-making and the administration of finance and investments, to have sufficient time to allocate to investment direction. The greater the percentage of time taken by those other responsibilities, the less the percentage of time and resource available for consideration of investment matters and the greater is the need for an investment committee that reports either to the finance committee or directly to the trustee governing body.

At the University of Washington, for instance, where the professional staff have delegated authority to make investment decisions that are implemented through outside managers, the investment committee reports to the Finance and Facilities and Audit Committee. The investment committee has two members of the Board of Regents and five outside investment professionals who are experienced in various different asset classes. The committee is an advisory body that meets quarterly to discuss strategy and annually for an asset allocation overview.

It is by no means inevitable that trustees should delegate their investment responsibilities to a committee if they, as a body, have the time and the resource in terms of investment skills, experience and current knowledge. The University of Pennsylvania developed a unique model, described by the chairman of the investment board at the time as 'benevolent despotism.'[7] The chairman of the investment board, and equity manager, was John Neff, former managing partner and Senior Vice President of Wellington Management Company. He credits the model to Paul Miller, who was chairman of the Board of Trustees from 1977 to 1985.

Miller and Neff believed in an approach to endowment management that was low cost, enjoyed the confidence of trustees, employed differing investment strengths on the board, a single equity manager and a superior investment approach. In Neff's view, the investment committee is 'the point where most large endowments break down . . . the typical investment committee is a disparate group of people with different viewpoints and skills in investing . . .' What is needed is a good cocktail of personalities, skills and experience, as is the case with any good team.

Neff argued that confidence of the trustees 'to withstand occasional stretches of pain' was crucial and 'using benevolent despots is the most efficient way to run not only countries but also endowments.' He also argued for a 'systematic enduring approach' to management. On Neff's retirement, however, the University was unable to find an alumni willing to contribute as much, and they started the process of hiring outside managers. More than investment sophistication, Russell Olson cites as key criteria for investment committee members: high moral character, common sense, a flexible mind, an ability to consider new concepts and ideas, a willingness to accept risk and to learn.

The Meyer Foundation has five trustees with strong business credentials and no investment committee. The trustees are lifetime appointments, which encourages long-term thinking, and they meet once a month. This keeps the trustee board current on the background to investment strategy so that decisions can be well-informed and promptly executed.

In the case of the Meyer Foundation investment decisions are not only constantly reviewed but are integrated with grant-making. The Meyer Foundation board also meets annually with its investment managers to consider asset strategy, with some input from a consultant. The board has a long-term, partnership-type relationship with those managers who have significant freedom for action within given parameters. This type of relationship encourages feedback from managers that might not be in their short-term interest but cements a long-term business relationship, such as a recommendation to reduce assets managed by themselves when the asset class is overvalued.

Many endowments and foundations of any size will not, however, have access to quite the same array of investment skills, knowledge, experience and, crucially, time among those on the governing board. Most will have an agenda of grant-making, daily operations, policy formulation, governance and personnel issues that will crowd out investment considerations. Few will have sufficient investment experience. So delegating investment policy to a dedicated investment committee is clearly for them the optimum way forward.

Delegation first requires terms of reference. Terms of reference are the constitution of the committee. The terms of reference should establish the type of committee and the number of members, and it should make clear the accountability and authorization for action and for documented monitoring of the committee's proceedings. Terms of reference are not an investment policy statement (IPS) but production of an IPS should be a headline requirement of the terms of reference, signed-off by the trustees, if it does not already exist as an integral part of the charter.

The number of members of the committee needs to be a balance between a larger number providing volume and variety of input, and a smaller number that will tend to be more decisive and easier to contact, especially at short notice. The number will therefore depend on the type of input needed as well as the availability of suitable candidates. If the committee is making either tactical or selection investment decisions, it must be readily available at short notice and with a degree of frequency that would not be practical with a larger number of members.

The question is what constitutes a large number and how frequently the constituents of the investment committee change. Some consider the optimum number to be one, along the lines of John Neff's benevolent despotism, so anything above one is too large. Placing unfettered responsibility on one person may aid flexibility but it may also lead to hasty and ill-considered judgments. But an odd number of members ensures a casting vote. Five members is sometimes regarded as a perfect balance between breadth of view and need for prompt decision. Too frequent rotation of constituent members loses valuable experience before it can prove useful; and too long on a committee may jeopardize fresh thought.

The NACUBO and Commonfund surveys are interesting.[8] They show 8 to 10 as the average number of investment committee members in the case of universities and colleges, but the NACUBO survey also gives a range. The full sample average range is 3 to 50 members but the latter figure must be an outlier! What is clear with committees is that the larger they become the more susceptible they are to dangerous crowd behavior and the more vulnerable to John Maynard Keynes's concern that 'worldly wisdom teaches that it is better for reputation to fail conventionally than to succeed unconventionally.'

If the day-to-day investment decisions are being made by an executive Chief Investment Officer (CIO) and professional staff, then the role of the committee will be different. In that case the role will be strictly strategic and supervisory in nature. The biggest danger with such a committee is micro-management of the professional staff. Such a committee can provide a guiding hand and a sounding board for the professional staff. Members of such a committee may be especially helpful also in providing contacts and feedback where they are themselves investment professionals. Counter-productive is committee involvement in the day-to-day decisions that are the responsibility of the CIO, who can only be held accountable for the decisions that the CIO and staff make.

The constituents and character of the committee is therefore at least as important as the number of members. The need for members who have sufficient understanding of the investment issues to induce debate and invoke independent and contrary views is critical to a constructive contribution. No investment interest or, at the other end of the scale, too much investment conflict are to be avoided on committees but members with intelligent enquiring minds, who are not investment professionals, can bring a welcome perspective and balance. The chairman, however, should be an investment knowledgable person and the committee members should be chosen by the chairman for a sufficient period of years service to become fully engaged, but not so many as to become entrenched.

Some committees comprise well-known businessmen or outside investment professionals with time on their hands who have much to offer, both with wise advice and with useful contacts. Time availability is important. There is no value in having figureheads who have no time to contribute and cannot attend meetings regularly, even by telephone conference call. Conference calls by phone or video are perfectly acceptable media with a well-functioning committee who know each other well, especially when it obviates delay in meeting or deciding because an in-person meeting cannot be held promptly.

The Commonfund Benchmarks Study shows, not surprisingly, that in the largest funds 8 out of 10 members of the committees surveyed are investment professionals. This drops to less than half the committee for funds of $100 million in size and only a third of the members in the smallest funds. More than half of the investment professionals on committees also have alternative asset experience.

Personal chemistry is important in a committee, created by a cocktail of personalities who make two plus two equal five as a team with no domination by any one member. Independent thinking and vigorous debate are healthy, indeed necessary, but enmity is not helpful. Committees, like any team, must want to come together. Skepticism is also important. This means recognizing when policy is following the herd or 'this time its different.' Chemistry between the committee and the professional staff of an endowment is also critical to a constructive working environment.

Proper organization of the investment committee is essential to its effectiveness. Committees should be provided with briefing papers ahead of time to allow thoughtful deliberation, leading to a better contribution at the meeting and less time wasted in defining rather than solving investment problems. The decisions of the committee should be recorded and revisited at the subsequent meeting for analysis of what went right and what went wrong. Ideas should be followed up by reports. The generation of ideas without practical application is an academic exercise.

Frequency of meetings should also be considered. The Meyer Foundation meet monthly and they find that this keeps the committee in touch. Others will choose to meet quarterly and yet others less frequently. The answer is sufficient frequency to keep in touch and make effective and timely decisions. Most committees meet 4 to 10 times a year, with dates scheduled 12 months in advance to secure a high level of attendance.

Finally, there is the question of committee focus. The committee should be clear of its terms of reference and the items for their agenda. Regular monthly or quarterly tactical or policy review meetings should include such items as asset allocation; future strategy; spending policy; performance measurement; governance matters; staff issues. Annual meetings may focus solely on long-term strategy, and *ad hoc* meetings may cover such matters as investment consultant or manager selection or termination.

9.4   INVESTMENT STAFF

Any endowment fund must have an individual responsible for the physical implementation of investment strategy. In the very smallest endowment, that may be a trustee or an administrator of the endowment who may do no more than buy a charity mutual fund for the intergenerational funds and leave the operating reserves in the bank.

Endowments tend to add professional investment staff as funds grow in size and complexity. While the Commonfund Benchmark Study of universities and colleges in the USA shows an average of just over one full-time equivalent member of staff dedicated to investment at all funds, the average rises to between 12 and 13 for funds with assets of over $1 billion in size.

The number and type of professional staff in any endowment must depend partly on cost. A smaller endowment may simply not be able to afford a high level of internal resource. Smaller endowments can leverage the highly professional and experienced resources that consultants and fund managers can offer, albeit for a fee. The Commonfund Benchmark Study shows clearly that consultants' fees are correlated by size, with smaller institutions paying on average 25 basis points and the largest paying only 2 basis points of the fund size.

Dedicated investment staff can add value to the investment process at any level of the operation; however, the roles of the in-house staff must be clearly defined. At one level in-house professionals may be managers of managers, actively involved in formulating investment strategy and in judging and selecting the managers through whom the strategy is effected. At another level they may be primarily involved in administration of the investments, liaising with investment managers, bankers and custodians and in preparing investment information for the investment committee but not necessarily involved in investment direction.

The number and type of staff in an endowment will depend on the size of the fund, the number of managers used, the costs involved and the preferred model of strategy implementation. The move of endowments of all sizes toward more sophisticated investments, including hedge funds and private equity, has increased the burden of due diligence and monitoring. Keith Ferguson, CIO of the University of Washington, believes that there is no substitute for visiting managers on site to understand how they operate. Such due diligence is time-consuming but worth while.

There are essentially three investment models for implementation of strategy, and they are mostly a function of size.

The first model is for the smallest of funds. These funds will generally employ an external investment manager to recommend and effect both strategy and selection decisions through the medium of one generalist or a selection of specialist funds. The investments in this model may all be in one fund, commingled with the assets of other endowments that have similar objectives. The external manager may draw on different funds from within his own organization, reflecting different asset classes and skill sets, to effect strategy implementation creating for the endowment a fund of internal funds.

Trustees of such a small entity may have no investment experience and rely entirely on the judgment of the chosen asset manager. A consultant may help to establish strategy, recommend a generalist manager and monitor the results. The manager will make tactical asset class moves at his discretion within the generalist fund but within parameters set by the investment committee on the advice of a consultant, where asset strategy is through specialist funds. In-house staff may in this model have prime responsibilities elsewhere, such as administering grant-making. Investment may be only a part-time and entirely administrative role.

The second stage in size and complexity of fund takes the endowment into the second model. This stage moves the endowment from generalist to specialist management. It involves adding other funds or managers, either for manager diversification or to gain access to other investment specializations. The vehicles may all still be commingled funds but this begins to require some sifting of manager or asset class expertise, by the staff or the investment committee, again with the help of a consultant if the in-house resources are not sufficient. If the assets are large enough, the endowment may have a segregated portfolio of assets, which means holding individual securities. A common variant of this model is to have an external manager of domestic bonds and/or equities and to buy in funds to cover the international or alternative asset classes.

What distinguishes the second from the first stage model is the move from generalist to specialist investment management and separation of the function of tactical asset strategy and specialist security selection. The in-house professional staff must be able to prepare sufficiently effective information for the investment committee to be able to make that tactical decision or have sufficient investment experience, and the confidence of the committee, to do so themselves. And the committee must contain sufficient professional experience to be able to make judgments in this area.

Consultants have generally promoted the view that they are best placed to determine asset strategy and help to select specialist managers because there is no value added in tactical asset allocation and there is no one asset manager who excels in all asset classes. However, some consultants began to discover that there was little money in advising on the most critical aspect of asset strategy and many have moved into asset management as a fund-of-funds provider. Managers of larger assets have countered by offering separate asset allocation advice alongside specialized security selection teams. The wheel has begun to turn full circle, at the larger fund stage two level, back toward the days of 'balanced' asset management, when an asset manager performed all the functions as described in stage one for the larger as well as the smaller funds.

The third stage model is the development of a full in-house capability. This involves a full-time, in-house group of asset managers who manage segregated portfolios of securities on a day-to-day basis, although there can still be some funds even if these are confined to alternative asset classes. This model involves the employment of highly qualified, full-time investment professionals. In this model both asset strategy and selection decisions are made in-house. In this model the investment professionals are not distracted by the demands of other clients, they only have one client to satisfy. They are fully dedicated to the endowment or foundation and must be sufficiently remunerated and incentivized to perform.

The staffing decision to be made in this model is the allocation of responsibilities. Should the investment staff be generalists with an involvement in different asset classes or should they be specialists on each asset class? To some extent that decision is again a function of size. Smaller resources implies the former, generalization; larger resources allows the latter, specialization. Generalists will have broader knowledge and be less inclined to fight their corner when it comes to deciding which specialist areas of the portfolio should lose funds to more attractive opportunities. Their wider perspective might mean a more effective contribution to the asset allocation question. But they may not have the same degree of expertise in efficient markets where there is sophisticated and dedicated opposition. So it may prove more difficult for generalists to add alpha in specialist areas.

At this third level of operation the greater question may be what is the business model, rather than the investment model. Foundations and endowments in this position must make the decision as to whether highly paid asset managers can ever sit alongside academics in the same organization on a fraction of the pay. The alternative is a separate management company.

The Yale Investment Office is part of the university and outsources investment management to external fund managers like many other endowments. Exceptional returns have come from a mixture of asset allocation and manager selection. Many, if not most, of the Yale Investment Office staff are Yale alumni and compensation rates are approved by university committees.

Harvard University, like the University of Texas, uses a different business model. The Harvard Management Company is a separate entity from the university and manages a high proportion of funds in-house. The Harvard Management Company has consistently provided investment returns that have significantly raised the contribution of the endowment to Harvard University's operating budget, but despite this there was criticism of the levels of compensation of the best performing managers, which eventually led them to leave.

9.5 RISK TOLERANCE AND CONTROL

In Chapter 4 we defined endowment fund risk as:

a measure of the likelihood and the extent to which an endowment's resources fail to meet its financial objectives during its expected life.

This general definition should be honed, in the investment policy statement, to meet the specific needs and resources of the fund in question. The Big Sister Foundation of Boston, for instance, having outlined the very long-term nature of its time horizon in respect of its capital, defines itself as 'moderately conservative' on risk because of the required contribution of annual income to the operating budget. It defines risk in their terms as:

1. The Investor recognizes that higher returns involve some volatility and is willing to tolerate declines in the value of this portfolio of up to 15% in a given year.
2. The Investor would accept losses as often as two out of ten years to achieve higher returns.

These statements are to aid understanding of the Investor's risk tolerance and are not intended to be limitations on actual results or benchmarks triggering specific action.[9]

A stated policy on risk, even if risk is not quantified, is essential to an endowment. And the importance of the statement may not lie just in controlling too much risk but too little. We have seen in previous chapters that long-term return can be prejudiced by taking too little risk, especially through holding too much cash. This is probably the natural bias of endowments for two reasons. The first is that prudence is associated with not losing money more than with not maintaining real asset value. The second is the natural personal bias of some successful people on committees who, as private bankers will confirm, are often inclined not to risk their capital having risked their lives in building their wealth and many sublimally apply the same thinking in their role as trustee.

As a practical matter in implementing strategy, investment committees must take a broader stance on risk in terms of non-delivery of return. Not only does this involve investment considerations but operational ones too. So part of the committee's job is to ensure that internal controls and procedures are in place and functioning properly, especially covering business-critical catastrophic events. This monitoring must extend to dealers and custodians, to separation of duties to good audit trails and independent monitoring procedures.

9.6   OPERATIONAL ASSET MANAGEMENT

Operational assets are like an internal deposit bank. At the University of Washington cash represents 20–25% of the operating reserve assets, much of the pool is in intermediate-term Treasuries and corporate bonds but 25% is also in equity-type securities. Operating assets are a stable pool of funds which is constantly growing and many colleges and universities, including some of the largest, use the Commonfund cash management program.

The previous chapter emphasized the point that too much permanent cash for the given operational needs can reduce unnecessarily the overall endowment return. It showed that raising the volatility level marginally can add significantly to that overall return and can flatten, especially at points in the economic and financial cycle, the expected risk to return line.

These are two different points and they need to be managed in two different ways. The first matter, raising the return on operational assets as a permanent move, is purely operational reserve management. The operational funds available to different departments of an endowment organization such as a college or university, or allocated to an account of a foundation designed for immediate grant-making, must be sacrosanct. But there is scope for duration and volatility management if the operating budget period allows scope. Funds for operations must be separate from the funds that are used to change the overall risk profile of the endowment where tactical asset allocation or gradual portfolio shift is employed in the management of the intergenerational assets.

9.7   INTERGENERATIONAL ASSET ALLOCATION

Strategic asset allocation of the intergenerational assets is the principal role of the investment committee. As such it should be the committee's principal focus. The investment policy statement should outline the parameters and targets for asset allocation based on the inputs discussed in Chapter 8 such as real and nominal return objectives; risk parameters and minimum acceptable return; budgeted operational and intergenerational needs; social and ethical investment and governance issues.

Some foundations say in their policy statement that the time horizon for their investments is perpetual. Others chose a finite period. The primary objective of the University of Texas, for instance, is:

> to preserve the purchasing power of LTF assets by earning an average annual real return over rolling ten-year periods or longer at least equal to the target distribution rate, plus the annual expected expense... The secondary fund objective is to generate a fund return in excess of the policy portfolio benchmark and the average median return of the universe of college and university endowments with assets greater than US$1 billion as reported by Cambridge Associates over rolling five year periods or longer.

The San Diego Foundation has a long-term (over five years) and medium-term (three years) objective. The long-term objective is for the asset value, net of contributions and withdrawals, to exceed a specified composite index, to outperform the median representative foundation or endowment fund and to produce a minimum annual compound return of 5% in excess of inflation. In the medium-term objective, the total foundation return should exceed a custom-made index (specified in the policy statement) and outperform the medium fund in a comparable peer group. It must also outperform specific targets for various asset classes.

These are all statements that are clear about objectives and time periods and specific benchmarks that are different from each other and particular to the needs of each institution. But while each one also specifies a peer group comparator, this may be questionable as a measure of performance unless the peer group constituents each have the same objectives, risk profiles, time horizons, cash inputs, spending rules, fund-raising abilities and if the comparison is effectively a strategy comparison (the constituent parts of the portfolio being measured differently).

The statement on asset allocation should specify acceptable and prohibited asset classes or financial instruments. It is quite common, for instance, to prohibit short sales, commodities and derivatives, especially in leveraged form. But the question must always be asked why such strategies are included or excluded. Commodities, in some form, can be an effective inflation hedge. Short sales and derivatives can reduce volatility and enhance return.

The statement may also define maximum and minimum commitments in each class and selections of investment in each class. For instance, strategy parameters for domestic publicly listed equities might be a range of 20% to 40% with not less than 25% of that portfolio in small capitalization stocks and no more than 10% in any one stock (or index percentage plus or minus one half). Private equity, hedge funds or real estate might be limited to smaller and lower ranges, but there should be some rationale for all these decisions.

The question that trustees need to ask themselves is why the limit is 20% and not 25%? Why 50% and not 60%? Sometimes these parameters are arbitrary, but they should not be. They should be based on stress-tested scenarios that determine minimum expected losses and highest likely areas of long-term return. And policy parameters should be reviewed at regular, but not necessarily frequent, intervals because they can become out of date. This is especially the case when parameters are set and then market capitalization indices are used as benchmarks. If, for example, there is a parameter that limits a portfolio to 10% in an industrial sector, and that sector moves from 5% to 15% of the benchmark index, a manager becomes even more unfairly constrained in ability to outperform that benchmark.

Strategic asset allocation may require the input of a consultant to help the process of thinking and provide input on asset class risk and return expectations even where the resources are available in-house to do this exercise. Where the resource is not available within an endowment or foundation, an experienced consultant can usually draw on high levels of in-house information and knowledge to run simulations and answer 'what if' questions to help to determine the probabilities of meeting or failing to meet minimum acceptable returns. The consultant can also help the process of determining spending policy, which is an integral part of the asset allocation decision.

Foundations are tied to a 5% spending rule (subject to possible legislative change) which severely limits the scope for asset strategy flexibility in determining the balance between current and intergenerational needs. The Commonfund Benchmarks Study shows that the average spending rate for all foundations they surveyed was 6% of funds although special factors, such as a prolonged bear market and multi-year programs of grant, seem to have kept this rate higher than stated policy objectives.

Nearly two-thirds (but down from 80%) of the respondents in the Commonfund survey use a 12-quarter moving average of the fund's market value to determine the value to which the spending rate is applied. Many larger funds use a longer term, or a different policy altogether, with more focus on escalation of spending by applying inflation indices. More than half of the funds adopt the principle of maximizing intergenerational equity and the average percentage of the operating budget funded by endowment income was 11%. Funds that have fallen below their historic dollar values are known as 'underwater funds'. In some States spending is forbidden for these funds, and in others only income can be spent.

Apart from selection of asset classes in the strategic asset mix, there is methodology to be considered. Should strategy be implemented passively through indexed portfolios or actively managed with a view to achieving alpha (separating added value from pure market risk)? Should assets be managed with beta exposure to achieve pure market returns or by neutralizing market return and focusing on alpha? Or is the optimum using a 'portable alpha' approach, as we discussed in Chapters 6 and 8? Is the best approach 'bottom-up' (portfolio weights are driven by selection of securities) or 'top-down' (choose asset classes, markets and sectors then select securities consistent with the macro-overview)? Should the process be quantitative (using computer-generated screens and algorithms to choose markets and stocks) or judgmental (humans have brains or at least gut instincts)?

Quantitative versus judgmental can be difficult to delineate. Most active management processes rely on computer screens and models to help to make judgments, and most black boxes have models that are constantly tweaked because relationships change and formulae must be adjusted. Either way the endowment must be convinced by the process and it is difficult to escape the conclusion that since most processes need some judgment and most judgments need a discipline, the definition between quantitative and qualitative can sometimes be a gray area.

'Bottom-up' is a process for selection of securities according to a discipline. It is not a process for strategy decision. 'Bottom-up' with a proven discipline may or may not be a better way to select a portfolio of equities than attempting to develop a 'top-down' strategy. Each must be judged on its merits but both must be integrated into a portfolio strategy that recognizes common factor elements across the whole endowment fund.

There is evidence to show that there are times when active management tends to outperform passive, and that the reverse is true. There is also evidence to show that not all managers 'are average' and that some of the disciplines adhered to can add value over time. As we saw in Chapter 3, indexation by market capitalization, rather than by fundamentals, is the ultimate momentum strategy. The cycle of active and passive outperformance implies that a momentum approach is valid at times, and a contrarian at others. That means that the decision between active and passive may be cyclical, not a one-off and for-all-time judgment unless it is part of a consistent program for implementing market directional decisions.

The previous chapter covered the process of deriving strategic asset allocation from the objectives of the fund and relating this to resources, spending and scenarios. It covered the need to formulate a strategy that is specific to the endowment in terms of that endowment's culture, needs, risk profile and resources. This makes each endowment unique, and requires care when deciding measures of performance and relevant comparators or 'benchmarks'.

Chapter 8, 'Understanding Strategy', also covered the issues of portfolio rebalance once initial policy is established. A process must be established for a rebalancing mechanism and if no rebalancing is to be done, which may for whatever reason be appropriate, a justification for no action should be provided in the Investment Policy Statement.

9.8   BENCHMARKS AND PERFORMANCE

The word 'benchmark' means a point of reference used in estimation, derived from a survey mark which indicates a known location and elevation. In investment, benchmarks can be useful indicators for analysis of average returns from asset classes or investment styles. They can also be useful comparators for measurement of achievement of targets, but, when used as targets, one issue is the link between policy and benchmarks and benchmarks and behavior. Those who are not investment professionals do not always understand the extent to which benchmarks drive investment behavior because of subliminally perceived business risk to the manager.

Benchmarks in asset management may take any one of a number of forms. Most often they represent an average, usually market capitalization weighted, of a given universe. They may represent the whole of one universe or a subset of that universe as a measure of specialization, such as small or medium capitalization stocks, or energy or technology stocks. Such benchmarks may represent a target to be achieved or a minimum to be beaten. That minimum may be an index average or a higher level such as the top quartile of performers in a universe or an average plus a margin of expected achievement.

Modern Portfolio Theory (MPT) suggests that the market-capitalization-weighted index is the lowest risk portfolio in a given asset class. Laurence Siegel argues in *Benchmarks and Investment Management*[10]: 'you can't design a simple, rule-based judgment-free portfolio that is demonstrably more efficient than the cap-weighted benchmark.' That may or may not be true. It is perhaps too soon for the fundamental indices that we mentioned in Chapter 2 to disprove this point.

Siegel argues that 'the best choice of an index is one that, simultaneously, is useful as a benchmark for active management, can be used as the basis for index funds, and can provide proxies for asset classes in asset allocation'. He suggests that this implies the following characteristics: completeness, investability, clear published rules and good governance, accurate and complete data, acceptance by investors, availability of derived tradable products, low turnover and related transaction costs.

Siegel has concerns about absolute return as a benchmark alternative to market indices. He says that a good benchmark is generally one for which an index fund or tracking portfolio can be constructed. Because there is no asset other than cash which pays an absolute return, Siegel's concern is the lack of information that arises from there being only a cash-based comparator. He comments that there is a great deal of active risk in absolute return investing, so he is not optimistic about efforts to earn an absolute return.

Siegel does, however, acknowledge an alternative view expressed by Peter Bernstein. This is a focus on liabilities as a benchmark. Bernstein's perspective is that 'traditional benchmarking for active portfolio managers is contrary to the client's best interest'. Bernstein argues the case for a liability-driven, or absolute return, benchmark which 'can circumvent to the extent poss- ible the dangerous conflicts of interest in traditional arrangements that fester between manager's risk and owner's risk'. Bernstein suggests as a benchmark an immunized portfolio with zero tracking error to the fund's liability return. He argues for 'determination of the required return of the total portfolio and the degree of volatility the client can live with in the search for that required return'. He suggests 'a much looser set of marching orders for managers' encouraging greater latitude in their investment decisions with less fear of being 'wrong and alone'.

Siegel then suggests a case for two benchmarks. One is a traditional policy benchmark that uses a combination of asset classes that could be held through indexed subportfolios, albeit with a smaller weight in equities. The other is liability focused as 'a conceptual reference point', recognizing that the real purpose of a foundation or endowment is to fund its operations.

Operational and intergenerational assets are held to meet different objectives. One endow- ment may take cash as its benchmark for operational assets because the operational budget timeframe is very short term. Another endowment may take a five-year operating view, imply- ing that a duration mixed portfolio of relevant asset classes would be more appropriate than pure cash. Either objective, however, can be met by a predefined investable index or composite of indices.

For intergenerational assets, a combination of long-term real asset class weightings is the more appropriate benchmark. This might imply a combination of inflation-linked securities, equities, commodities and real estate in the policy portfolio as a proxy for asset strategy. The long-term historic characteristics of such a policy mix should be assessed and both policy and selection alpha should be monitored going forward. The ultimate judgment for an endowment is how much it exceeds the minimum expected return, reflected in the spending rule over both the short and longer terms.

Benchmarks for measuring the achievement of strategy is one thing, but measuring the spe- cific performance of fund managers is another. Performance measurement is partly a numbers game but it also involves a qualitative assessment, especially of people in their continuity and their commitment to the business and the client. An organization is only as good as the people within it. Manager change is a key warning factor for possible change in performance.

When measuring performance, the scope for error and misrepresentation in the calculation and presentation of numbers, both absolute and relative, is considerable. In recognition of this, the CFA Institute has developed the Global Investment Performance Standards (GIPS), which combine the former AIMR Performance Presentation Standards and the Global Investment Performance Standards.

The objective of GIPS is a worldwide standard for the calculation and presentation of investment performance in a fully transparent, fair and comparable format to ensure accurate and consistent presentation of performance information. It requires investment managers to include all fee-paying discretionary portfolios in composites of similar investment strategies and/or objectives for a minimum period of five years, or since inception, and to be measured and presented on a prescribed basis.

GIPS is a standard; it is not a benchmark *per se* but it is a standard that trustees should require, and if this requirement cannot be met, an explanation should be given. Even then, as Charles Ellis comments,[11] 'Measurements of a portfolio investment performance do not, at least in the short run, "mean what they say". Performance measurement services do not report "results". They report statistics.' He observes that these statistics are 'samples drawn period by period from a most unusual and continuous process – the process of managing complex, changing portfolios of securities in the context of a large, dynamic, always changing and often turbulent free and competitive capital market'.

This message from one who has had at least as much experience as any, and certainly more than most in assessing managers and their performance, is that recognizing measurement as statistics helps an understanding that these numbers are only approximations. This means that there is sampling error in the calculation and difficulty in knowing the validity of the result relative to the period in which it is measured, given choices of starting and ending dates, given factors that may apply in one period and not in another, and given all the variables that affect the condition of the sample being measured – not least the conditions of the mandate and the risk that has been taken. Ellis also quotes Professor Barr Rosenberg's estimate that it would take 70 years of observations to show conclusively that 200 basis points of incremental return was due to skill rather than to chance.

The ultimate performance comparison is routed in human psychology as part of the competitive instinct: peer group comparison; who wins the race or at least comes in the top 25% of all entrants? Such comparison, as with all else we are considering in this book, needs thought.

First, is the peer group truly representative? Are the others trying to do exactly the same thing and in the same way with similar resources? Who is really making the decisions and so who is being measured? If a committee sets the portfolio risk level and monitors the manager against all-comers, then the appropriate adjustment for handicap must be applied. And what of the peer group? In the alternative asset management world, for instance, quite apart from the differences in types of strategy, the half-life of a hedge fund has been estimated at five years. How is the survivorship bias accounted for in any composite index that purports to measure hedged fund returns? Peer group review needs careful analysis, and this is usually the role of the investment consultant.

Finally, it is hardly consistent for a trustee to measure a manager against a well-known index on a quarterly basis and then ask that manager to make active bets rather than follow the benchmark, unless the manager is required to make minimum index-deviations. These are defined in terms of minimum allowed tracking error (the difference between manager and index return). This would at least ensure that strong active positions (bets against the index), reflecting real investment conviction, are taken in the portfolio. Manager risk will be defined as deviation from the index so managers will necessarily tend to track the index to a greater or lesser degree. That may be exactly what is required and may even be defined in a manager's mandate by reference to maximum tracking error, but the implication of the requirement needs the trustee's full understanding and recognition.

9.9 CONSULTANTS

Interpretation of performance statistics is one of the roles of investment consultants. They may use this information to advise on fund manager and investment style selection, drawing on proprietary databases of managers, and, where necessary, on the termination of managers. They may assist the process of selection and subsequently provide a monitoring service. This would involve performance measurement and peer group comparison.

Consultants may also provide asset allocation input using their databases of past returns and volatilities of return and risk premia derived from historic numbers. This may or may not incorporate advice on spending strategy, using estimates of likely future returns and 'what if' simulations to stress test different assumptions.

Consultants should be selected for their knowledge, experience and understanding of the issues of endowments and foundations. There will be those that have skills in other areas but understanding endowment fund needs is a different story from the needs and cultures of other funds. The investment committee should assure themselves that the individual presenter is the person who would be 'in the hot seat' when advising the committee, not just a marketing person. Personal chemistry is important to the conviction with which the committee will rely on the advice.

The committee should assure itself that the consultant has no conflicts of interest with other clients and, when satisfied, should ask for references. Clients of consultants who will provide references should be asked about the type and the substance of the advice they were given, to ensure it is comparable, the promptness with which issues were covered and the dedication of the staff. They should be asked whether in hindsight they might have made a different choice. The remuneration of the consultant should preferably be by fee, which may involve a retainer. Fees obtained through retrocessions from managers whom the consultant recommends is less good practice.

In few other professions than consultancy is the phrase 'time is money' more true. A working relationship for continuing advice should have clear written terms of engagement and agreement on fees. Endowments that employ consultants on project work should be very specific in their brief, which should also be written and should agree with the consultant various discrete stages of work with fee cut-off points.

9.10   SELECTION OF ASSET MANAGERS

One of the first choices to be made is a decision between active and passive management. There is no avoiding the strategic asset weighting decision and rebalancing but there is choice over how this is implemented. As we have seen earlier in the book, market capitalization indexation may be the least-cost method of achieving market direction but it has flaws and strategic decisions must still be made as to which markets and why.

Whatever the investment merits of different managers, trustees of endowments and foundations will usually want to satisfy themselves that managers must be one of the following: (1) registered with the requite domestic regulatory authority – in the USA under the Investment Companies Act 1940; (2) a bank as defined in that act; (3) a qualified insurance company; (4) other persons or organizations registered under their respective national laws. In some of the asset areas these national laws may be in offshore countries that may have less stringent regulatory environments than the USA or the UK. This does not invalidate the managers; it simply places more pressure on trustees or staff of an endowment to ensure a comprehensive due diligence process than might otherwise be the case.

The Commonfund Benchmarks Study shows the clear correlation of fund size with number of external investment managers employed. The most recent study[12] shows that the average educational endowment employs 12 managers but the largest, over $1 billion in size, have nearly

70 and the smallest just 2. Generalist or 'balanced' asset managers may be most appropriate for smaller endowment funds, but even larger endowments have adopted an approach known as 'strategic partnerships' with only one firm. Smaller fund portfolios can be constructed on a segregated basis (meaning they hold individual securities) with relatively high levels of specialist asset class risk but having a relatively low overall portfolio risk. For instance, the global element of an equity portfolio may have only 10 to 15 stocks in Asia, which is a fraction of the number held in the average specialist Asian equity fund. But combined appropriately with other domestic and international stocks, that portfolio may be no more exposed to average volatility risk than one that substituted those 20 stocks with a specialist fund.

Such generalist funds can be constructed very specifically to meet an endowment fund's needs, including, where relevant, taxation considerations. Where investment knowledge and skill are lacking within the endowment itself, this can be supplied wholly by the generalist manager and implemented in a 'tailor-made' portfolio for the relevant institution. Such precision cannot necessarily be achieved so precisely using pooled funds and can only otherwise be achieved by the largest endowment organizations.

Pooled funds have advantages and disadvantages over a segregated account. They tend to attract the better fund managers in an asset management organization but the funds may have to carry higher levels of cash balance because of client turnover. They can have cost advantages although pooled fund fees can also tend to bear heavy marketing charges in the management fee which can offset the economies of scale. As ever, it is a question of objective assessment.

Selecting generalist managers is a different proposition from selecting specialist managers. Generalists need to demonstrate a clear approach to asset, sector and geographic allocation as well as security selection. One approach may simply be to invest proportionately in a given asset and geographic allocation and to add alpha entirely through sector or security selection skills, either using the manager's own or others' commingled or pooled vehicles, or using separate stocks.

If that is the approach, the manager must demonstrate, through performance attribution, that it can add value in this way. Conventional performance attribution of managers of balanced funds shows that few managers add value on timing of asset class shifts. But as we considered in Chapter 2, 'Language of Return', attribution measures precise timing and while timing may not add-value on a time-weighted basis, even suboptimal timing of asset class shifts can still make a positive contribution to compounding overall wealth.

An alternative generalist approach is a focus on an investment style and the selection of assets, countries, sectors and securities based on that style without reference to any benchmark weighting. A global value fund, for instance, will find value on the criteria appropriate to its investment approach. It will simply ignore securities that do not pass the screen, however large those companies may be in an index. In the late 1980s, a number of funds that were managed on strict value criteria had no stocks in Japan at all, at a time when the Japanese stock market represented more than half the weight of the international stock indices. Selection by style is best made alongside another type of manager with a different investment style to achieve some measure of style diversification. Value and growth styles, for instance, can each be out of favor for very long periods of time.

The 'strategic partnership' approach allies an endowment fund to a large asset management organization which has a broad range and global reach in investment skills and considerable depth in manager, research and administrative resources. This was the approach adopted by MIT in the mid-1970s to great effect but, to quote Dr Allan Bufferd, Treasurer of MIT, who was involved in that process: 'the idea was to go with one firm with a broad selection of skills – not specifically a balanced manager.' MIT, operating without a consultant for the process, spent extensive contact time with candidate organizations, eventually selecting Wellington Asset Management. One of the factors that helped in the relationship was that Wellington was located only two subway stops away from MIT, clearly a positive for communication at a time when communication was not as easy as today.

One example of the benefit of a close working relationship was the way in which Wellington was able to present to MIT the case for investment in Japan in 1980. MIT had an investment committee that comprised primarily of senior business leaders with exposure to the international marketplace. These individuals had open minds to considering new ideas. During the 1980s MIT expanded its alternatives program and established other long-term relationships to the one it has maintained to this date with Wellington.

Russell Olson quotes recent success with strategic partnerships, albeit with pension plan sponsors rather than endowment funds, and the reasons given for that success are equally applicable: tactical allocation handled within broad limits; favorable fee rates from a large account; partners providing a consulting resource; reduction of complexity through dealing with one entity.

For funds that are at stage two or three in size and complexity, strategic asset allocation and security selection are quite separate activities. Once asset allocation is decided, the question is the selection of a specialist manager. The overriding goal of manager selection in these cases is to try to obtain the world's best managers in each asset class. This implies no constraint on location or type of manager and complete objectivity. The benchmark for each specialist manager should be the index fund that replicates that asset class. If that index fund cannot be bettered by an actively managed alternative, then an indexed portfolio, Exchange Traded Fund or derivative alternative should be used to effect the appropriate market decisions.

The universe of available managers in every asset class and every geographic location is enormous and some method must be found for screening a search. Such screens should involve characteristics of performance (with care, given the generally low correlation between historic and future performance) and fund size; organizational resource (asset managers, research, back-office and compliance); both investment and business philosophy and style; stability of personnel.

While past performance may genuinely be no guide to the future, the clues to the future lie in investment philosophy and style and in the people and process. This should be the focus of investment manager search. A fund manager should be chosen for evident commitment to a discipline, which will work in some environments and not others, with a clear process linking discipline to implementation and a process for identifying and explaining the source of both negative and positive alpha.

The choice of people, at the end of the day, is almost invariably a matter of chemistry. Russell Olson[13] makes the point with the interviewing of managers that 'articulateness has a low correlation with investment capability' and 'in 20 to 30 minutes, a committee's interview can be little more than superficial'. He concludes that even a 'beauty contest', whereby a short-list of managers is interviewed following a process of screening through inviting a 'request for proposal' (RFP), which is a long questionnaire, is a suboptimal method for selecting investment managers. He suggests that the RFP should be tailor-made for each manager – a longer process for the endowment but one designed to allow each manager to tell his own story comprehensively.

An alternative is to combine both: to use a standard RFP for the first level of screen and to screen the short-list with tailor-made questions. A common base for performance numbers, with a sufficient investment history and frequency of data interval and assurances of no extraneous factors – including no manager or style or mandate changes – is an essential part of the process.

This is not simply to judge outperformance but to assess style of return. Information ratios (which show relative added value) as well as extent, timing and character of performance deviation from benchmarks – and indeed the peer group – all paint a picture and help to confirm that what a manager says is in fact what a manager does.

Once a manager is hired, terms of agreement should be enshrined in the Investment Management Agreement. This contract outlines the investment objectives for the manager, parameters of the investment universe and, if applicable, the limits of percentages that can be invested in any one sector or, more particular, any one security. It covers the contract period and general rules of engagement – including communication and meetings, performance criteria, termination procedures and other general matters of corporate governance. Most particularly the agreement covers the matters of manager fees.

Selection of asset managers is one thing and termination is another. Termination is never lightly undertaken, and it must be due to more than temporary loss of performance. In fact temporary loss of performance in a good manager is often a signal for selection. There are three main reasons for the termination of a manager.

The first reason is that the asset class or investment style no longer fits the need of the fund. A strategy change to exclude an asset class, for example, would lead to manager obsolescence. Change or 'drift' in investment style is a related reason for change. A manager may be hired to be a 'value' manager on the basis of a strong philosophy and resources and process devoted to this type of investment. If the manager begins to buy growth stocks because growth is in fashion, then this should be grounds for immediate divorce.

A second reason for termination is loss of trust. This could arise in the event of significant evidence of sustained lack of internal control or lack of transparency in the dealings of the manager on behalf of, or with, the endowment. It would certainly arise in the event of dishonesty or fraud or serious regulatory breach. Hopefully such matters are less probable if due diligence in the process of manager selection had been adequately done, but scandals still occur and one side of an asset management business can suffer collateral damage from issues in another.

The third reason is loss of confidence. Loss of confidence can arise from various circumstances. One example is change of control or of business direction of the manager. Change of control or of business direction can lead to a change of culture, distraction from the business and loss of key people. Lack of control of business success can also lead to hubris which itself can cause cultural change and unsettle a relationship. Decline in performance and relationship, in hungriness for the business, can also simply occur with the passage of time.

Finally, most investment management firms rely on a few key but still mortal individuals. Illness, death and retirement can have a major impact on continuation of comparable investment service.

9.11 COSTS

Implementing asset strategy brings with it a number of different types of cost. Asset management fees are only just one of them. Costs can have a major impact on overall return. The Commonfund Benchmark Study identified the average cost of managing investment programs for all the endowments on their survey as 71 basis points (0.71% of the assets under management). Surprisingly the cost for funds over $1 billion in size was similar to that for funds under $10 million: 65 and 68 basis points respectively.

Other costs include consulting charges for asset allocation advice, legal fees and transaction charges for implementation of investment decisions. Security dealing usually incurs commissions payable to agents and a 'spread' that is taken by a market maker. In the UK, 'commission-sharing agreements' can use commissions that are payable out of an endowments transactions to pay only for third-party research.

Commission sharing is an alternative, agreed by the UK regulator (FSA) and being watched by the SEC, to a less acceptable practice known as 'soft dollars'. 'Soft dollars' are commissions given by asset managers to brokers to pay for a wide range of third-party services used by asset managers. These services have included 'performance measurement services' commissioned from consultants by asset managers but not disclosed to the clients. In the case of commission sharing, the broker who executes the trade is paid separately for execution and required to pass on the balance to providers of pure research. Stamp duty and regulatory levies are other costs that are payable in many markets.

High levels of turnover in securities markets can have a significantly detrimental impact on overall return but high turnover combined with high levels of skill can more than justify high transaction costs. The problem comes when high levels of turnover are combined with low skill levels. High turnover can bring costs in brokerage commissions and custody charges for handling and retaining securities in safe keeping. These fees are generally both fixed and volume related. Other custodial costs include collection charges for claiming income payments and for special services including payment to subcustodians for overseas securities.

Cash management charges and charges for foreign exchange transactions, low interest rates on deposits, and fees for performance measurement, accounting and auditing – all these detract from the return that an endowment receives, and they need to be monitored.

Investment management fees may not even be the largest part of the total expense ratio (TER) of the management of a fund. But management fees come in many different guises. Fees to watch are fees on fees, where a manager charges an overall fee and a fee within funds that are included in the portfolio. Front or back-end loads are fees charged on some mutual funds and trail fees are retrocessions paid to a third party out of the fees of a mutual fund as a marketing reward. Section 12(b)(1) fees are fees up to 0.25% of a mutual funds assets that can be charged for advertising and promotional expenses. This is an allowable practice but one eschewed by many mutual funds to the benefit of their clients.

All these charges may be perfectly legitimate but they should all be disclosed and an endowment should be mindful that fixed charges are certain while performance is not. Endowments should also request 'Most-Favored-Nation' status. This requests that the endowment should be entitled to at least as good a fee as any other comparable client of the manager.

In 1927, when investment management was a fairly new profession, Scudder, Stevens & Clark distributed a pamphlet to their clients and prospective clients. This was republished in 1977 and included by Charles Ellis and James Vertin in their compendium *Classics, an Investor's Anthology* published in 1989.[14] The following is a paragraph from this pamphlet:

> The client may regard our fee merely as an insurance premium paid by him for the safeguarding of his investments. In reality it is much more than that. As a charge against principal it has practically no effect on income or, eventually, upon principal itself. In return for each year of continuous professional service in his interest, the client pays us but $\frac{1}{2}$ of 1% of the average dollar value of his capital. If during a year of depression we do no more than save that capital from a shrinkage of $\frac{1}{2}$ of 1%, or in normal times increase it over and above that amount, our services cost nothing. In point of fact, during the last eight years the average annual gain to the client through investments made under our supervision has more than ten times exceeded the amount of our fee. We therefore believe this fee to be not only an equitable charge for our services but a profitable expenditure on the part of the client.

This form of fee, based on a percentage of the market value of assets under management, is the most common practice with traditional asset classes and is known as 'ad valorem' or 'asset based'. Such fees are normally charged in bands of value with break-points at various levels. A typical institutional fee would be a fixed amount whatever the size up to $20 million with a lower percentage on the amount of assets between $20 million and $50 million and a lower percentage still on the band between $50 million and $100 million and so on. At some point they become negotiable.

Commodity-type products, such as passively managed funds, attract commodity-like fees. These tend to be low, single basis points depending on the size of the fund but are higher for markets that are more difficult to replicate and rebalance. Enhanced indexation and active management raises the level of fee as the price for research resource and the potential reward for excess return.

Fees on specialist funds are conventionally higher than on balanced accounts – a system without logic unless the balance account is so large that the overall fee more than covers the combined discounts that would be applied at that size on the various specialist components. That has generally not been the case, with the result that balanced account management has effectively been offering specialist portfolios at a discount with no fee for asset allocation. It is hardly surprising that asset managers in the 1980s invested little or nothing in the asset allocation process and the role was taken over by the investment consultants.

Implicit in the scale of ad valorem or asset-based fees is the concept that larger funds need more resources to manage, even if this is not necessarily in proportion to the added fee charged. Ad valorem fees have generally been the norm in conventional asset management but this has changed in some areas under the influence of performance or incentive fees that are the norm in alternative investment strategies.

The justification for performance fees is that they should align the interests of managers with the interests of clients and so incentivize the behavior the client wants to see: alpha generation. Performance fees are usually part of a two-tier structure involving a base fee to cover overheads and a performance element based on added value to the client. Added value is calculated by reference to a benchmark which, in absolute return strategies, is usually cash plus a margin. This sets a 'hurdle rate' that should be met before there is any excess return on which the performance fee is to be calculated.

These fees come in various guises. They may be base plus a performance element without limit, or to a level which is the normal ad valorem fee if certain hurdles are achieved. They may be ratcheted, capped, or leveraged. They may be subject to an override called a 'high water mark'. A high water mark ensures that the performance fee is charged on return from the last high point of performance or from an accumulated hurdle rate, not just return from a previous point in time when the market may have fallen to create a lower base. This prevents paying fees to a volatile fund which adds no value over time.

The high water mark may be the last peak of performance or it may be based on accumulated hurdles of a rate of interest which acknowledge that a manager should not be rewarded on the risk-free element of the return. If there is a catch-up provision once a hurdle rate is achieved, then there should be a policy enshrined in the management agreement on how the catch-up operates and whether the manager receives a proportion of the catch-up amount during that period.

For alternative asset classes, performance fees are the norm. The fees for hedge funds are usually a base 1% or 2% of assets under management and 20% at a minimum of the return over a certain hurdle rate (which in some cases is zero). Funds of hedge funds work on different fee rates. They are typically 'one and ten' (1% ad valorem and 10% of profit) on top of the fees charged by the underlying hedge funds although the 1% may be reduced by retrocession from the constituent funds. Some hedge funds can charge more than 20% of the excess profit because of a long record of exceptional return.

In the case of private equity funds, there must be clarity as to when the performance incentive begins. Investors should receive back their capital and at least a risk-free return before such fees should be calculated, or even more, deducted. In the case of illiquid asset classes where return of capital and profit is delayed till final realization, as in the case of real estate and private equity, the performance fee pay-out should also be delayed unless some fee clawback system can be arranged.

9.12   CUSTODY

There is more of a legal than a practical distinction between custodian bank and master trustee, even if this was not always the case. A custodian bank is a security holding agent. In the case of a trustee arrangement, title to the investments resides with the bank on a 'directed trustee' basis. It was once the case that trust banks tended to manage a high proportion of private investments on a discretionary basis, as well as control the administration, but independent investment managers increasingly began to take over management of institutional funds from trust banks and insurance companies in the 1970s. Multiple investment managers and multiple asset classes need a common platform for administration and cash management. This is perhaps best provided by a Master Trustee as custodian of the assets.

The custodian should be selected by the investment committee on the advice of the staff after a process of investigation. The custodian provides safekeeping for securities and cash arising from transactions made with authorized dealers on a delivery-versus-payment (DVP) basis, even if today such a custodian does not tend to hold paper script but a computer record of holdings in a central depositary.

Master Trustees may offer other than pure safekeeping facilities. The trustee will handle collateral on repurchase agreements and required margin on derivatives. The trustee will offer security lending where the endowment's securities are lent out to short-selling funds for a fee that is then shared between the bank and the endowment. Foreign exchange transactions will be handled through the Master Trustee. Risk and performance analysis and attribution may also be offered.

Reporting to the endowment is a key part of the custody service. Asset statements, statements of transactions and other records of investment activity, records of dividends and interest, dealings with brokers and subcustodians of foreign securities are all in a day's work for a custodian bank.

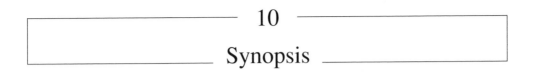

10
Synopsis

The first act's doubtful, but we say, it is the last commends the play.

ROBERT HERRICK (1591–1674)

Endowments and foundations are a unique type of long-term fund and they are unique in themselves: each fund has its own ethos, objectives, risk constraints and governing body of people who legally own, and direct the management of, the underlying assets. Endowments and foundations generally have the longest term vision of any known funds but must still walk a tightrope of responsibility between the demands of the present and a duty to the future with little or no 'lender of last resort'.

Investment strategy for endowment funds is a holistic process, which means that it is a process of forming a whole that is more than the sum of its component parts. Modern Portfolio Theory may have taken the theory of strategy beyond simply finding the best combination of money-making ideas. But strategy for endowments is even more than simply finding the diversified mix which hopefully provides the theoretical optimum portfolio return for every point on the axis of risk.

Ultimately endowments are subject to Micawber's Rule, which equates investment return and other income with spending rates and endowment growth. Investment strategy must therefore be an integral and iterative part of a strategy that takes into account other income, current and future spending policy and intended endowment and spending growth. The need to reinvest in the endowment simply to stay in line with inflation, which is called maintaining intergenerational equity, can be seriously underestimated. At a time of low prospective nominal returns it is easy to retain high nominal spending rates and to underestimate the capital sum that is needed to sustain the activities of the endowment.

Understanding strategy must begin with understanding both the fundamental principles of investment and one of the commonest but least understood words in the language of investment: *return*. Spendable return may usefully be defined as the economist Sir John Hicks defined the word 'income': 'the wealth which can be consumed in a year which leaves unchanged the quantum of wealth left to generate the same income in the following year.'

The amount that is available to be consumed during the year is equivalent to total return less the amount that should be reinvested to maintain intergenerational equity. The quantum of wealth that is left at the end of that year to generate the same return in the following year is 'intergenerational equity' – that is the capital that can sustain the same level of return in real (inflation-adjusted) terms.

Inflation creates a money illusion that can lead to overspending of current return to the detriment of the future because of insufficient reinvestment for wealth accumulation through compounding reinvested return. Disinflation can also create an illusion of spendable value when valuations adjust and provide one-off returns that cannot be consumed if Hicksian 'well-offness' is to be sustained.

Consideration of Albert Einstein's eighth wonder of the world, the power of compound interest, exposes both the dilemma between spending now or growing for the future and the focus on relative return rather than absolute return. The use of time-weighted return, which is a device for measuring funds with different cash flows comparably but not a measure of wealth accumulation, may sometimes obscure this underlying fundamental objective.

Financial return is created through entrepreneurial activity and financial intermediation. The central bank sets the price at which money is lent to the government and this establishes the risk-free rate of interest from which other rates are derived. Time is money and the future is uncertain creating a premium for risk which is amplified, in the case of non-government assets, by the economic cycle.

Guesstimating the future effectively requires analysis of the sources and drivers of return and of the validity of past relationships; it is not simply about extrapolating past returns. Planning involves recognizing future uncertainty through scenario analysis rather than single point estimates. It is more than the weighted average of most likely outcomes. As Keynes wrote: 'The assumption of arithmetically equal probabilities based on a state of ignorance leads to absurdities.'

Return cannot be divorced from risk. The Chinese term for risk is a combination of the character for danger and that for opportunity and risk is something to be managed not just minimized. There is a long history in the development of the mathematics of risk that culminated in twentieth-century modern portfolio theory (MPT). This theory first formally quantified financial risk as variance of return from the mean or average return. In other words, risk was volatility.

One of the main developments of MPT is that security returns have three elements: an underlying element of market return; an element that is leveraged to the market (beta); and an element that is independent of the market, called alpha. Alpha, which can be positive or negative, defines the source of value added to (or detracted from) a benchmark by active management of portfolios.

Another feature of MPT is the shift in thinking toward the non-correlation of asset class returns as a measure of diversification, not just spreading risk over a large number of investments. From this developed the analysis of common factors between asset classes and securities and the analysis of portfolios by themes and by styles.

While MPT has expanded the thinking on risk, simply equating risk to volatility is not sufficient when it comes to the mission of endowments. We define endowment fund risk as 'a measure of the likelihood and the extent to which an endowment's resources fail to meet its financial objectives during its expected life'. This definition follows the Sortino approach that risk for an endowment is failure to meet a minimum acceptable return. And the definition implicitly assumes that endowment fund risk takes into account factors other than simply the volatility of return.

Risk is benchmarked to the liability demands on a fund over both operational and intergenerational time horizons. This implies that risk is particular to a given fund and not general, and that the same conditions of risk can have different implications for different funds depending on a fund's objectives and liabilities. And this definition takes into account both the timing and duration of the impact of risk.

Spending Rules dictate the percentage of an endowment that can be consumed today at the expense of tomorrow. Intergenerational equity is maintaining sufficient value in the endowment to sustain grant-making in real terms for future generations. There is a symbiotic relationship between investment return, other income, current spending and growth of the endowment and therefore of the ability to spend in future. Inflation tends to distort spending ability by creating illusory income and capital gain. The illusory part of the income, in the Hicksian sense of the word, should be reinvested to maintain an endowment's real value and thereby to maintain real spending power.

Change in consumer prices can also cause illusory spending power through valuation change. A perpetual bond yield which halves through a halving of inflation doubles the price of the bond for no increase in income generation. It is an illusion to presume that the 100% rate of capital return on such a bond is now available for current expenditure. Rather, some of the 100% total return from that bond still needs to be reinvested to maintain the sustainable, consumable real income from the bond.

A spending rule that is purely a percentage of an endowment's net asset value provides some discipline but is not a complete answer. A better approach is to relate a percentage of the endowment value to the minimum acceptable return escalated by a price deflator component to account for the change in value of money. An upper limit spending rate also provides protection for intergenerational equity. In effect this approach generates a reserve in good times which can be drawn on in poor return times to maintain grant-making ability.

Until the second half of the twentieth century, few asset classes were available for investment by endowment funds. MPT and other financial developments changed the way in which conventional assets were viewed. MPT also helped to expand the categories of asset and the financial instruments available, and to change the approach to portfolio management.

Assets can be classified by use and by characteristics. The classification by use distinguishes between operational and intergenerational assets. The former are short-duration investments to cover, with a high degree of certainty, both the daily operating needs of an endowment over the budgeted period and the tactical and risk management needs of an endowment's portfolio managers. Such assets provide managers with a way, when necessary, to deleverage portfolio risk caused by the more volatile intergenerational asset base – the long-term endowment.

Intergenerational assets meet the longer term need to preserve or enhance intergenerational equity. They are long-duration, often illiquid, higher return assets mostly with equity-like and long-term inflation-protection characteristics.

The asset classes within the operational and intergenerational classifications can behave like chameleons: some fixed income bonds can behave like equities while others will behave like cash or real estate depending on the financial background. Some equities behave more like commodities than other equities, or even like bonds. The behavior of all will also vary as scenarios change. It is therefore the characteristics of these asset classes appropriate to different potential scenarios that will determine their relative portfolio weight in the total portfolio at any particular point in time.

One other ingredient to endowment strategy is the ethos of the endowment and its social policy toward acceptable investments. Some endowments have strong internal policies with rigid screens to exclude what they regard as antisocial investments, but external pressures may also influence 'socially responsible' parameters to investment, even if this is not outlined in an endowment's original constitution. And since the law today is society's resolution of the social issues of yesterday, some issues of today's governance best practice may influence the laws of tomorrow.

Today's laws are clear about the fiduciary responsibilities of trustees in balancing risk and return without jeopardizing the interests of beneficiaries. While a study by the United Nations's Environment Programme Finance Initiative concluded that there was a threat to share price performance if ethical questions were ignored, it was also agreed that while corporate leaders have to think beyond just making profits, toward how they affect society, it is not their job to save the planet. And a session of the World Economic Forum concluded that good corporate governance and corporate citizenship should simply make good business sense.

Investment strategy involves assessing resources, quantifying objectives and marrying those two with a flexible plan which manages the risk that objectives might not be met. Quantifying objectives involves both a relatively precise budget covering the endowment's operating time horizon, usually a period of one to five years, and a more general long-term, intergenerational objective that is measured in real terms.

The budget will set the level of minimum acceptable annual return required to cover day-to-day operations, including grant-making and administration, and from this will be derived the required level of operational assets. A second element of operational assets arises from investment management transfers and occasional tactical reduction of portfolio risk out of intergenerational assets at appropriate points of the financial cycle. The allocation to different asset classes within intergenerational assets, within the long-term endowment, will be driven by the analysis of valuation criteria and of economic and financial scenarios. The objective with intergenerational asset classes is to 'avoid losers', to diversify among potential winners and to follow a discipline of rebalancing based on relationships, not on returns or fixed weights.

This approach to rebalancing may be contrarian, but not on the grounds that returns themselves are necessarily mean reverting. It is based on the evidence that relationships tend to regress to a mean for given scenarios. Relative valuations can become stretched beyond reasonable limits for any given scenario. 'Avoiding the losers' involves reducing portfolio weight from such asset classes into others where relationships are undervalued, or at the least normal, for the prospective most likely scenarios.

Implementing strategy for an endowment fund involves establishing principles and philosophy and structure and process. Structure and process set the parameters and procedures through which the endowment's mission and objectives are implemented by asset strategy. Structure and process are defined in the Investment Policy Statement (IPS).

Key to implementation is people – those involved on the board of trustees, on the investment committee, in the staffing of endowments and in service provision such as investment management, legal counsel and other consultancy. The key is the right skill and experience, balance and chemistry of people on committees, in the staff and in service providers – especially asset managers.

Implementation involves deciding, monitoring and changing allocation between and within operational and intergenerational assets to balance current and future spending needs and to reflect external scenarios. It involves determining the investment management model appropriate to the size and sophistication of the endowment. It includes assessing styles of asset management and parameters of risk, selecting advisers and custodial relationships. It also requires identification of, and negotiation on costs, especially the remuneration of asset managers. It includes monitoring the achievement of objectives and measuring results both quantitatively and qualitatively.

Implementation needs careful consideration of the benchmarks used for guiding strategy and for measuring investment management and other achievement. Benchmarks inevitably drive investment behavior so both the first- and the second-order effects of benchmarking must be assessed. But performance measurement is about more than simply investment management results. It includes accountability for the outcomes in the broadest sense and at all levels: of the governing body itself, the investment committee and the service providers.

References and Reading Matter

Preface

1. Graham, B. (2003) *The Intelligent Investor* (revised edition). New material by Jason Zweig. New York: Harper Business Essentials.
2. Professor Tobin, quoted in Swensen, D.F. (2000) *Pioneering Portfolio Management*. New York: The Free Press; Simon & Schuster.
   Must read: *The Intelligent Investor* by Graham and *Pioneering Portfolio Management* by Swensen.

Chapter 1: Introduction

1. Wood, Struthers & Co. (1932) *Trusteeship of American Endowments*. New York: Macmillan.
2. Swensen, D.F. (2000) *Pioneering Portfolio Management*. New York: The Free Press; Simon & Schuster.
3. Yale Endowment Report (2005).
4. Moggridge, D. (1983) *Collected Writings of John Maynard Keynes*, Volume XII: 'Economic Articles and Correspondence. Investment and Editorial.' London. Published for the Royal Economic Society by The Macmillan Press; 'Memorandum for Estates Committee, King's College, Cambridge. 8 May 1938. Post Mortem on Investment Policy.'
5. *Collected Writings of John Maynard Keynes*, Volume XII: 'Letter to F.C. Scott, 7 June 1938'.
6. *Collected Writings of John Maynard Keynes*, Volume XII: 'Memorandum for Estates Committee, King's College, Cambridge. 8 May 1938. Post Mortem on Investment Policy.'
7. Wood, Struthers & Co. (1932) *Trusteeship of American Endowments*. New York: Macmillan.
8. Wood, Struthers & Co. (1932) *Trusteeship of American Endowments*. New York: Macmillan.
9. The Ford Foundation in the 1960s (July 1962) *Statement of the Board of Trustees on Policies, Programs and Operations*. Published by the Ford Foundation. (Library of Congress Catalog Card Number 62-18670.)
10. *Harvard Management Company* (2001) and (1994). Harvard Business School case studies.
11. *Yale Endowment Report*. (2004).
12. Schiller R. (2000) *Irrational Exuberance*. Princeton, NJ: Princeton University Press.

13. Sandra J. Champion, AIFA President, Champion and Partners, Inc. (undated) *Leaving a Lasting Legacy*.
14. Dimson, E., Marsh, P. & Staunton, M. (2002) *Triumph of the Optimists: 101 Years of Global Investment Returns*. Princeton, NJ: Princeton University Press.
15. Bernstein, P. (1996) *Against the Gods*. New York: John Wiley & Sons Inc.

Must read: Chapter on 'Long Term Expectations' in Keynes's *General Theory*; *Irrational Exuberance* by Shiller; *Triumph of the Optimists* by Dimson, Marsh & Staunton; *Against the Gods* by Bernstein; Pioneering Portfolio Management by Swensen.

Chapter 2: Language of Return

1. Graham, B. (2003) *The Intelligent Investor* (revised edition). New material by Jason Zweig. New York: Harper Business Essentials.
2. Soros, G. (1987) *The Alchemy of Finance. Reading the Mind of the Market*. New York: Simon & Schuster.
3. Shiller, R. (2000) *Irrational Exuberance*. Princeton, NJ: Princeton University Press.
4. Rogers, F. & Strehle, G. (2005) *Sources of Endowment Growth at Colleges and Universities, 2005*. Common Fund.
5. *Managing Education Endowments* (1968) New York, NY: The Ford Foundation.
6. UK Charity Commissioners: *Guidance on Total Return Investing* (see website).
7. Swensen, D.F. (2000) *Pioneering Portfolio Management*. New York: The Free Press; Simon & Schuster.
8. Wilkie, A.D. (1981) *Indexing Long-Term Financial Contacts*. London: Institute of Actuaries.
9. Ramsey, P. (1968) *Tudor Economic Problems*. London: Victor Gollancz.
10. Swensen, D.F. (2000) *Pioneering Portfolio Management*. New York: The Free Press; Simon & Schuster.
11. Gave, C. (1999) *Indexation and the Allocation of Capital*. London: Gaveco.
12. This quote is sometimes attributed to Mark Twain because it appears in his posthumously published autobiography. But Mark Twain attributed it to Benjamin Disraeli as 'there are three kinds of lies: lies, damned lies and statistics'. Disraeli's biographer, Lord Blake, says there is no evidence that this remark was made by Disraeli but another English politician, Leonard Henry Courtney, gave a speech on proportional representation in New York in 1895 in which the following was said: 'After all, facts are facts, and although we may quote one to another with a chuckle the words of the Wise Statesman, "Lies–damn lies–and statistics" still there are some easy figures which the simplest must understand but the astutest cannot wriggle out of.'
    (*Source*: www1c.btwebworld.com/quote-unquote/p0000149.htm)

See also: Jastram, R.W. (1977) *The Golden Constant, The English and American Experience 1560–1976*. London: John Wiley & Sons Inc.; Homer, S. & Sylla, R. (1996) *A History of Interest Rates*. New Brunswick, NJ: Rutgers University Press.

Chapter 3: Elements of Return

1. Swensen, D.F. (2000) *Pioneering Portfolio Management*. New York: The Free Press; Simon & Schuster.

2. Dimson, E., Marsh, P. & Staunton, M. (2002) *Triumph of the Optimists. 101 Years of Global Investment Returns*. Princeton, NJ: Princeton University Press.
3. National Bureau of Economic Research (1938) *Some theoretical problems suggested by the movements of interest rates, bond yields and stock prices in the United States since 1856*. New York.
4. Keynes, J.M. (1973) *Collected Writings*, Volume VII: 'The General Theory of Employment, Interest and Money'. London: Published for The Royal Economics Society by Macmillan Publishers.
5. Mottram, R.H. (1929) *A History of Financial Speculation*. London: Chatto & Windus.
6. Shiller, R. (2000) *Irrational Exuberance*. Princeton, NJ: Princeton University Press.
7. Bernstein, P. (1996) *Against the Gods*. New York: John Wiley & Sons Inc.
8. Markowitz, H. (March 1952) 'Portfolio Selection', *Journal of Finance*, Volume 7, Number 1. New York: American Finance Association.
9. Keynes, J.M. (1973) *Collected Writings*, Volume VII: 'The General Theory of Employment, Interest and Money.' London: Published for The Royal Economics Society by Macmillan Publishers.

Must read: *Portfolio Selection* by Markovitz.

Chapter 4: Understanding Risk

1. Bernstein, P. (1996) *Against the Gods*. New York: John Wiley & Sons Inc.
2. Adams, J. (1995) *Risk. John Adams*. London: UCL Press.
3. Montier, J. (2002) *Behavioural Finance*. Chichester: John Wiley & Sons.
4. Mandlebrot, B.B. & Hudson, R.L. (2004) *The (Mis)Behaviour of Markets, A Fractal View of Risk, Ruin and Reward*. London: Profile Books Ltd.
5. Sortino, F. (2001) 'From Alpha to Omega', in Sortino, F. & Satchell, S. *Managing Downside Risk in Financial Markets*. Oxford: Butterworth Heinemann.
6. Montier, J. (2002) *Behavioural Finance*. Chichester: John Wiley & Sons; Erb, Harvey & Viskanta (1994) 'Forecasting international equity correlations.' *Financial Analysts Journal*, Nov/Dec.
7. Lowenstein, R. (2001) *When Genius Failed: The Rise and Fall of Long Term Capital Management*. London: Fourth Estate.
8. Keynes, J.M. (1973) *Collected Writings, Volume VII*: 'The General Theory of Employment, Interest and Money'. London. Published for The Royal Economics Society by Macmillan Publishers.
9. Clarkson, R. (2001) FARM: A financial actuarial risk model, in F. Sortino & S. Satchell, *Managing Downside Risk in Financial Markets*. Oxford: Butterworth Heinemann.
10. Denbo, R.S. & Freeman, A. (1998) *Seeing Tomorrow; Re-Writing the Rules of Risk*. New York: John Wiley & Sons Inc.

Chapter 5: Spending Rules

1. Ennis, R.M. & Williamson, J.P. (1976) *Spending Policy for Educational Endowments*. Commonfund Institute.
2. Cary, W.L. & Bright, C.B. (1969) *The Law and Lore of Endowment Funds*. New York: Ford Foundation.

3. Commonfund Benchmarks Study. (2005) *Educational Endowments Report*, Commonfund Institute.
4. Sedlacek, V.O. & Clark, S.E. (2003) *Why Do We Feel So Poor? How the overspending of the 90s has created a crisis in higher education*. Commonfund Institute.
5. Swensen, D.F. (2000) *Pioneering Portfolio Management*. New York: The Free Press; Simon & Schuster.

Chapter 6: Assets for Strategy

1. Schneider, W., DiMeo, R. & Cluck, D.R. (1997) *Asset Management for Endowments and Foundations*. McGraw-Hill. ISBN 0-7863-1070-7.
2. Cary, W.L. & Bright, C.B. (1969) *The Law and Lore of Endowment Funds*. New York: Ford Foundation.
3. Dimson, E., Marsh, P. & Staunton M. (2002) *Triumph of the Optimists*. Princeton, NJ: Princeton University Press.
4. Takahashi, D. (1996) *AIMR Conference on Managing Endowment and Foundation Funds*. Alternative Assets: Pros and Cons or Endowments and Foundations. Charlottesville: Association of Investment Management and Research.
5. Hutton, L. & Strauss, M. (2005) *Asset Allocation: The Case for Diversified Inflation Hedging Strategies*. Commonfund Institute.
6. Brooks, C. & Kat, H.M. (2001) *The Statistical Properties of Hedge Fund Index Returns and Their Implications for Investors*. Working Paper. London: Cass Business School.

See also: Ridley, M. (2004) *How to Invest in Hedge Funds. An Investment Professionals Guide*. London: Kogan Page; Lake, R.A. (1996) *Evaluating and Implementing Hedge Fund Strategies*. London: Euromoney Books.

Chapter 7: Legal, Social and Ethical

The John Wesley quote is the title of four consecutive addresses quoted by John Hancock in his introduction to: *Corporate Social Responsibility* (2004) Kogan Page. ISBN 0-7494-4147-X

1. Cadbury, A. (2002) *Corporate Governance and Chairmanship – A Personal View*. Oxford: Oxford University Press.
2. Smith, A. (1776) *The Wealth of Nations*. (1930 edition by Edwin Canan). London: Methuen & Co.
3. Berle, A.A. & Means, G.C. (1932/1968) *The Modern Corporation and Private Property*. New York: Harcourt, Brace & World.
4. Berle, A.A. (2004) 'The Impact of the Corporation on Classical Economic Theory.' *Journal of Economics*; published in T. Clarke (ed.) *Theories of Corporate Governance*. New York: Routledge.
5. Henderson, D. (2001) *Misguided Virtue*. London: The Institute of Economic Affairs.
6. Friedman, M. (1962) *Capitalism and Freedom*. Chicago: University of Chicago Press.
7. Yale Advisory Committee on Investor Responsibility: *Academic Year 2003–2004 report*.
8. Sparkes, R. (2002) *Socially Responsible Investment: A Global Revolution*. Chichester: John Wiley & Sons.

9. CC14. *Investment of Charitable Funds*. UK Charity Commissioners website.
10. Vogel, D. (2005) *The Market for Virtue: The Potential and Limits of Corporate Social Responsibility*. Brookings Institute Press.

   See also: Clarke, T. (2004) *Theories of Corporate Governance*. New York: Routledge; 'Useful Guidelines – Charities and Social Investment.' UK Charity Commissioners website:
   www.charity-commission.gov.uk/supportingcharities/pdfs/casi.pdf

Chapter 8: Understanding Strategy

1. Wood, Struthers & Co. (1932) *Trusteeship of American Endowments*. New York: Macmillan.
2. Walsh, J & Gribbon, D. (1984) *The J. Paul Getty Museum and Its Collections: A Museum for the New Century*. Report to the Trustees. Quoted in D.M. Darst (2003) *The Art of Asset Allocation*. New York: McGraw-Hill.
3. Sedlacek, V.O. & Clark, S.E. (2003) *Why Do We Feel So Poor? How the overspending crisis of the 90s has created a crisis in higher education*. Commonfund Institute.
4. MacKay, C. (1980) *Extraordinary Popular Delusions and the Madness of Crowds*. Original publisher: Richard Bentley. London, 1852. New York: Harmony Books and Crown Trade Paperbacks.
5. Bufferd, A.S. (2003) *Asset Allocation in a Universe of Choices*. Presentation to the Investment Management Forum for Endowments and Foundations. Scottsdale, AZ.

Chapter 9: Implementing Strategy

1. Joseph Rowntree Charitable Trust. *Statement of Investment Policy*. The Garden House, Water end, York, YO30 6WQ. (01904 627810)
2. The Jessie Noyes Foundation, 6 East Street, 12F, New York, NY 10016. (212 684 6577) (noyes@noyes.org)
3. Bufferd, A.S. (2003) *Asset Allocation in a Universe of Choices*. Presentation to the Investment Management Forum for Endowments and Foundations. Scottsdale, AZ.
4. Olson, R.L. (2003) *Investing in Pension Funds and Endowments*. New York: McGraw-Hill.
5. The David and Lucille Packard Foundation: *Code of Conduct and Statement of Values for Board of Trustees*.
6. Swensen, D.F. (2000) *Pioneering Portfolio Management*. New York: The Free Press; Simon & Schuster.
7. Neff, J.B. (1996) 'Managing an endowment Fund: The University of Pennsylvania Model.' *Proceedings of the AIMR Seminar on Managing Endowment and Foundation Funds*, 25–26, March 1996. Philadelphia, Pennsylvania: Association of Investment Management and Research.
8. *NACUBO Endowment Study* (annual). Prepared by TIAA–CREF for National Association of College and University Business Officers. Commonfund Benchmarks Study, 2005. Commonfund Institute.
9. The Big Sister Foundation of Boston: *Investment Policy Statement*.
10. Siegel, L. (2003) *Benchmarks and Investment Management*. Charlottesville: Association of Investment Management and Research.

11. Ellis, C.D. (1985) *Investment Policy. How to Win the Loser's Game*. Homewood, Illinois: Dow Jones-Irwin.
12. Commonfund Benchmark Studies (2005).
13. Olson, R.L. (2003) *Investing in Pension Funds and Endowments*. New York.
14. Ellis, C.D. & Vertin, J.R. (1989) *Classics: An Investor's Anthology*. The Institute of Chartered Financial Analysts, Homewood, Illinois: Dow Jones-Irwin.

Must read: *Investment Policy* by Ellis; *Classics I* and *Classics II* by Ellis.

Glossary

This glossary is designed to be simple and to cover the investment language most likely to be heard by trustees of endowment funds. Inevitably this includes a few economic, legal, accounting and statistical terms.

ACT – *see* Advanced Corporation Tax.

ADR – *see* American Depositary Receipt.

AIBD – *see* Association of International Bond Dealers.

AIM – *see* Alternative Investment Market.

ALM – *see* Asset/Liability Matching.

APR – *see* Annual Percentage Rate.

APT – *see* Arbitrage Pricing Theory.

Absolute return – measures the actual appreciation or depreciation of an asset as a percentage movement to the purchase price in nominal terms. Absolute real return is absolute nominal return deflated by inflation price indices. Absolute return investment strategies are 'market neutral' or 'non-directional' strategies, meaning they seek to add value to a risk-free or cash return irrespective of the direction of markets. (*See* Relative return.)

'A' shares – ordinary shares that do not give the owner voting rights.

Accretion – increase in value of an asset due to natural changes outside the control of market forces, e.g. livestock.

Accrual – a payment event occurring in this period but not settled until the next period, applies to income receivable but not yet paid and added to a price on a bond when exchanged.

Accumulation units – units of a fund whose earnings are retained within the unit thus increasing the value.

Active management – management to outperform a benchmark index, whether the benchmark is cash (absolute return) or an index that is representative of an asset class. The fund manager will select investments that are different in proportion, or even different from those in the index in such a way that the combination selected will provide a higher rate of return, or a lower risk or both, than the index itself.

Active reward – the incremental return on a portfolio due to active management. (see alpha).

Active risk – the portfolio risk in excess of the risk on the benchmark, measured as tracking error.

Ad valorem – usually refers to management fees and means they are charged as a percentage of the value of the fund.

Advanced Corporation Tax (ACT) – early installment of UK Corporation Tax deducted from gross dividends and offset against a full year's corporation tax.

Alpha – a measure of the risk-adjusted performance or excess expected return. Alpha is synonymous with misvaluation. A stock with positive alpha is one that is undervalued relative to others with the same systematic risk. A manager who 'adds alpha' generates return in excess of a benchmark portfolio.

Alternative Investment Market (AIM) – a 'junior' market for listing companies in the UK.

Alternative investments – investments other than listed securities and vehicles of listed securities such as unit trusts or mutual funds, and cash deposits. A name ususually given to investments in commodities, private equity, real estate and hedge funds.

American Depositary Receipt (ADR) – a US dollar-denominated security issued by a US depositary bank representing a share listed in another country. It allows US investors to buy international shares without having to buy the relevant currency first and to open an overseas brokerage account.

American option – option that can be exercised at any time before expiry. (*See* European exercise or Bermudan exercise.)

Amortize – the process of writing off debt, or accounting for large payments, over a period of time by putting aside periodic fixed amounts.

Annual Percentage Rate (APR) – true rate of interest on a loan.

Annuity – a series of regular payments usually bought with a lump sum.

Arbitrage – simultaneous purchase and sale of different but related investments with a view to exploiting a price differential between them to generate a risk-free profit.

Arbitrage Pricing Theory (APT) – developed in the 1970s, APT asserts that expected returns are derived from the expected returns of an unknown number of underlying factors.

Arithmetic mean – also known as a 'simple average', is the sum of a series of numbers divided by the number of items in that series i.e. $(2 + 3 + 4 + 5 + 6)/5 = 4$. (*See* mean.)

Asian option – an option that has an exercise value that depends on the average value of the underlying instrument over a given period of time.

Asset allocation – investing between different asset classes within a portfolio to achieve an optimum balance or risk and reward. Strategic asset allocation is long term and usually related to the liabilities of the fund. Tactical Asset Allocation (TAA) seeks to exploit perceived short-term anomalies between asset classes.

Asset-backed investment – an investment that pays interest but is backed by tangible assets as collateral. (*See* Covered bond and SPV.)

Asset/Liability Matching (ALM) – matching assets that provide similar cash inflows with pre-determined cash outflows (such as for pension funds)/analysis of a company's, or institution's, liabilities and assets to determine the financial position and health of the company.

Asset strip – buying a business to sell off the underlying assets for more than the purchase cost of the business.

Asset swaps – sale of the bond element of a convertible security while retaining the option element. (*See* Synthetic instruments.)

At best – the process of buying or selling a security in the market 'at best' indicates that the transaction is carried out immediately at the best current price available.

At-the-money – when the exercise price is equivalent to the spot price of the underlying security, or in the case of a mortgage pass through, the coupon rate is the same as the prevailing mortgage rate.

Attribution analysis – analysis of returns attributable to the difference between elements of the portfolio return relative to elements of the benchmark index return which disaggregates the difference in to allocation effect, selection effect and an interaction effect. The last term arises because the differences are multiplicative rather than additive. (*See* Contribution analysis.)

Authorized investment fund – a UK fund that is authorized by the Financial Services Authority to be marketed to the public.

Authorized share capital – maximum number of shares that a company can issue specified in a company's articles of incorporation.

bp – *see* Basis point.

Back door listing – the process whereby a company obtains listing on an exchange by acquiring or merging with another company that is already listed.

Back end (or 'exit') charge or load – a charge by fund managers on a sale of units in a fund. The charge becomes due only upon 'exit' from the fund. (*See* Front-end load.)

Back office – part of the office of a financial institution which administers business. (*See* Front office.)

Back testing – testing past data to discover patterns that may have predictive ability.

Back to back loans – the process of repaying one loan by taking a new loan.

Backwardation – a position in which the price of a security or derivative is lower at the more distant delivery date than at the current delivery date. Government bonds with a fixed coupon higher than the prevailing base rate usually show signs of backwardation as the par value is less than the spot price.

Balanced fund – an investment fund that spreads the capital and therefore risk across a wide range of asset classes such as cash, shares, bonds and property. The opposite to a balanced fund is a specialist fund.

Balloon loan (bullet loan) – a loan that has one large redemption amount on maturity but a low coupon in the meantime ensuring a lower capital outlay. The redemption amount is typically covered by securing refinancing and obtaining a new loan.

Barrier option – an option that terminates when it reaches a given barrier.

Base currency – the currency in which a portfolio is measured. Usually, but not always, the currency of domicility of the investor.

Base rate – an interest rate set by the country's central bank (or government) which reflects the cost of borrowing at zero risk. A change to the base rate has an immediate knock-on effect to the rest of the money markets.

Basis – the difference between the price of a future and the current (spot) price of the underlying instrument (hence basis risk, market risk arising as a result of this difference).

Basis point (bp) – one basis point is equal to 1/100th of 1%. Used in the description of yield.

Bear – an individual who holds a view that the market will decline.

Bear market – widespread decline in prices, opposite of a bull market.

Bear spread – an option spread designed to be profitable if the underlying investment declines in price.

Bear trap – a signal indicating the end of a rising trend that proves to be false.

Bearer security – security that is evidenced by possession of the certificate of title.

Behavioral finance – the application of psychology to the behavior of financial markets and market participants.

Bellweather – a bond or stock the price of which moves closely with market trends.

Benchmark – a standard of comparison against which the performance and risk of a fund, or any component of a fund, can be compared. Benchmarks of relative performance are generally market capitalization-weighted indices. Absolute performance is usually measured against a risk-free asset. (*See* Risk-free assets.)

Bermudan exercise – provision that allows the exercise of an option several days before expiry of the option.

Beta – a quantitative measure of the volatility of a security or fund relative to the market as a whole. A beta below 1 shows that the security or fund is less volatile than the market. Above 1 it is more volatile. A beta of 1–2 implies a +12% return for a +10% market return.

Bid–offer spread – the difference, or range, between the price one can buy and sell the same security at any given time. The spread represents the 'fee' that the market (broker or fund) takes to carry out the trade.

Bid price – the price at which securities or funds are bought by a market maker. Bid price might include a 'back-end' charge on funds sold back by an investor to the fund's manager.

Big board – New York Stock Exchange. (*See* Wall Street.)

Binomial – method used to calculate a return using a binomial tree that analyzes expected outcomes.

Black–Scholes option pricing model – refers to a model of option pricing developed in 1973 by the two Nobel prize-winning economists who gave the model its name. The model incorporates the time value of money, the period to exercise of the option, the exercise price of the option and, crucially, a term for risk defined as volatility. This term assumes that the price or value of the underlying asset moves in a random way that can be captured by statistics as a normal or bell curve which gives a symmetrical pattern of risk.

Block – a large holding of shares in a company or fund. A block trade is the purchase or sale of a large position in one trade rather than an accumulation over time.

Blue chip – any share in a large, well-established company with steady and long-term profits and dividends.

Bollinger bands – a band defined by a trading range based on standard deviations from moving average.

Bond ratings – used to determine and to group those bonds with similar credit worthiness. The rating is usually a series of letters with AAA being the most credit worthy and C being the least. (*see* Credit rating agencies.)

Bond – a security that may pay interest and repays capital at a specified future point in time. A bondholder is a creditor of the entity which issues a bond and ranks ahead of equity holders on liquidation of the entity. Long-term bonds are generally those with a life of more than 10 years.

Book value – the value of an asset (or liability) as recorded in the company's accounts. The book value may or may not reflect the current market price. (*see* Mark-to-market.)

Bottom up – style of asset management whereby securities are selected using factors at the company, rather than the macro- or micro-economic, level.

Bound influence regression – a regression technique that underweights the most influential observations.

Brady bonds – named after Nicholas Brady, US Treasury Secretary in the early 1990s. These were bonds issued by the Mexican Government in restructuring its debt. Now evolved into an IMF/World Bank scheme for restructuring Emerging Market sovereign debt backed by US Treasuries.

Building societies – UK equivalents of US 'Savings & Loans', which provide finance for housing.

Bull – an individual who holds a view that the market will rise.

Bull market – widespread rise in prices. Opposite of a bear market.

Bullet loan – see Balloon loan.

Business to Business (B2B) – business between two businesses rather than between a business and an end-customer or client of a business.

Buy & Hold – a strategy of purchasing investments for the long term rather than trading them for short-term profit.

CAPM – *see* Capital Asset Pricing Model.

CBO – *see* Collateralized Obligations.

CD – *see* Certificate of Deposit.

CDO – *see* Collateralized Obligations.

CDS – *see* Credit Default Swap.

CEER – *see* Certain Equivalent Expected Return.

CFRR – *see* Cash Flow Rate of Return.

CLO – *see* Collateralized Obligations.

CMBS – *see* Commercial Mortgage Backed Securities.

CMO – *see* Collateralized Obligations.

CTAs – Commodity Trading Advisers.

CTD – *see* Cheapest to Deliver.

Cable – exchange rate between sterling and the US dollar. The origin of the term is said to derive from the first cable telephone line between the UK and the USA across the Atlantic. Perhaps also due to confirmation of trades by telex, which was often described as cable.

Call option – the buyer of the option has the right to call (buy) the underlying security from the seller.

Call premium – the price of an option or difference between price at which a company can call its bonds and the face value of the bonds.

Callable bond – a bond that allows the issuer to repurchase the bond at a specified price and time before maturity.

Calmar Ratio – similar to the Sterling Ratio in using drawdown as a measure of risk. Calmar Ratio = Fund's 3-year annualized return/maximum drawdown over past three years.

Cap – a derivative instrument that protects against rising interest rates.

Caplet – an option that provides a cap.

Capital Asset Pricing Model (CAPM) – a method for valuing stocks by looking at the risk and the expected return. The CAPM implies that the total return on a security will be equal to the risk-free return plus the security's beta times the expected excess return. An investor will demand a greater return if the risk is greater and the CAPM will show which stocks offer better return for a given amount of risk.

Capital charge – a management charge made to the fund's capital rather than the growth it has produced.

Capital gain – profit on sale of an investment. Short- or long-term gains are taxed differently in the USA and the UK, so the definition is important to entities that are not tax-exempt.

Capital markets – the markets in which debt and equity – that is, bonds and stocks or shares – are issued and traded. The 'primary market' describes the market where such instruments are first issued (*see* IPO or Initial Public Offering) and the 'secondary market' describes their subsequent trading.

Capital protected – a fund that carries a guarantee that the capital sum invested will be safe and incur no losses. The guarantee comes at a price as the techniques used to insure against capital losses ultimately affect overall portfolio performance.

Capitalization – a company or fund's capitalization is the sum of the value of all the issued shares. It represents the total value that the market places on the company.

Carry trade – an arbitrage trading technique where money is borrowed at a low rate of interest and then used to buy fixed income securities with a higher interest rate.

Cash – assets with a maturity of less than one year which are liquid and regarded as risk free, such as Treasury Bills, Certificate of Deposit (CD), balances at highly rated banks (cash at bank).

Cash equivalents – investments that can be quickly and easily converted to cash, usually with maturities no longer than 180 days, e.g. Bank bills, Treasury notes.

Cash Flow Rate of Return (CFRR) – internal rate of return or dollar-weighted rate of return.

Certain Equivalent Expected Return (CEER) – the expected reward which, if it was known with certainty, would give the same satisfaction to an investor (utility) as the risky investment that is being considered.

Certificate of Deposit (CD) – a certificate issued by a bank declaring that a certain amount has been deposited at a certain interest rate for a certain duration of time.

Chartist – an individual who monitors the price movement of stocks and markets on charts to determine potential predictive patterns or trends to exploit for trading. (*See also* Technical analyst.)

Cheapest to Deliver (CTD) – the cheapest security to deliver against expiry of a derivative contract.

Chinese Wall – a system of controls and procedures to ensure that there is no conflict of interest between different departments within a financial institution. At its most simple a Chinese Wall will be a physical barrier stopping employees from obtaining access to sensitive information such as deploying employees in different offices, e.g. stockbroking and investment management.

Chinese-ing – taking a reverse position in merger arbitrage to exploit a merger deal breaking down.

City – generic term, derived from the 'City of London' which is also known as the 'Square Mile'. Originally the City was the area of London administered by the Corporation of London, representing a financial district or group of mostly wholesale more than retail financial activities in the UK. Often now refers simply to all financial activities in London including banking, investment management, insurance, etc.

Closed-end(ed) fund – a commingled fund, usually in the form of a company that is listed on a stock exchange, where capital is raised by initial subscription, and occasional subsequent share issue, but is otherwise closed to further investment. Those who invest in such a fund either exit through trading on a stock exchange if the fund is listed or have to wait till some predetermined date when the fund is liquidated and investors repaid. (*See* Open-ended fund.)

Closed period – period prior to a company's release of results during which directors may not deal in the company's shares.

Coefficient of Determination ('R' squared) – the fraction of variance in the dependent variable that can be explained by the independent variable. The fraction is expressed as a number between 0 and 1, with 1 being a perfect explanation.

Collar – conditions in a deal structure (or option) which define limits such as upper and lower limit of interest rate on a floating rate note.

Collateral – security pledged as guarantee of repayment.

Collateralized Obligations – Collateralized Bond Obligation (CBO): investment grade bond backed by a pool of junk bonds. Collateralized Debt Obligation (CDO): an investment grade security backed by assets that are loans, bonds or other forms of debt. Collateralized Mortgage Obligation (CMO): a bond that is structured to pay different rates of return according to different levels of risk backed by the same investment or basket of investments. The investments behind the CMO can be corporate loans (where the CMO becomes known as a Collateralized Loan Obligation or CLO); bonds; asset-backed securities; or credit default swaps, which are derivative instruments linked to the risk of corporate default. Synthetic CDOs, known as SCOs, comprise credit default swaps and are not backed by cash bonds. The pricing of CDOs depends on the perceived correlation of price movements between the underlying assets. Pricing depends on the risk of default of any one of the basket of underlying assets.

Collective investment schemes – combinations of securities into a fund such as a mutual fund, investment trust, Limited Partnership, OEIC. (*See* Commingled fund.)

Commercial Mortgage Backed Securities (CMBS) – securities secured by loans with commercial rather than residential property.

Commercial paper – short-term, unsecured (less than 270 day maturity) company finance in the form of promissory notes.

Commingled fund – a pooled investment fund also known as a collective investment vehicle or a common fund.

Commodity Trading Advisers (CTAs) – describes a hedge fund style of investing whereby futures contracts, either on physical commodities or financial instruments, are used to create leveraged directional positions. Also known as 'Managed futures'.

Commission sharing – a process whereby commission paid to brokers not identified as being for pure execution, is specifically allocated as payment for research, on the instructions of the client, to third-party providers of that research. One of the brokers may be the financial institution that executes the trade.

Common factor – a factor which influences the risk and return of a number of different securities and is therefore common to them. Examples of common factors are industry groupings (oil for instance), currency exposure, degree of leverage.

Commodity – a tradable physical item that can usually be processed and refined such as sugar, coal, gold, etc. (See CTA.)

Common stock – security that represents ownership or 'equity' in a corporation. Common stocks rank after all other creditors but receive the benefit of profits of the corporation after all other claims.

Compliance – the process of complying with laws and regulations and internal rules.

Compound interest – reinvestment of interest that earns more interest, which is reinvested. Continuous compounding is interest compounded continuously rather than at fixed intervals.

Confidence region – a statistical term which describes a range of values within which it can be determined with a given degree of confidence that a random value will fall. For instance, within a normal distribution, a 66% confidence region, in which a variable may be expected to fall 66% or two-thirds of the time, is one standard deviation from a mean. So if an average annual return is 10% with one standard deviation equal to 12%, in every two out of three years one can expect a return of 10% plus or minus 12%. The confidence region is therefore −2% to +22%.

Consensus forecast – an average of analysts forecasts.

Consol – perpetual UK Government bond.

Contango – forward prices exceed current (spot) prices.

Contribution analysis – disagregation of total return figure for total portfolio in to component parts. Found by multiplying return of each of the component parts of the portfolio by the weighting in the portfolio and adding up the result, which equals the overall return.

Conversion ratio – number of shares with which a convertible bond may be exchanged.

Convertible – a bond or preferred stock or share that pays interest but includes an option to convert into underlying common stock or equity at a predetermined price and time.

Convertible arbitrage – Anomalies may appear between the price or value of the convertible and the underlying common stock or equity. Convertible arbitrage seeks to exploit these anomalies. A number of hedge funds specialize in this field.

Convexity – a measure of bond price sensitivity to underlying interest rates change but to the extent that the change is non-linear. (*See also* Duration.)

Core portfolio – the majority of a fund's assets invested in such a way as to control risk tightly, especially market risk. The balance of the fund's assets can then be invested in a non-core or 'satellite' portfolio which will incur much greater risk in the pursuit of above market returns (alpha).

Corporate bonds – bonds issued by corporations. They exhibit all the usual qualities of Government bonds but the issue size is usually less, as is the credit rating.

Corporate governance – issues associated with the management practices, company structure, board structure. The investor is usually most concerned with the level of influence the shareholders have over the running of the company and the degree to which the non-executive directors protect shareholder interests.

Correlation – a statistical term giving the strength of a linear relationship between two random variables. If two stocks or stock indices are said to be correlated then the prices will move together in the same direction.

Counterparty – the person or organization (Principal) who issues a security in the primary market or is on the other side of a trade in the secondary market (*see* Capital markets). Counterparty risk is the risk that the counterparty fails to meet the financial obligation, resulting in loss of all or part of the transaction.

Coupon – a bond's interest rate. The coupon may be fixed, floating or zero rated and, depending on the issuance, will be payed at different times/frequency. (*See also* Strips.)

Covariance – the tendency for different investment returns to have similar outcomes. The magnitude of covariance is a measure of the extent to which the returns move together.

Covenant – clause in a loan agreement and status of tenant of a property: good covenant being a secure and credit worthy tenant.

Covenant Information Ratio – an agreement between a client and a money manager on the information ratio (*see* Information Ratio) the manager is expected to produce.

Covered bond – a bond that is backed by mortgage portfolios or public finance loans that are ringfenced from the operations of the issuing intermediary (bank) but stay on the balance sheet of the issuer so that investors have recourse to both the underlying assets and the assets of the intermediary. In the case of traditional mortgage-backed securities, the bonds are issued by a Special Purpose Vehicle (SPV) and the assets are removed from the balance sheet of the issuer.

Credit Default Swap (CDS) – a financial contract between two parties where the buyer pays a periodic fee to the seller in order to purchase 'insurance' in case of a credit event on the underlying security.

Credit derivatives – financial instruments used to mitigate or to assume specific forms of credit risk.

Credit event – any event whereby the perceived credit-worthiness of an institution (company, government, supra-government) is changed, such as a default on debt repayment. Most usually a credit event will be reflected by a rating agency, such as Moody's, changing the credit rating of a company.

Credit rating – measure of credit quality, usually of a bond, assessing likelihood of default. Measurement is by a rating agency such as Standard & Poor's or Moody's.

Credit risk – the risk of a third party defaulting on its obligations. Measured by credit score.

Credit spread – difference in yields between instruments of different credit quality.

Cum dividend – 'with dividend' a share that is trading so that the buyer rather than the seller will receive the next dividend payment. (*See* Ex-dividend.)

Cumulative return – returns from different continuous periods accumulated by multiplying together.

Currency carry-trade – the process of borrowing money in a foreign country where interest rates are low and investing in a second country with higher interest rates. This seems like an easy way to make money but there is additional risk exposure due to the possibility of adverse movements in the currency exchange rate.

Currency overlay – independent management of currency exposures implicit in a cross-border portfolio of assets.

Currency risk – the risk borne by an investment in a security that is denominated in a foreign currency due to a negative movement in that currency against the base currency. The 'actual' value of the security may not have fallen but after currency exchange rates are applied the investment has lost value.

Cushion bonds – bonds selling at a premium having a higher than average coupon, which cushions the price against volatility.

Custodian – any financial institution that keeps physical custody of share certificates and other legal documents on behalf of clients for safe-keeping.

Cyclical stocks – those stocks whose market valuation changes as the business cycle changes. Typically, any company whose predominant activity is business to business will be cyclical.

DCF – *see* Discounted Cash Flow.

DWR – *see* Dollar-Weighted Return.

Dead cat bounce – a temporary upward reversal of a trend fall in prices.

Debenture – a debt security backed by the credit of the issuer and providing payment of interest at given intervals.

Debt – loans or bonds issued as debt, such as mortgages. The debt ratio is the ratio of the debt issuer's obligation to the issuer's assets.

Dedicated portfolio – a portfolio of securities structured to meet a set of given liabilities.

Default risk – the risk a company, or institution, might default on its debt obligations. Default is failure to pay interest or repay principal on the date specified.

Defeasance – termination of the rights and interests of bondholders.

Deflation – the opposite to inflation, where prices of goods and services fall over time. Not to be confused with disinflation.

Delivery – settlement of financial transaction by exchange of the underlying instrument, such as futures, for cash. Physical delivery is settlement by a specific underlying instrument.

Delta – equivalent to the hedge ratio: the sensitivity of the price of an option to change in the price of the underlying asset.

Delta one arbitrage – arbitrage between groups of, or single, securities where the delta (*see* Delta) is neutral.

Denomination – face or nominal value.

Depositary – central agency for depositing securities usually allowing transfers to be effected by computerized book-entries rather than physically exchange certificates.

Derivative – a security, the price and value of which is linked to, or derived from, another asset, currency or commodity.

Dilution – diminution in the proportion of a company's earnings to which a share is entitled.

Directed commission – a client may request the fund manager to deal through a given stock broker to generate commission to pay for a service.

Directed trust – a custodian with investment responsibility such as for cash reserves.

Discount – extent to which a price is below its value.

Discounted Cash Flow (DCF) – a mathematical analysis used to compare similar investments by taking future income and discounting it to a present value.

Discount factor – the number by which cash flows are multiplied to obtain a present value.

Discretionary fund – fund that the trustee or manager has the discretion to manage without reference to the client for investment decisions.

Disinflation – the process of a fall in the rate of inflation. There is still inflation in the economy but the rate of inflation falls. As example, if three months ago the rate of inflation was 4% and now it is only 3% then it can be said that there is disinflation in the economy even though prices are still increasing.

Disintermediation – withdrawal of funds from an intermediary to invest directly.

Distressed debt securities – bonds or other securities where the rating has fallen below investment grade. Also known as Junk bonds. The fall in rating will be due to the issuing entity being perceived to have difficulty meeting its obligations to pay interest. This may be an entity that is in, or close to, bankruptcy or, in the USA, is filing for protection under Chapter 11 of the US Bankruptcy Code. Chapter 11 allows the company to continue to trade. Distressed debt is also the name given to a hedge fund style that exploits anomalies in distressed debt.

Distribution – payments to investors of either income or realized gains; statistical terms describing an array of data.

Diversification – the reduction is risk that is obtained either simply by spreading a portfolio across many different investments or, more particularly, by investing in assets that are not positively correlated.

Dividend – the proportion of a company's profits paid out to shareholders, usually declared as dividend per share.

Dividend cover – the number of times a company could pay its most recent net dividend out of its profits after tax.

Dividend yield – the division of the dividend rate by the share price. The dividend yield represents the return on investment at the current market price, assuming the dividend does not change.

Dollar cost averaging – investing the same amount of money each month so that more shares are bought when prices are depressed and fewer when prices are high leading, in a volatile market, to an average 'in-price' that is lower than a straight average of the all the prices that have been paid.

Dollar-Weighted Return (DWR) – also known as the internal rate of return or cash flow rate of return (CFRR). *See* internal rate of return (IRR) and time-weighted return (TWR).

Double tax agreement – agreement between countries that tax paid in another country can be offset against domestic tax on the same income to prevent double taxation.

Downward deviation – a calculation that accounts for those returns that fall below a minimum acceptable return (MAR).

Dragon – once referred to the economies of the second wave of newly industrialized Asian nations such as Indonesia, Philippines, Thailand, or China.

Drawdown – in hedge fund terminology, a drawdown is a decline in values from local peak to local trough. In banking and capital terminology a drawdown is the amount of money paid out of a total sum committed but not yet paid.

Drop lock – level at which a floating interest rate becomes fixed.

Due diligence – investigation into a company or individual's background and financial reliability.

Duration – weighted average term to maturity of the cash flows of a bond. Duration measures the sensitivity of a bond to changes in interest rates. It measures the amount of time taken for an investor to receive half the present value of all future payments from the bond using the bond's yield as the discount factor. A bond duration of 4 means that bond price will change by approximately 4% for every 1 percentage point change in yield. Higher coupon bond tend to have lower durations; zero coupon bonds have durations equal to their maturities. 'Partial duration' and 'key rate duration' are measures which focus on exposure to changes in, respectively, the par yield curve or the spot yield curve. (*See* Yield curve.)

EAFE – The Europe, Australia and Far East Index from Morgan Stanley Capital International. A market-capitalization weighted index used as a benchmark by US institutions to represent the universe of non-domestic listed investment equity opportunity in the major international markets.

EBITDA – Earnings Before Interest, Tax, Depreciation and Amortization. This is used as a cross-border comparison for companies that have different accounting rules and tax regimes. (*See* Enterprise value added.)

ECU – *see* Euro.

EDGAR – Electronic Data Gathering, Analysis and Retrieval System. The SEC's electronic system for receiving and displaying US company filings.

EGM – Extraordinary General Meeting. A meeting called to consider and authorize special events that normally require 75% of the voting shares to pass.

EPS – *see* Earnings Per Share.

ERISA – Employee Retirement Income Security Act.

ESOP – Employee Stock Ownership Plan.

ETFs – *see* Exchange Traded Funds.

EVA – *see* Enterprise Value Added.

Earnings – profit available to shareholders after all expenses, including preference dividends, but before extraordinary items.

Earnings Per Share (EPS) – A company's share price divided by earnings per share after tax but before extraordinary items. Historic EPS refers to the last published earnings. Forward EPS refers to the current share price divided by the forecast earnings per share.

Economic value added – *see* Enterprise value added.

Economic rent – profit in excess of a normal competitive level.

Efficient frontier – a series of points that mark the optimal set of portfolios, in terms of highest return to variance, across the spectrum of risk.

Emerging growth – countries or companies that are at an early stage of 'economic take-off'.

Emerging markets – stock markets in countries that are deemed to be developing economies.

Endowment – the permanent funds of a non-profit-making institution. A 'true' or 'permanent' endowment refers to those assets, the use of which is restricted by mandate of the donor. Quasi-endowments are assets that carry no restriction as to their use. 'Term' endowments are restricted for a period of time.

Enhanced indexation – creation of portfolios that replicate index returns with an element of added alpha. The correlation of return with the underlying benchmark will be very high but the return will be enhanced.

Enterprise Value Added (EVA) – Enterprise value is a measure of a company's value. Calculated as market capitalization plus debt and preferred shares, minus cash and cash equivalents.

Equity – common and preferred stock representing the ownership of a company and entitled to all the financial benefits of a company after those with a prior claim, such as creditors and loan holders, have been paid. The term may also include convertible and warrant holders.

Ethical funds – *see* Socially responsible investment. Those funds whose investment choices must meet predetermined criteria with regard to the activity of the company and to environmental and social considerations.

Euro – European currency unit (formerly ECU).

Eurobonds – bonds that are traded internationally.

Euro-dollars – US dollars deposited and traded internationally. Euro-dollar deposits are those that are deposited with a bank outside the USA.

European option – option that can only be exercised on final expiry date.

Event driven – a hedge fund strategy that takes advantage of price movements on corporate events such as mergers.

Exceptional items – *see* Extraordinary items.

Excess return – the return in excess of a risk free rate. Also describes the return in excess of a benchmark return.

Exchange Traded Funds (ETFs) – exchange traded group of securities structured as an open-ended fund but usually representing an index.

Excise tax – IRC Section 4940 requiring US foundations to pay 2% tax on net investment income including gains. The tax rate falls to 1% (with 1% to grant-making) if the average payout over five years exceeds the mandatory payout. (*see* Mandatory payout.)

Ex-dividend (XD) – a share is traded 'xd' during a period before a dividend is paid in order to have time to identify those on the share register to whom the dividend should be distributed. The share price will reflect the amount of dividend payment due.

Ex-rights – acquisition of shares without the right to shares recently issued in a 'rights issue'. (*see* Rights issue.)

Exempt funds – funds designed for institutions that are exempt from tax.

Exercise price – price at which an underlying security may be bought from (in the case of a call) or sold to ('put on') the seller of the option. (*Same as* Strike price.)

Ex-gratia – an extra payment that the payee is not contractually bound to make. An ex-gratia payment might be made where it is felt that services or conditions are such that the payee has a moral, rather than legal, obligation to offer payment.

Exit charge – see 'back end' charge levied on redemption of shares or units.

Expected return – the mean of the probability distribution of potential returns; average of possible returns weighted by their probability of occurring.

Expected value – the mean or average.

Extra-Market Covariance (XMC) – the risk in return due to extra-market common factors. Market or systematic risk, specific risk and market timing risk are the other elements of portfolio risk. (*See* Portfolio risk.)

Extraordinary items – gains or losses that arise from events that are not part of normal trading activity. Different from 'exceptional items', which are gains or losses arising from normal trading activity but are outside the normal range of size.

FISBO – for sale by owner, implying a sale that involves no sales commission and therefore is better priced.

FHLMC – *see* Federal Home Loans Mortgage Corporation.

FOREX – foreign exchange.

FRA – *see* Forward Rate Agreement.

FRN – *see* Floating Rate Note.

FSA – Financial Services Authority, the UK's financial regulatory authority.

Face value – the value of a bond that is shown on the bond certificate (par value or nominal value). The face value is usually the amount payable upon maturity and not the market value; however the market value and the face value will converge as the day of maturity draws nearer.

Factoring – acquisition of a company's receivable accounts and collection of the debt.

Fallen angel – a bond that has been downgraded from investment grade to junk.

Fannie Mae – Federal National Mortgage Association (FNMA). Government sponsored but privately owned corporation that purchases mortgages from lenders and provides a secondary market in federally guaranteed or insured as well as conventional mortgages (*see also* Freddie Mac.)

Fat tail risk – higher incidence of events at the extremities of a distribution than a normal distribution would imply.

Federal funds – Banks' non-interest-bearing deposits at the Federal Reserve.

Fed funds rate – US interbank borrowing rate for overnight money and an indicator of Federal Reserve monetary policy.

Federal Home Loans Mortgage Corporation (FHLMC) – provides a secondary market in conventional residential mortgages. (*See also* Fannie Mae.)

Federal Reserve – the Central Bank of the USA, established in 1913, decades after the previous Central Bank was closed down. The system is governed by the Federal Reserve Board.

Feeder fund – a fund that is used to 'feed' money into another. It is a way of raising money in one jurisdiction, using one fund structure to invest in another which may already be established.

Fibonacci studies – a form of technical analysis using charts and numeric relationships to anticipate changes in trend.

Fiduciary – a person or an entity that bears legal responsibility for the investments of others. Trustees of a fund are therefore fiduciaries of the fund.

Financial engineering – creating new financial products and company structures from existing products and structures to achieve a different result.

Financial leverage – borrowing or debt.

Financial risk – risk attributable to debt in the structure of an entity.

Fiscal year – an accounting period that covers 12 consecutive months. Sometimes referred to the 12 months ending in March because this is the tax year in the USA and the UK as distinct from the calendar year which ends on December 31.

Fitch – a rating service for municipal, corporate and agency bonds.

Fixed income/interest – any investment that supplies a fixed flow of income such as a bond or annuity. The term is applied, somewhat confusingly, to the bond markets as a whole even though many bonds do not provide a 'fixed' rate of interest being either zero interest or floating rate.

Fixed income arbitrage – a hedge fund strategy that exploits anomalies in the fixed income markets such as yield curve anomalies and volatility differences.

Flash report – early data before final figures are confirmed.

Flip-flop note – a note that allows switching between different types of debt.

Flotation – listing of a company's shares on the stock market.

Floater – a bond that has a coupon that fluctuates with changes in a designated interest rate.

Floating lien – general lien over assets. (*See* Lien.)

Floating Rate Note (FRN) – a 'floater' where the interest rate moves in line with market rates. Inverse floaters: coupon varies inversely to interest rates.

Floorlet – an option that has an interest rate floor.

Forward cover – purchase or sale of currency in future to offset a known cash flow.

Forward exchange rate – exchange rate that is fixed today for exchange of currency in the future.

Forward pricing – fund dealing price based on valuation of a fund using next available prices. (*See* Historic pricing.)

Forward rate of interest – the interest rate that can be secured now but will take effect in the future.

Foundation – an entity that is funded by an endowment to support a not-for-profit activity. Community Foundation – type of US foundation formed by broad-based community support from multiple sources; Corporate Foundation – receives its income from a company; Family Foundation – private foundation supported by a single family; Operating Foundation – conducts its own programs rather than making grants to others and must follow specific rules; Private Foundation – non-governmental, non-profit-making organization established to provide social, educational, religious or other charitable activities for public good primarily through making grants (tax exempt under Section 501(c)(3) of the Internal Revenue Services Code). Foundations can be perpetual or limited life.

Forward Rate Agreement (FRA) – an over-the-counter derivative under which a fixed rate is paid and a floating rate received, the difference being settled on the termination date.

Franked income – dividends from UK companies where UK corporation tax has been paid by the company.

Freddie Mac – *see* Federal Home Loans Mortgage Corporation (FHLMC).

Free cash flow – cash flow from operations less capital expenditure and dividends paid; cash not required for operations or reinvestment.

Free float – the percentage of a listed stock's market capitalization that is not owned by a long-term holder and is therefore readily traded in the market. For instance, if a government holds 25% of a listed telecommunications company, the free float is 75%.

Front-end load – charges or commissions deducted at the beginning. Back-end and 'no load' are self-explanatory.

Front office – revenue generating sales, trading and management part of an organization.

FSA recognized funds – funds from external jurisdictions recognized by the FSA: Bermuda; Cayman Islands; Guernsey; Isle of Man; Jersey; and Luxembourg.

Full service lease – lease whereby the lessor maintains the property or equipment.

Fully diluted – adjustment to earnings per share assuming all warrants and convertibles are exchanged for common shares.

Fund of funds – portfolio of funds rather than securities.

Fund size – the sum of the values of all assets in a fund.

Fundamental analysis – the process of valuing a company by looking at its financial position and principal activities.

Futures contract – a derivative security. An agreement to sell or buy a fixed amount of the underlying security at some point in the future at a fixed price. Unlike forward contracts, futures are generally traded on an exchange and are marked-to-market frequently.

Future value – the value of present dollars at a future time. $P(1 + R)T$, where P is the present dollar amount, R is the rate of interest and T is the number of compounding periods.

GDP – *see* Gross Domestic Product.

GNMA – *see* Ginnie Mae.

GNP – *see* Gross National Product.

Gamma – rate of change in the delta of an option for a given unit of change in the price of the underlying asset.

Gearing – the ratio of a company's debt to assets. A highly geared company will have a lot of debt compared to its assets and thus is potentially a higher risk investment. Some funds are geared, meaning they borrow money to invest.

Geometric mean – is the nth root of the product of a series of numbers, minus 1. It is used in taking an average of returns over time and found by calculating 1+ the first period's return times 1+ the second period's return up to the nth or last period. The geometric mean is then found by taking the nth root and deducting 1. This is the average used when looking at returns from securities and funds.

Gilt – a UK Government bond so called because traditionally the bond certificate had gilt edges, hence: gilt-edged – now a generic term assigned to an investment with extremely low risk and high security.

Ginnie Mae – Government National Mortgage Association (GNMA). A wholly owned US Government corporation within the US Department of Housing and Urban Development. GNMA packages mortgages guaranteed by the Federal Housing Authority.

Global macro funds – hedge funds that trade long and short primarily in asset classes and currencies, including commodities, which represent global themes in financial markets. These are 'directional' strategies, that is they aim to identify and exploit expected directions in the markets concerned and often use leverage to enhance the potential return.

Global portfolio – a portfolio that includes domestic and non-domestic (international – *see* EAFE) securities.

Golden hello – a guaranteed bonus payment made to attract personnel; parachute: termination payment on company take-over.

Greeks – the term given to the symbols used in options terminology for measuring exposures.

Greenmail – repurchase of shares by a company from a corporate raider at a higher price to protect itself from take-over.

Gray market – purchase and sale of securities before they are publicly issued.

Gross Domestic Product (GDP) – a country's aggregate goods and services produced domestically, not including external revenue. GDP is an important indication of the health of the economy.

Gross National Product (GNP) – a similar economic indicator to GDP, but plus income earned from overseas investments and minus income earned domestically by overseas investors.

Growth investor – an investor who seeks capital growth above a steady income.

Growth style – a style of investing where the principal aim is to profit from the increase in price of a stock as the company grows. (*See also* growth stocks and Income investing.)

Growth stocks – those stocks which are deemed to offer capital gains from an increase in the share price due to growth in the underlying company. Growth stocks are sometimes defined by price to book ratios.

Guarantee – commitment by a third party to underwrite a debtor's obligations.

Guaranteed fund – a fund which promises to provide at least a minimum return. The fund usually enters into a legally binding agreement with a third party to ensure this.

HEPI – College and University Higher Education Price Index. A US domestic measure of price movement in the goods and services purchased by universities and colleges.

Hang Seng index – the principal share index of Hong Kong.

Hard dollars – a term for payment of expenses by fund managers by cash amounts rather than 'soft dollars'.

Heaven-and-Hell bonds – dual currency bond that has a capital repayment in a different currency from the interest payments.

Hedge – the taking of one investment position in order to offset potential losses arising from another position. Hedging is offsetting risk.

Hedge funds – funds that attempt to 'hedge' out the risk of the primary investments by entering into a series of positions, some of which will be short. Hedge funds differ from 'vanilla' investment funds because they are permitted to take short positions. Hedge funds tend to specialize in certain types of strategy and often use leverage in their strategies. The strategies are generally absolute return strategies and the fees tend to comprise both a management and a performance fee.

Hedge Ratio – ratio of the market value of shares sold short to the full conversion value of the long position. (*See* Delta.)

High-yield bond – *see* Junk bond.

High-water mark – a level of return, usually an accumulated hurdle rate, which must be exceeded before a performance fee may be paid.

Historic pricing – fund dealing price based on valuation of a fund using latest available historic prices. (*See* Forward pricing.)

Holding company – company that holds stock in other companies, especially subsidiaries.

Hurdle rate – a rate of return that is deducted from the portfolio return to find the basis on which a performance fee will be charged in a given year. Minimum acceptable return on a project.

ILBs – *see* Inflation-Linked Bonds or Index-Linked Bonds.

IPO – *see* Initial Public Offering.

IRR – *see* Internal Rate of Return.

Implied volatility – *see* Option.

Immunization – constructing a portfolio of assets that offsets or hedges liabilities, usually by matching the duration of assets with that of liabilities.

Incentive fee – *see* Performance fee.

Income investing – a style of investing where the principal aim is to earn a regular income from the investment from dividends and fixed income coupon payments. Any capital gains from the investments are seen as a bonus. (*See also* Growth investing.)

Income stabilization reserve – a reserve created as a smoothing device to subsidize spending when income is short.

Income stocks – stocks that have a high income yield.

Income unit – a unit of a unit trust that pays out an income as opposed to being reinvested.

Income yield – annual (or annualized) dividend or interest from a security or fund as a percentage of market price. (*See* Redemption yield.)

Indenture – formal legal agreement.

Index – a notional representation of the performance of a basket of shares. Examples of the most widely known indices are the Dow Jones Industrial Average, the S&P 500 and the FTSE 100.

Indexation – 'passive' management of a portfolio so that the portfolio moves in line with an index.

Index fund – a fund that is structured to mirror an index. It can be created in different ways. One is 'full replication' where every stock in the index is bought for the fund in direct proportion to its size in that index. Another is 'statistical sampling' where a sample of stocks is bought in appropriate proportions to mirror the movement in the index within a high degree of tolerance.

Index linked – *see* Index fund.

Indifference curve – when applied in investment, a line joining all investment outcomes that are equally satisfying to the investor.

Inflation – the general or average increase in prices over time. The usual method of calculating inflation is to take a basket of known goods and services and monitor the prices to determine the percentage increase over one year. (*See also* Disinflation and Deflation.)

Inflation-Linked Bonds or Index-Linked Bonds (ILBs) – interest and capital repayments linked to the Consumer Price Index. Also called inflation-indexed bonds. First launched by the UK Government in 1980. Now exist in Australia, Canada, France, Italy, Sweden and the USA (see TIPS).

Information Ratio – the ratio of expected excess return to risk as calculated by standard deviation. Most often the information ratio is used to measure a fund manager's performance against a benchmark. A positive information ratio equates to positive alpha. Information Ratio = (Fund's annualized return – Benchmark return)/Annualized standard deviation of fund's relative returns.

Initial charge – charges made 'up-front' by fund managers on unit trusts and OEICs.

Initial Public Offering (IPO) – the first time shares of a company are offered for sale to the public. The IPO takes place in the primary market and any subsequent trading in the shares is in the secondary market.

Insider dealing – using price sensitive information to gain an unfair advantage in the buying or selling of securities.

In specie – in kind rather than in money. Refers to distributions of portions of securities, rather than cash, held within a fund to investors in that fund pro-rata in proportion to the investors' interest' in the fund.

Intangible assets – non-material assets such as patents, technical expertise. (*See* Tangible assets.)

Interest rate sensitivity – a measure of how sensitive the price of a security, usually a bond, is to a change in the base rate of interest.

Intergenerational equity – the real capital value of an endowment fund that remains, after crediting return and deducting current spending in the ensuing period of measurement, sufficient to maintain the real value of equivalent or greater spending in future.

Intermediate bond – medium term; maturity between 5 and 12 years.

Intermediation – investment through a financial intermediary which mediates between savers and lenders.

Internal Rate of return (IRR) – the interest rate that discounts all cash flows from an investment, including the end value, back to a present value which is equal to the initial cost of the investment. The Net Present Value is the Present Value less that initial cost. The IRR is therefore the interest rate that causes the NPV to be zero.

In-the-money/Out-of-the-money – an option term describing the difference between the strike price of an option and the current value of the underlying investment. (*see* option.)

Intrinsic value – value of an option on expiry.

Inverted yield curve – *see* Yield curve.

Investment grade bonds – bonds whose credit ratings according to the three major bond rating agencies (Moody, S&P, and Fitch) are BBB or Baa or better.

Investment trust – in the UK an investment trust is a closed-end fund listed on the UK stock exchange. In Japan, and other Asian countries, investment trust is the term that is used in translation for open-ended (mutual) funds.

Isoreward contour – a line joining all portfolios that offer equal total return.

Isovariance contour – lines that join portfolios with constant variance.

Jeopardy investments – speculative investments.

Jensen's Alpha Ratio – a risk-adjusted performance measure that shows the average return above the CAPM, given the portfolio's beta and the average market return. It distinguishes between those managers who have achieved outperformance through a high beta portfolio in rising markets and those who have created alpha from active management. Jensen Measure = Fund's return − (Risk-free rate + Fund's beta × (Market return Risk-free rate)).

Junk bond – a bond whose credit rating is below that of investment grade (BBB rating by Standard & Poor's; Ba by Moody's), the issuer of which is more likely to default on repayment. Junk bonds are high risk and potentially high return.

Knock-out option – an option which has reached its expiry date and is now worthless.

Kurtosis – a statistic that measures the extent of the peaks and tails (flatness) of a probability distribution. Positive kurtosis (leptokurtosis) is associated with returns that are peaked in the center but have fatter tails (where the surprises are), suggesting consistency of return most of the time but more outliers. Negative kurtosis (platykurtosis) implies a flat distribution where most of the probability is neither around the mean nor in the tails, and so returns are not consistent.

LBO – *see* Leveraged Buy-Out.

LIBID – London Inter-Bank Bid Rate of Interest. (*See* LIBOR.)

LIBOR – London Inter-Bank Offer Rate is the interest rate at which banks are prepared to lend to one another and is an international barometer of the current interest rate market. Often interest rates are quoted as 'LIBOR plus 50 basis points'. If LIBOR for the day is 5.0% then this is 5.5%. Banks and institutions who can borrow at, or close to, LIBOR typically have credit ratings of AA.

LSE – London Stock Exchange.

Laddering – reducing market risk by owning a series of bonds of different durations.

Large cap fund – a fund that consists of common stocks with a large market capitalization. (*See* Market capitalization.)

Launch date – the inception date of a fund.

Leading economic indicators – compendium of economic indicators that are deemed to be an early indicator of the underlying trend in the economy.

LEAPS – Long Term Equity AnticiPation Securities. Put or call options with expiration dates as far as two and a half years in the future.

Leptokurtosis – *see* kurtosis.

Level term assurance – a simple life assurance policy that will pay a one-off lump sum on the death of the assured.

Leverage – a measure of the extent of exposure to liabilities. Funds can either borrow money to invest or can buy derivatives contracts without actually having the capital to cover the positions. Gearing and leverage are synonymous terms.

Leveraged Buy-Out (LBO) – debt financed take-over of a company. (*See* Management Buy-Out.)

Liabilities – the opposite of assets. All loans, debt, bonds issued, etc.

Lien – lenders claim or security over assets.

Life assurance – an insurance policy that pays out upon the death of the holder.

Limited liability – financial liability limited to the amount invested.

Limited partnership – a form of business organization that provides some of the partner's limited liability. The General Partner orgnanizes the business while the limited partners provide the capital.

Liquid assets – assets that are readily convertible into cash.

Liquidity – a term that describes the convertibility of an instrument into cash.

Liquidating dividend – dividend that represents return of capital.

Liquid market – a market that sees a significant amount of trading activity and can therefore accommodate and fill a large order quickly and without causing large price movements.

Liquidity premium – additional reward for investment into a security that cannot easily be converted into cash. Also, the difference between the forward and spot rates of interest.

Liquidity risk – the risk that, at any given time, there will be insufficient liquidity in the market to absorb a trade without moving the price significantly, or simply a failure to cover short-term financial obligations. For very large position sizes relevant to the market it is prudent to discount the market price when marking the position to market. Exactly how much of a liquidity discount should be applied depends on the volatility and depth of the market.

Liquidity spread – interest rate spread due to lack of liquidity.

Load – a sales charge made on purchase of a fund.

Long position – a position where the investor owns the investment as opposed to a short position where the investor owes, and must deliver in a set amount of time. Long positions can relate to securities, options, futures, volatility or other indices, etc.

Long-only management – a management style wherein the fund can only take long positions.

Long/short funds – a hedge fund strategy in which one security is bought and another similar security is sold to exploit an anomalous price differential between them.

Look-back option – an option that has an exercise value dependent on the maximum or minimum value of the underlying instrument during the life of the option.

MBO – *see* Management Buy-Out.

MBI – *see* Management Buy-In.

MER – *see* Management Expense Ratio.

MFM – *see* Multiple Factor Model.

MPT – *see* Modern Portfolio Theory.

Macro funds – *See* Global macro funds.

Managed futures – a style of hedge fund management that uses derivatives to implement strategy. (*See* Commodity Trading Advisers.)

Management Buy-In (MBI) – acquisition of a business by investors who inject new management. (*See* Management Buy-Out.)

Management Buy-Out (MBO) – acquisition of a company's equity by existing management normally using debt and often with the involvement of a private equity company.

Management Expense Ratio (MER) – The ratio of the managers fees and other expenses to the total value of a fund. (*See* Total Expense Ratio.)

Mandate – the fund's objectives that are agreed by the manager and the client. The mandate will outline the risk/return objective of the fund and the sectors in which to be invested. If there are any investments that the client prohibits the manager from making, then these will be detailed in the mandate.

Mandatory payout – IRC Section 4942 requiring Foundations to make qualifying distributions equal to 5% of the value of non-charitable assets.

Margin – there are two quite different financial meanings to this word. One is profit as a percentage of revenue; another is the proportion of the value of a trade, usually a derivative, which is deposited with a market maker or agent as collateral. Margin may be 'initial' margin, i.e. that which is deposited when the trade is initiated, or 'variation' margin, which is the added amount to be deposited as protection when the value of the trade goes against the investor.

Mark-to-market – value an investment at the same price at which an identical investment is traded on the open market.

Market capitalization – a measure of market size, often represented by indices especially for listed stocks, found by multiplying the number of securities in a universe by the market price of each security. Equity indices are usually split in to large, mid and small (or even micro and other) company capitalization indices. The definition of large, mid and small cap company is usually made not in terms of absolute nominal value but proportion or number of stocks in the universe: the top 100 stocks by size being large, the next 100 being mid and the remainder being small or the top 25% being large, the bottom 10% being small.

Market inventory fund – a fund that is used by a client with multiple managers who are required to trade with the inventory fund before dealing with outside brokers in order to save the client transaction costs.

Market neutral – balanced long and short positions giving no net exposure to the general movement in the underlying market (a hedge fund style or strategy).

Market risk – risk that is due to movement in the market as a whole. Also known as systematic risk.

Market timing – the process of picking the moment in which to buy or sell securities in order to profit from short-term market price movements.

Marketable securities – publicly traded securities such as bonds and equities, which are readily convertible to cash in the secondary market.

Master trust – a pooling of assets, which may include several independent trusts, through one trust. Master trustees are generally banks that may handle the administration of investments of multiple managers of any one client.

Maturity premium – the premium paid for risk in the yield on a bond when the capital is repaid over longer periods. The risk is an adverse change in the rate of interest during the life of the bond.

Mean – an average; the most common mean is the arithmetic mean, which is the total of a set of numbers divided by the number of numbers in the set. The geometric mean is the nth root of the product of n numbers. So the geometric mean of two numbers, 1 and 4, is the square root of 1×4, which equals 2. A non-stationary mean is one that changes rather than remaining static, and this applies to many economic time series.

Mean reversion – tendency of a series of numbers to return to the average of that series.

Mean/variance – a ratio of mean expected return to the variance of return. Can also refer to a style of investment management which assumes that investments deviate from an average but tend to return to that average over time.

Median – the middle point of a distribution which is the 50th percentile. (*See* quartile).

Merger arbitrage – a style of hedge fund management that exploits market anomalies in mergers between the listed equity of the two companies or, in a take-over, between the aggressor and its target. Some merger arbitrage focuses on agreed mergers where the market has priced in the terms but left a small discount for the time value of money and the modest risk of the merger not being approved. Some arbitrage is more speculative and targets prospective mergers that have not yet been agreed between all parties.

Mid cap fund – a fund which comprises securities of medium market capitalization sized equities. (*See* Market capitalization.)

Mid price – mid point between the bid and offer price.

Mode – statistical term denoting the most likely value of a random variable. In a normal distribution, the mean, median and mode are the same.

Modern Portfolio Theory (MPT) – a theory of portfolio optimization based on risk/reward trade-offs.

Momentum – used to describe a trading strategy which assumes that a trend will continue until it reverses or runs out of momentum. The basis of the old stock market adage: 'Run your profits but cut your losses.'

Money market – the market in which short-term financial instruments are traded, such as Certificates of Deposit (CD) and Treasury Bills.

Money Center Bank – major bank in the USA which provides general banking services.

Money supply – the total amount of money in an economy (see an economics dictionary for elaboration of this concept).

Money-weighted return – Internal Rate of Return.

Monte Carlo simulation – an analytical technique for calculating the probability distribution of possible outcomes where many simulations are run in which uncertain variables are assigned random numbers and the outcome is monitored to suggest the values that are more likely. The simulation takes its name from Monte Carlo, which is famed for its casinos.

Moody's – US credit ratings agency which provides assessments as to the credit worthiness of corporations and governments.

Mortgage-backed security – a security that pays interest and principal from an underlying mortgage.

Mortgage bond – bond secured against an asset.

Most Favored Nation – refers to fees charged by investment managers and ensures that a client receives at least as good a fee basis as any comparable client of the manager.

Multiple Factor Model (MFM) – based on arbitrage pricing theory, the model states that return on a security is equal to the weighted sum of returns on a set of common factors which affect that security plus the security specific return. (*See* Multiple regression.)

Multiple regression – a statistical means of explaining how a set of independent variables drive the movement of a dependent variable. Used, for example, to explain the impact of different economic and financial factors in an investment strategy.

Municipal bond – bonds issued by US States generally, and historically exempt from Federal, State and local income taxes.

Municipal notes – short-term obligations, 12 months or less maturity, issued by US States.

Multi-strategy fund – a fund that follows an asset allocation process to diversify across investment styles and strategies.

Mutual fund – a US open-ended pooled fund of securities priced and traded on a daily basis. (*See* Open-ended fund.)

NASDAQ – National Association of Security Dealers Automated Quotation System. Electronic stock exchange established in 1971 run by the National Association of Security Dealers.

NAV – *see* Net Asset Value.

NPV – Net Present Value. *See* Internal Rate of Return.

NYSE – New York Stock Exchange.

Naked option – an option that is not used to hedge an asset or other option. *See* option.

Net Asset Value (NAV) – total assets less total liabilities; the sum of all the mark-to-market values of the constituent securities of a fund divided by the number of units outstanding.

New issue – a security recently issued to raise additional funds for the issuing company.

Nifty Fifty – 50 growth stocks favored by institutions in the 1960s and 1970s.

No-load fund – a mutual fund with no front-end or back-end commission charge. (*See* Front-end load and Back-end load.)

Nomad – nominated adviser for listing companies on a stock exchange.

Nominal interest rate – interest rate expressed in monetary terms from which may be deducted the rate of inflation to assess the real interest rate.

Nominal value – the face value of a security rather than the market value. (*See* Face value.)

Nominee – an individual or a company who assumes responsibility for a security but where the legal ownership is held by someone else.

Non-core portfolio – *see* Core portfolio.

Normal distribution – a probability distribution that has equal areas either side of the mean, having the shape of a bell hence known as a 'bell curve'.

Normal portfolio – the optimal long-run portfolio.

Normalization – process of transforming a set of numbers by adjusting them by a constant (such as deducting a mean of a set of numbers from each of those numbers in order to standardize them).

OEIC – Open-Ended Investment Company. A commingled investment vehicle equivalent to a unit trust but with the legal form of a company which issues shares at a single price based on Net Asset Value. (*See* Open-ended fund.)

OTC – *see* Over the Counter.

Odd lot – a block of securities that is less than the unit of trading.

Off-balance sheet finance – finance that is not shown as a liability in a company's accounts.

Offshore financial center – financial center that is free of many of the taxes and regulations of traditional 'onshore' centers. Sometimes referred to as 'Tax Havens'.

Off-market – a transaction is said to be 'off market' if it is negotiated outside of a formalized marketplace such as a stock exchange. Over the counter transactions are off market.

Offer price – the price at which the market is willing to sell a security. Also known as the 'ask price' as the market is asking for the amount.

Omega – symbol used to denominate the standard deviation of active return.

On-the-Run-Treasuries – the most recently issued Treasury securities.

Open-ended fund – Mutual Fund, Unit Trust or Open Ended Investment Company (OEIC), where investment is by subscription and redemption and the price is equal to the Net Asset Value (total assets divided by number of stock units, shares or trust units) less a 'spread' for transaction costs.

Opening price – the initial price of a security or market at the beginning of the day.

Open interest – the number of outstanding option or futures contracts on an exchange.

Operational risk – risk that arises from failed internal business systems, people or procedures.

Opportunity cost of capital – expected return forgone.

Optimization – the process whereby assets are combined in a portfolio so as to provide the optimum prospective risk to return trade-off. Also known as 'mean-variance optimization'.

Option – a right to buy or sell a security at a given price at a given future point in time. A European option can only be exercised at the expiration of the option. An American option confers the right to exercise at any time during the life of the option. An 'in-the-money' option is where the exercise price is inside the current market price of the underlying asset. 'At the money' is equal to the market price and 'out of the money' means that the exercise price is outside the current market price of the underlying asset. A 'naked option' commits to delivering underlying assets that are not held (short). (*See* Black–Scholes option pricing model.)

Ordinary shares – shares in a company that give the holder ownership interest in the company and dividend and voting rights.

Outperformance – obtaining a higher rate of return on an investment than the benchmark.

Outlier – a data observation that is outside the normal range of observations.

Out of the money – an option that has no intrinsic value. (*See* Intrinsic value and option.)

Over the Counter (OTC) – a trade that is not implemented through an official market exchange.

Overlay strategy – addition of a managed portfolio of derivatives, usually futures, on top of an existing investment portfolio. An example is currency overlay on top of a global bond portfolio. The underlying portfolio manager may select the optimum portfolio of bonds denominated in any of a number of currencies. The currency overlay manager would then manage the exposure of the portfolio to currencies.

Overweight – a fund is said to be 'overweight' a particular sector or asset class if it has a larger proportion of total equity assigned to that particular sector or class than the market.

PBR – *see* Price to Book Ratio.

PEG (Price to Earnings Growth) Ratio – the Price to Earnings Ratio (*see* PER) divided by the earnings per share growth rate. The PEG Ratio is used to value growth stocks. The lower the PEG value, the better value are the shares.

PER – *see* Price to Earnings Ratio.

PPP – *see* Purchasing Power Parity.

Pair trading – also known as relative value arbitrage, this trading strategy takes advantage of different valuations for similar stocks. If two similar stocks which usually display a high level of price correlation momentarily become uncorrelated, there might exist a chance to profit when they eventually become correlated again.

Par value – nominal value (*see* Face value).

Pass-through-securities – notes or bonds backed by a package of assets.

Passive management – investment management style which aims to follow a particular index by investing in the index constituents. As the aim is to follow the performance of the index once the initial investments have been made, the management is said to be 'passive' as the fund needs only occasional re-balancing.

Payback period – time taken for an investment to recover its initial capital.

Payout ratio – dividend as a percentage of earnings per share.

Penny shares – shares that are trading at below 10p are sometimes referred to as penny shares.

Percentile – ranking of 1% of a given sample distribution. Quartile is the 25th percentile.

Performance analysis – evaluation of returns in relation to a benchmark to determine levels of skill.

Performance attribution – *see* Performance measurement.

Performance contribution – *see* performance measurement.

Performance fee – a fee paid to the investment manager based upon the performance of the fund. This can take many forms including: rewarding for excess return relative to a benchmark; incorporating a 'hurdle' rate, which is a figure (often in an absolute return fund this is the risk-free rate of interest) that must be achieved before the performance calculation begins; incorporating a 'high-water mark', which is a level that must be exceeded before the next performance payment is made.

Performance measurement – analytical techniques for evaluating the absolute and relative performance of portfolios. Performance contribution is identifying the contribution of returns from components of the portfolio. Performance attribution measures the amount by which each decision contributes to the difference between the return from the portfolio and the return from the index, i.e. the attribution of each decision to the 'alpha' of the portfolio, from asset allocation, sectors and stock selection and from market timing.

Permanent endowment – gift to be invested to generate return rather than capital to be spent.

Phi – the change in the premium of an option for a unit change in interest rates.

Placing – the sale of newly issued securities to a group of investors.

Poison pill – strategy to frustrate the take-over of a company such as through an issue of securities that convert into those of the acquiring company.

Poison put – right to redeem a bond at par before a take-over.

Political risk – the risk arising from uncertainty in the political environment due to the chance that the government might enact a law that would be detrimental to an investor's interests.

Pooled investment – also known as 'Collective investments', are funds in which many individuals have 'pooled' their money in order to invest more efficiently. Most funds are pooled investments.

Portable alpha – combination of alphas in a portfolio, representing active risk, which is left after indentifying the beta of the portfolio. Beta is generated by a portfolio invested in index instruments, leveraged to meet portfolio liabilities, to catch pure market exposure.

Portfolio – a group of securities or funds.

Portfolio activity – is defined as the lesser of the total cost of all purchases or the total proceeds of all sales divided by the mean value of the fund (fund at the beginning plus fund at the end of the period, divided by two). *See* Portfolio Turnover.

Portfolio construction – the process of determining where funds should be invested within a set of investment classes and how much to invest.

Portfolio risk – there are four principal components of portfolio risk in classic financial theory: extra-market risk; systematic risk; market timing risk; specific risk. As described in Chapter 4, this book looks at portfolio risk primarily in terms of likely failure to meet objectives with those risks described in classic financial theory as potential contributory factors.

Portfolio theory – theory of how to select securities for a portfolio to achieve the optimum combination. (*See* Modern Portfolio Theory.)

Portfolio turnover – defined as the total cost of all purchases plus the total proceeds of all sales in a period divided by the mean value of the fund (fund at the beginning plus fund at the end of the period, divided by two). Turnover by this definition includes both purchases and sales made simply for 'activity' reasons (*see* Portfolio activity) and purchases and sales arising from new money into or out of the fund. The relationship between the two is 'Portfolio activity' times 2 plus or minus new money into or out of the fund equals 'Portfolio turnover'.

Position – a market commitment. If a trader or fund owns shares in a company then it is said that the trader 'has a long position'.

Pound/dollar cost averaging – investment of regular sums giving an average in-price to an investement that is lower than the arithmetic average of the price over the period.

Pre-emption right – shareholder's prior right to buy stock whether newly issued in the primary market or sold by another investor in the secondary market.

Preference shares/Preferred stock – shares that rank ahead of ordinary shares in the payment of dividends and in the event of liquidation and usually do not have voting rights. They tend to have fixed and relatively high dividends and are usually cumulative: preference holders must be paid current and historic dividends before ordinary holders receive ordinary dividends.

Prelims – first release to the stock market of a company's results for that financial year.

Premium – the excess return demanded for risk; difference between share values and a convertible bond; the amount of money paid into an investment fund on a continuing basis.

Present value – *see* Internal Rate of Return (IRR).

Price correction/Market correction – a larger than usual price movement which arises from the general perception that the market, or security, is incorrectly priced as valued against similar markets/securities.

Price to Book Ratio (PBR) – a stock's market capitalization divided by its book value. The PBR of a stock shows how much of a premium the market is adding above and beyond the book value of the company, as shown in its financial statements. A low PBR might indicate an investment opportunity. PBR is not always a reliable indicator of value because a company might have assets not recorded 'on the books' such as intellectual property in technology companies. Furthermore, growth stocks may have high PBRs, especially where the company is in an industry, such as services, which is not capital intensive.

Price to Earnings Growth (PEG) Ratio – the price to earnings ratio divided by the rate of growth of earnings. Shares that have a low price to earnings ratio but a high rate of earnings growth are attractive and have a low PEG Ratio.

Price to Earnings Ratio (PER) – a widely used method of weighing up the attractiveness of an investment calculated by dividing the current (or future estimated) earnings into the current market price of the security. A PER of 15 means that at current price and assuming the earnings remain constant the share will have 'paid for itself' in 15 year's time.

Primary market – *see* Capital markets.

Prime brokers – intermediaries in the equity (and increasingly the currency) market who provide credit lines and administrative resources for fund managers and others, including hedge funds and banks, to deal with other counterparties such as market makers.

Prime rate – the interest rate that banks charge their best customers for short-term loans.

Principal – capital invested or amount of debt that must be repaid.

Private equity – capital that is made available to companies but does not result in formal securities being listed on a relevant exchange. Private equity is usually raised by start-up companies needing to develop their product or service to sufficient level before an initial public offering.

Private placement – equity or debt that is offered to certain investors but is not offered to the public and does not therefore require registration with regulatory authorities. Lehman Brothers Bond Index.

Program-related investment – a UK term of social investment by a charity, not covered by the normal fiduciary obligation to maximize financial return and not considered to be an investment by the UK Charity Commissioners or Inland Revenue.

Program trading – securities bought or sold in batches, such as a basket of index stocks.

Property Unit Trusts – Inland Revenue exempt mutual funds holding direct property.

Prospectus – registration document which outlines the terms of a new issue of securities. In the USA, it highlights the much longer statement that must be registered with the SEC.

Proxy – a written agreement given by the shareholder, or fund member, to someone else to vote at shareholders' meetings.

Purchasing Power Parity (PPP) – valuation of two currencies based on the relative changes in inflation such as to equalize the price of goods traded between two countries.

Put option – a derivative: the buyer of a put option has the right to 'put' an underlying security on the seller of the option, i.e. to sell it to them. A 'Put spread' comprises a long–short position with put options. *See* option.

'Q' ratio – the ratio of the market value of an asset to its replacement cost.

Qualified investor – an institutional investor qualified by the Securities and Exchange Commission (SEC) to trade private placement securities with other qualified investors without notifying the SEC.

Quantitative management – an investment management style that uses statistical and numerical methods, usually computer driven, to determine investment opportunities while paying particular attention to risk/return.

Quartile – the performance of similar funds is recorded in a league table with four divisions or quartiles. If a fund is said to be in the top quartile it is performing better than those in lesser quartiles. (*See* Percentile.)

REITs – *see* Real Estate Investment Trusts.

RFP – *see* Request for Proposal.

ROE – *see* Return on Equity.

ROI – *see* Return on Investment.

RPI – *see* Retail Price Index.

RSI – *see* Relative Strength Index.

'R' squared – the amount of a portfolio's total return explained by movements in the market. 'R' squared is quoted as a percentage. (*See* Coefficient of determination.)

Rally – a sustained rise in the price of a security or market.

Ramping – buying securities to artificially raise their price.

Range – the difference between the highest and lowest prices in any given time period.

Ratchet option – option that periodically locks in profits.

Real assets – tangible assets.

Real estate – land, buildings or other commercial structures.

Real Estate Investment Trusts (REITs) – a pooled investment vehicle that invests in direct property and is traded on a stock exchange. REITs are generally exempt from tax if 95% of the income is distributed.

Real return – nominal return adjusted for inflation. The formula for adjustment is: 1+ nominal return/100 divided by 1+ Rate of inflation.

Rebalancing – process by which asset distributions that move outside a given change because of price movements are rebalanced to the weighting given by long-term asset strategy benchmarks.

Red herring – preliminary prospectus.

Redemption fee – a fee charged when an obligation, including a unit in a mutual fund, is redeemed for cash.

Redemption yield – the internal rate of return, including both income and capital change, between the time of issue or purchase of a security and the date at which the security is redeemed and the capital repaid to the investor (*see* Income yield). Redemption yield represents total rate of return.

Refunding – replacement of current debt with new debt.

Regression analysis – a statistical technique that attempts to discover relationships between variables of a function in order to predict future values.

Regulatory capital – amount of capital that financial organizations are required to hold by regulation.

Regulation D ('Reg D') – privately issued securities in the USA hedged with short positions in the listed equity of the same company until the privately issued securities can be publicly traded.

Regulation Q – limit on rate of interest paid by banks on savings.

Reinvestment risk – the gross redemption yield on a bond assumes that coupons are reinvested at the same yield over the life of the bond. If interest rates fall during the life of the bond, then coupons will be reinvested at lower yields and the risk is therefore that the gross redemption yield is not achieved.

Relative return – the return of an investment relative to the return of a benchmark which is representative of that group of investments. For US equity management, for instance, the S&P

500 index is a commonly used general benchmark. Other indices would be used to measure more specialist US equity mandates.

Relative Strength Index (RSI) – technical analysis indicator gauging stock price movement relative to its past trend, used to indicate imminent change in trend.

Relative value arbitrage – a style of management for hedge funds which seek to go 'long' and 'short' baskets or pairs of securities, either in similar or in dissimilar industries, to exploit perceived differences in value where the value should be largely determined by common factors. (*See* Pair trading.)

Repurchase agreement (Repo) – purchase of securities (particularly Treasury) from a dealer with agreement that the dealer will buy them back at a specified price.

Request for Proposal (RPF) – a questionnaire produced by an institution or its consultant to be completed by a prospective investment management company.

Reserve currency – currency that is acceptable to the central banks of other countries as part of their reserves.

Residual risk and return – also called unsystematic or diversifiable risk or return, that which is uncorrelated with the risk and return on the market portfolio.

Retail Price Index (RPI) – a measure of inflation, calculated as the change in price of a particular basket of items.

Rights issue – an issue of new shares, at a discounted price, to existing shareholders in proportion to their holdings in the company.

Retained earnings – a company's earnings that are retained rather than paid out by way of dividend.

Return – real; nominal; absolute; relative; total, etc. (*See* Chapter 2.): internal rate of return, money or dollar-weighted return and time-weighted return.

Return on Equity (ROE) – the last 12 months net income from a company divided by the most recent share capital or earnings as a proportion of book value of equity.

Return on Investment (ROI) – income before interest as a percentage of assets.

Rho – rate of change of an option price to every one basis point move in interest rates.

Rights issue – issue of securities to existing equity stockholders.

Risk-adjusted performance – a measure of the performance of a fund adjusted so as to allow two or more funds with different overall risks to be easily compared.

Risk budget – assessment of total risk taken in generating return. 'Good' risk adds value to risk-adjusted return; 'bad' risk detracts value.

Risk-free assets – any assets, such as Government securities, that have a known rate of return but have no chance of defaulting on the payments. Normally a Treasury Bill, the interest on which is the risk-free rate.

Risk neutral – not exposed to risk.

Risk premium – the premium payable for risk over the risk-free rate of return. The bond maturity premium is the premium investors require for holding long-rather than short-dated stock. The equity risk premium, measured using historic data (ex post), is the total return from investment in equity relative to the total return from either Treasury Bills or, as sometimes used, Long-dated Government bonds. It is measured by comparing either the geometric or the arithmetic mean of annual returns. The former tends to be lower than the latter, depending on the level of volatility in returns. The arithmetic mean is used as the basis for a forward-looking (ex ante) assessment of the risk premium because the compounded (geometric) average is distorted by volatility.

S&P 500 – the Standard & Poor's 500 index is one of the main US indices of the largest 500 US companies.

SCO – *see* Collateralized Obligations.

SEC – Securities and Exchange Commission; the primary regulator of US financial markets.

SFC – Securities and Futures Authority; the UK financial market regulator.

SICAV – Société d'Investissement à Capital Variable. French form of mutual fund.

SOX – *see* Sarbanes–Oxley, Act 2002.

SPV – *see* Special Purpose Vehicle.

SRI – *see* Socially Responsible Investing.

SRO – *see* Self-Regulatory Organization.

STRIPS – Separate Trading of Registered Interest and Principal of Securities. A bond issued by the US government. The interest and capital components are separated and sold individually as zero coupon bonds.

Sallie Mae – Student Loan Marketing Association, a publicly traded US stock corporation which guarantees student loans traded in the secondary market.

Samurai bond – yen denominated bond issued by foreign borrowers in the domestic Japanese market.

Sarbanes-Oxley Act 2002 (SOX) – US legislation introduced to enhance accounting and auditing functions in a company.

Satellite portfolio – *see* Core portfolio.

Savings & Loans – known also as 'thrift', S&Ls are the US equivalent of UK Building Societies which provide finance for housing.

Scenario analysis – analysis of the future using different inputs to assess likely outcomes, especially used in asset-liability assessment.

Scrip issue – an issue of new shares free to existing shareholders in a company as an alternative to a dividend payment.

Seasoned issue – issue of a security for which there is already a market.

Secondary market – *see* Capital markets.

Sector – a sector is a notional group into which companies with similar business activities are placed. For example, the utilities sector will include gas, water and electrical companies whereas the pharmaceutical sector will include any manufacturers and developers of drugs.

Securities lending – lending of securities in a portfolio in exchange for a fee.

Security market line – a line representing the optimum point between expected return and risk.

Securitization – converting assets into securities.

Self-Regulatory Organization (SRO) – private organization that performs a regulatory function.

Senior debt – debt that must be repaid before subordinated debt in the event of liquidation.

Sensitivity analysis – analysis that measures the sensitivity of a change in outcome resulting from change to the inputs.

Serial bonds – package of bonds that mature over a series of years.

Settlement date – the date on which a trade is actually concluded and ownership in the security is transferred from seller to buyer, and payment is made from buyer to seller.

Share capital – the equity ownership of a company.

Share register – a list of the company's shareholders and the amount of their holdings.

Sharpe Ratio – a statistical measure showing the portfolio's return after the relevant portfolio risk has been taken into consideration. The Sharpe Ratio uses standard deviation to determine the reward (return) per unit of risk. The higher the Sharpe Ratio of a fund, the better its historical risk-adjusted performance has been. Sharpe Ratio = (Fund's return – Risk-free rate) / Fund's standard deviation.

Shelf registration – procedure that allows the filing of one document to cover a number of issues of the same security.

Short position – the process of selling a security without owning it in the first place. In effect the seller is left 'short' as he must re-enter the market at a later date and buy the security in order to deliver it to the buyer. A short seller is therefore hoping to benefit from falling prices.

Short selling – selling an asset, with a time delay to delivery, that is not held and will have to be bought to be able to deliver it to the buyer on the settlement date.

Significance – a statistical term that describes the probability that an outcome could have arisen by chance. Also used to describe an amount that is deemed significant as a percentage (also 5%) of the total sum under review.

Simple interest – an interest amount that does not accrue interest on interest.

Simulation – process of testing reality through the operation of a model that is built to have similar characteristics and thereby allow 'what if' scenarios to be assessed. Stochastic simulation is required when variables in the model are random. This involves running the model a number of times and changing one variable each time, building a frequency distribution of the outcomes.

Single price – based on mid-market valuation, the price at which units of a fund or securities are both bought and sold.

Sinking fund – fund established to retire debt before it matures.

Skewness – the degree of asymmetry of a distribution around its mean. A useful measure of positive or negative bias to a set of numbers. For instance, a set of performance figures may have positive average returns but negative skewness, indicating occasionally severe negative performance months.

Small cap fund – a fund that specializes in smaller market capitalization stocks. The definition of 'smaller', as of other sizes, varies. (*See* Market capitalization.)

Socially Responsible Investment (SRI) – an investment that meets strict criteria based upon ethical and environmental concerns.

Soft dollars – the use by fund managers of broker commissions on transactions to pay for third-party research and other services. Distinguished from Commission Sharing.

Sortino Ratio – a variation of the Sharpe Ratio, which uses downward deviation instead of standard deviation as the measure of risk. Sortino Ratio = (Fund's return − Risk-free rate)/Downward deviation.

Special Purpose Vehicle (SPV) – A separate legal entity established to hold assets or contracts/issue securities.

Specialist manager – a fund manager who specializes in one particular asset class and confines his/her investments to that class.

Specific returns – returns that are specific to a company and uncorrelated with the specific returns on other companies.

Spending rate – the annual amount of spending as a percentage of the beginning market value of the endowment fund.

Specific risk – risk that is uncorrelated to the market and therefore specific to the security.

Spending rule – guideline for determining the annual amount of funds available for spending in future.

Spot price – current price.

Spot rate of exchange – rate of exchange of currency for immediate delivery.

Spot rate of interest – interest rate that applies today on a loan made today.

Spread – the difference between the bid and offer prices is known as the spread. Generally a tight (narrow) spread will indicate that the security is liquid whereas a wider spread indicates less liquidity. But see credit spread.

Stag – subscriber to a security new issue aiming to sell at a profit when dealing begins.

Standard & Poor's – US credit ratings agency which provides assessments as to the credit worthiness of corporations and governments.

Standard deviation – a measure of the dispersion of a probability distribution. (*See* Confidence region.)

Standard error – a measure of the degree of uncertainty in an estimate because of disturbance in the data.

Standard rules – UK Trust Laws that govern the allocation of investment returns.

Statistical arbitrage – hedge fund style of investment that uses long/short positions in underlying securities which are similar.

Sterling Ratio – incorporates maximum drawdown as a measure of risk. Sterling Ratio = (Fund's 3 year annualized return / (Mean of maximum drawdown in each year −10%).

Stock borrowing – borrowing securities in order to sell them short.

Stock dividend – dividend in the form of stock rather than cash.

Stock split – division of existing stockholding; free issue of shares to existing holders to reduce the unit size.

Stop-loss – a market level at which an instrument is realized.

Straddle – an option spread involving a long call and a long put at the same exercise price.

Strategic asset allocation – *see* Asset allocation.

Stratified sampling – a technique of selecting a sample of a universe, such as of an index of stocks (rather than full replication, which is taking every member of that universe in direct proportion as to how it is held).

Strike price – price specified in an option at which the underlying instrument is to be bought or sold (*same as* Exercise price).

Style drift – change of investment style by a manager, e.g. a growth manager investing in value stocks or vice versa.

Subordinated debt – debt that is repaid after senior debt in a liquidation.

Survivor bias – bias in historic figures (usually performance numbers) because a component falls out of the universe, leaving only the surviving components.

Syndicate – a group of investors.

Synthetic instruments – investments of one type created out of others to have certain characteristics. For example, a synthetic future can be created from a simultaneous acquisition of put and call options. A synthetic call option can be created from a convertible security that has an option to convert into underlying equity but is valued as a straight bond because the option is a long way 'out of the money'. An arbitrageur can buy such a convertible and swap out the bond to create a cheap long-term call option (synthetic call). A synthetic put can be created from a convertible that is a long way 'in the money'. Such convertibles tend to trade above their value as a straight bond and arbitrageurs hedge out the equity exposure to give a modest positive carry.

Systematic – the reward and risk associated with the market.

Systemic risk – an event that has an impact on all investments in the same way. Major events can lead to all asset classes suffering from increased premia for risk, and thereby falling in price together rather than demonstrating the lower levels of correlation between them which are evident in more normal market conditions.

Swaps – an exchange of future payments between two parties. The most common type of swap is an interest rate swap in which one party agrees to provide a static rate of interest to another party in exchange for a floating (or variable) rate of interest. Swaps are widely used to 'sell on' the risk of a particular financial structure.

TAA – Tactical Asset Allocation. (*See* Asset allocation.)

TED spread – Treasury–Eurodollar spread.

TER – *see* Total Expenses Ratio.

TIPS – *see* Treasury Inflation Protection Securities.

TB – *see* Treasury Bill.

'T' statistic – a means of verifying the statistical significance of a calculation and the extent to which the answer is unlikely to be a coincidence.

Tangible assets – a company's property, plant and equipment after deduction of depreciation. (*See* Intangible assets.)

Tap stock – UK Government bond used by the Bank of England to control the gilt market by turning on and off the supply of stock to the market.

Technical analysis – a technique for identifying investment opportunities based upon mathematical and statistical analysis of historic data. In essence, technical analysis attempts to predict the future direction of the market by identifying patterns and trends in the historical data. A technical analysis practitioner may be referred to as a chartist.

Tender offer – general offer made to all shareholders to acquire a company's share capital.

Term deposit – any deposit of funds that has a defined time limit on the investment.

Term structure – any curve that describes a financial quantity as a function of time, notably interest rates (*see* Yield curve). The term structure of interest rates is the series of interest (or discount) rates at various intervals along the yield curve. It connects the discount rates on zero coupon bonds of different terms, i.e. periods to maturity. The yield curve is often deemed to indicate the market's expectation of interest rates, and therefore of likely monetary conditions, in the future. In practice, the yield curve can be influenced by other factors such as excessive demand for very long-dated Government bonds which may be in short supply. It is possible also to estimate future expected spot rates, known as forward rates, by comparing, for example, the rate for a 10-year bond with that for an 11-year bond and deriving the rate implied from end year 10 to end year 11.

Theta – time decay: the change in the option premium for a given change in the period to expiry.

Ticker – a symbol that identifies each traded security.

Tiger – the first newly industrialized economies of Asia: Hong Kong, Singapore, South Korea and Taiwan.

Time horizon – the period within which an investment goal is to be reached.

Time value – value of money over time; an integral part of option valuation.

Time-weighted return (TWR) – rate of return that gives equal weight to each time period for comparison of investment performance

Treasury Inflation Protection Securities (TIPS) – US Government bond with interest and capital repayment linked to inflation, first launched in 1997.

Tombstone – advertisement listing the underwriters to an issue.

Top-down – method of managing a portfolio by considering macro- and micro-economic factors as drivers of security selection. (*See* Bottom-up.)

Total expense ratio (TER) – the ratio of a fund's total costs to its total asset value. (*See* MER.)

Total return – income and price appreciation as a percentage of initial capital invested.

Tracker funds – funds that aim to 'track' an underlying index. (*See* Passive performance.)

Tracking error – a measure of how far a fund deviates from a underlying index. The tracking error is calculated as the standard deviation in the returns of the portfolio relative to the returns of the benchmark index.

Trade date – date on which a security is bought or sold. Value date is when it is settled.

Trading return – the returns gained through trading activities rather than through longer term investments.

Transaction costs – fees and commissions incurred on trading securities deducted from the value of the portfolio. Transaction costs generally involve: (1) a broker's commission; (2) a dealer's 'spread' – the difference between the buying and the selling price; (3) taxes associated with the trade such as stamp duty or VAT on commission costs; (4) any other costs incurred in completing an execution.

Treasury bill (TB) – US Government security maturing in less than one year.

Treasury bond – US Government security with maturity of 10 years or more.

Treasury note – US Government security with maturity of 2 to 10 years.

Treasury stock – common stock of a company which has been bought in by the company and held within the company's treasury.

Treynor Ratio – a return-to-risk ratio similar to the Sharpe Ratio where the excess return above the risk-free rate is divided by the beta of the return relative to the benchmark. Treynor Ratio = (Fund's return – Risk-free rate)/Fund's beta.

Trust deed – terms of a trust instrument or agreement between trustee and borrower outlining terms of the bond.

Trust for Application – charitable income that must be spent within a reasonable period of time.

Trust for Investment – permanent endowment to be used to generate return not to be spent.

Trustee investment – an investment authorized by the UK Trustee Investment Act as an investment for trust funds where the trust deed is silent on appropriate investments.

Trustee Savings Bank – bank managed by a body of trustees. Former trustee savings banks in the UK are now part of Lloyds TSB.

Turnover – *see* Portfolio turnover.

UCITS – 'Undertakings for Collective Investments in Transferable Securities'. A fund that is permitted to be marketed in all member countries of the European Union.

Unapplied total return – a UK charity concept which means the total investment return, both income and gain, less amounts previously applied for charitable purposes.

Unbundled – a service or product is said to be unbundled if the different component parts are managed/sold separately, usually with separate fees applying. An example, a stockbroker might offer investment advice but the trade execution might be carried out by a different company. The opposite is 'Bundled' implying the commission covers execution research etc.

Uncovered (naked) call – selling a call option when the underlying stock is not owned.

Underperformance – when a fund or portfolio's return is less than its benchmark's return.

Underwater funds – funds that have fallen below their historic dollar values which are the values of the contributions at the date of a gift to an endowment.

Underweight – when a fund's position in a company or sector is less than the equivalent position in the benchmark.

Underwriting – commission received for supporting a new issue of securities by a company. The support takes the form of undertaking to subscribe to any shares not otherwise acquired by investors.

Unfranked income – dividends or interest in the UK where corporation tax has not been paid by the company.

Unit trust – an investment fund that pools money for investing and issues units that represent a proportionate interest in the fund. A unit trust does not have a corporate structure so the investors are assigned 'units' rather than shares. *See* open-ended funds.

Universe – the list of all assets that are eligible for inclusion in a portfolio weighted by their market capitalization.

Unlisted security (market) – any security that is not listed on an organized stock exchange.

Unquoted security – *see* Unlisted security.

Unsecured – a liability not backed by an asset. (*See* Collateral.)

Unsystematic return – residual return, which is the part of return that is specific to a security and not associated with a movement in the market.

VAR – *see* Value at Risk.

VIX – an index that shows the expected volatility of the equity market over the next 30 calendar days, as is implied in at-the-money options on the S&P 500. VIX is calculated using the current prices of call and put options in individual stocks in the S&P 500 index which expire over the next two months. From this is derived a theoretical at-the-money implied S&P 500 market option with 30 days to expiry.

Value at Risk (VAR) – market risk measure; the minimum return likely to a given degree of confidence over a given period of time.

Value date – the date on which a trade settles. (*See* Trade date.)

Value stocks – stocks that appear to be undervalued on fundamental criteria. The valuation metrics used to identify such value stocks include such ratios as price to sales, price to earnings and price to book.

Vanilla – the simple or plain form of bond or derivative (vanilla option).

Variance – a statistical measure of risk. The squared deviation from the mean, which is the squared difference between the mean value and the observed value.

Variation margin – *see* Margin.

Vega – the change in the price of an option which results from a 1% change in underlying volatility, reflecting therefore the price of uncertainty.

Venture capital – capital investment usually in a start-up or early stage business which is subject to higher risk before the shares become listed on public markets.

Vertical spread – simultaneous purchase and sale of two options that differ only in their exercise price.

Volatility – a measure of the amount of movement in price around the average, usually measured by the statistic 'standard deviation' or by 'variance'. (*See also* VIX.)

Volatility arbitrage – purchase and sale of closely related options to exploit incorrectly priced option premia.

Wall Street – a district in New York which houses financial activity, principally the New York Stock Exchange (NYSE). The NYSE is also known by its price display system called the Big Board. (*See also* City.)

Warrant – a tradable security that confers the holder with the right but not the obligation to buy the underlying security at some point in the future. The main difference between a warrant and an option is that the warrant is issued by the company whereas the option is a derivative security created in the market. Warrants are effectively long-term options.

When-issued security – authorized but not yet issued.

White knight – the rescuer of a take-over target from an unwanted bidder.

Winsorization – the process of truncating outliers at a fixed number of standard deviations from the mean. This prevents unusual events having undue influence on the series.

Witholding tax – tax retained from dividends by companies at source and not reclaimable by foreign investors.

Writing options – selling options to receive premium.

XD – *see* Ex-dividend.

XMC – *see* Extra-Market Covariance.

Yankee bond – a US dollar denominated security issued by a foreign entity in the USA.

Yield – usually the return to a security from cash payments in the form of dividends and taxable as income. The term 'yield' is also used in other ways such as 'Earnings yield', which is the earnings per share over the share price expressed as a percentage. It is the inverse of a Price to Earnings (PE) ratio.

Yield curve – describes the change in redemption yield along a spectrum of time. The 'par' yield curve describes the yield on bonds along the curve based on a price of £100 per cent, i.e. where the income yield and the redemption yield are the same (*see* Duration). An 'inverted' yield curve is one where short rates are higher than long rates.

Yield to maturity – the yield a bond would give if it was held until maturity. This is different from the income yield (*see* Yield) and is the Internal Rate of Return that equates the cash flows of interest income and final repayment on redemption with the initial price.

Yield spread – the difference in yield between differently rated bonds of the same maturity structure.

Z bond – a type of CMO (*see* Collateral Obligations) bond called an accrual bond.

Z score – the number of standard deviations a given observation is away from a mean. Also a measure of financial health of a company, developed in 1968 by Dr Edward I. Altman, a Finance Professor at New York University's Stern School of Business.

Zero coupon bonds – those bonds that have no coupon and hence no periodic payment to the holder. Zero coupon bonds are issued at a discount to par and thus the yield to the holder is obtained within the capital returned at maturity. Zero coupon bonds can be created as a by-product of a Strip.

Index

Note: glossary entries are indicated by **emboldened page numbers**, Figures and Tables by *italic numbers*

Index compiled by Paul Nash